TUBERCULAR CAPITAL

STANFORD STUDIES IN JEWISH HISTORY AND CULTURE
Edited by David Biale and Sarah Abrevaya Stein

TUBERCULAR CAPITAL

Illness and the Conditions of Modern Jewish Writing

SUNNY S. YUDKOFF

Stanford University Press
Stanford, California

Stanford University Press
Stanford, California

Printed in the United States of America on acid-free, archival-quality paper

Library of Congress Cataloging-in-Publication Data

Names: Yudkoff, Sunny S., author.
Title: Tubercular capital : illness and the conditions of modern Jewish writing / Sunny S. Yudkoff.
Description: Stanford, California : Stanford University Press, 2018. | Series: Stanford studies in Jewish history and culture | Includes bibliographical references and index.
Identifiers: LCCN 2018019693 (print) | LCCN 2018038493 (ebook) | ISBN 9781503607330 | ISBN 9781503605152 (cloth: alk. paper)
Subjects: LCSH: Tuberculosis in literature. | Hebrew literature, Modern—20th century—History and criticism. | Yiddish literature—20th century—History and criticism. | Jewish literature—20th century—History and criticism. | Jewish authors—Diseases—History. | Tuberculosis patients' writings—History and criticism. | Tuberculosis and literature.
Classification: LCC PJ5012.T83 (ebook) | LCC PJ5012.T83 Y83 2018 (print) | DDC 839/.1093561—dc23
LC record available at https://lccn.loc.gov/2018019693

Cover design: Rob Ehle
Cover illustration: Drawing of the Hebrew poet Raḥel Bluvshtein by Aba Fenichel.

CONTENTS

ACKNOWLEDGMENTS

If the tubercular heroes of this book teach us one thing above all else, it is that writing is only nominally a solitary act. I am fortunate to have learned this lesson outside the sanatorium and with the support of many colleagues and friends around the world.

This project began at Harvard University, where I had the fortune to study with Ruth Wisse. I remain grateful to her for introducing me to Yiddish literature years ago, for pushing me to find the argument of a text, and for reminding me never to underestimate the possibility of humor. This book was also shepherded from its inception by the steadfast and kind encouragement of Werner Sollors. The resources of his wisdom are vast, as are the bibliographic references he always has at hand. Throughout the writing process, I also had the privilege to think with and learn from Karen Thornber, whose dedication to reading widely is a model for all. My thanks also extend to Ilana Pardes, whose sensitivity to the resonances of Hebrew have inspired many close readings, and to Irit Aharony, who taught me how to teach. This work also would not have come to fruition without the many lessons in interpretive elegance that I learned years ago from Joseph Sherman at the Oxford Centre for Hebrew and Jewish Studies. His passing has left an empty space in Yiddish literature.

The final chapters of this project were completed at the University of Chicago, where I had the pleasure of teaching and researching in the Department of Germanic Studies. I remain deeply appreciative for the support that was offered to me by colleagues both in the department and across the university. Special mention goes to Leora Auslander, Catherine Baumann, Faith Hillis, Anne Knafl, Bill Nickell, Eric Santner, Bożena Shallcross, Josef Stern, David Wellbery, and the dedicated students of the Yiddish Tish. My warmest thanks are also due to Na'ama Rokem, who asked the challenging, thoughtful, and playful questions that moved this project forward.

I had the privilege of completing this manuscript at the University of Wisconsin–Madison with help from colleagues in the Center for Jewish Studies; the Department of German, Nordic, and Slavic; and the English Department. Special thanks extend to Amos Bitzan, Rachel Brenner, Russ Castronovo, Skye Donney, Sabine Gross, Sara Guyer, Ronald Harris, Judith Houk, Dylan Kaufman-Obstler, Mark Louden, Venkat Mani, Todd Michelson-Ambelang, Pamela Potter, Simone Schweber, Judith Sone, John Torterice, Manon van de Water, and Marina Zilbergerts. I am also lucky to work alongside Tony Michels, whose commitment to Yiddish is guided by patience, curiosity, and deep wells of knowledge.

I have also benefited from the support of many institutions: the George L. Mosse/Laurence A. Weinstein Center for Jewish Studies at the University of Wisconsin–Madison; Harvard University; the Memorial Foundation for Jewish Culture; the Wexner Foundation; the Posen Foundation; the Vivian Lefsky Hort Memorial Fellowship of YIVO; and the Harvard Center for Jewish Studies. I also thank Amanda Siegel of the New York Public Library; Avraham Novershtern and Leybl Roitman of Beth Shalom Aleichem; Jeanne Abrams and Thyria Wilson at the Beck Archives at the University of Denver; Joachim Innerhofer and Sabine Mayr at the Museo Ebraico/Jüdisches Museum Meran; Rachel Abadi and Rina Bobman of the Degania Archives; the archivists of Machon Genazim, Machon Lavon, and the Central Zionist Archives; and Vardit Samuels and Elizabeth Vernon of the Harvard Judaica Collection. A version of Chapter 3 appeared as "Tubercular Capital: American Yiddish Literature at the Sanatorium," in *Literature and Medicine* 31, no. 2 (2013): 303–29. I am grateful for the permission of Johns Hopkins University Press to publish an expanded version here.

The insights of my friends and colleagues have also proved invaluable. Niv Allon and Ofer Dynes—your influences are evident and your kindness is cherished. Tatyana Gershkovich, Matt Handelman, Joela Jacobs, and especially my Madison colleague Hannah Vandegrift Eldridge—because of our book group my chapters were revised, my argument tightened, and my equilibrium maintained. My thanks are also due to Cori Anderson, Catherine Belling, Mollie Searle Benoni, Rachel Biale, Efrat Bloom, Mindl Cohen, Gennady Estraikh, Jordan Finkin, Mayhill Fowler, Itamar Francez, Liora Halperin, Kerstin Hoge, Avner Holtzman, Katie Kauss, Eitan Kensky, Jessica Kirzane, Olga Litvak, Caroline Luce, Anita Norich, Dana Olmert, Mihaela Pacurar, Philipp Penka, Shachar Pinsker, David Roskies, Adam Ehrlich Sachs, Rachel Seelig, Sasha Senderovich, Marina Sharifi, Sam Spinner, Giddon Ticotsky, Melissa Weininger, Saul Zaritt, and Wendy Zierler. I am also grateful to Ernest Gilman, who generously shared his work with me. I have learned a great deal from his thoughtful readings of the texts of the JCRS as well as from his collegiality. My thanks also extend to David Biale and Sarah Abrevaya Stein, whose editorial encouragement has allowed this book to see the light of day. I also thank Margo Irvin and Nora Spiegel of Stanford University Press for their attention to detail and for carefully guiding this project from book proposal to finished product. Support for this research was also provided by the Office of the Vice Chancellor for Research and Graduate Education at the University of Wisconsin–Madison with funding from the Wisconsin Alumni Research Foundation.

Finally, the merits of this book belong to my family. My father, Neal—finder of typos and advocate from the start; my mother, Judy—finder of warm boots and giver of pep talks; my brother and sister-in-law, Ben and Becca—finders of adventures and loving parents; and my in-laws, Marian and Rob—finders of great movies and model culture-vultures. Ten days after receiving the peer reviewers' comments, my son Theo entered this world. I could not have asked for a better companion during revisions. His smile was the answer for every writerly block. All my love, little man. And, finally, this book would not exist without my partner. Adam, you make everything better. You read every version ten times. And you never stop asking questions. This is for you.

NOTE ON TRANSLITERATION

The problems of rendering Yiddish and Hebrew texts into Roman characters are well documented. For Yiddish, I have relied on the standardized YIVO transliteration system. For Hebrew, I have used a simplified version of the Library of Congress transliteration system. For the names of most Yiddish and Hebrew writers, I have relied on the naming practices of *The YIVO Encyclopedia of Jews in Eastern Europe*, except where that spelling diverges from the one most commonly used by scholars (e.g., I. L. Peretz, when *The YIVO Encyclopedia* has Y. L. Peretz). In cases of lesser-known writers for whom standardized spelling of their names does not exist, I have rendered their names according to the formal transliteration systems mentioned.

The problems of identifying place-names are also manifold. Whenever possible, I have recorded place-names using the system employed by *The YIVO Encyclopedia of Jews in Eastern Europe*. In this system, major cities are spelled according to their common English variant (e.g., Warsaw, Jerusalem, and Kiev). An exception is made for Vilnius, which I refer to as Vilna, as is customary among Yiddish literary scholars. Smaller cities are rendered in standardized transliteration, and a note indicates where that place is located today.

Finally, unless noted otherwise, all dates follow the Gregorian calendar and all translations are my own.

TUBERCULAR CAPITAL

INTRODUCTION

Jewish Literature and Tubercular Capital

"Let it be a consumption," declares the protagonist of a 1903 short story by the writer I. L. Peretz, "at least something should happen."[1] The man behind these words is neither eccentric nor prone to hyperbole. Among the variety of characters populating Yiddish belles lettres at the turn of the century, he is decidedly typical. An aspiring writer, he is a recent urban transplant. He seesaws between moments of hopelessness and excitement, self-loathing and grandiose visions of his future. He is poor, hungry, and desperately seeking the attention of the Christian object of his affection. Even his cough is decidedly average, neither phlegmy nor blood-flecked. In fact, nothing about the scene portends any grave illness. Yet the brief cough emerges as a moment of potential action. "Zol zayn an optserung," he charges. "Let it be a consumption."

The present study takes its subject from this suggestive comment. What would have motivated a wish for a terminal disease? And what would such a diagnosis have afforded the ailing, secularizing, urbanizing Hebrew or Yiddish writer? The disease, of course, was far from physically ennobling. A diagnosis often accompanied brutal coughing fits, bloody hemorrhages, relentless fatigue, and physical emaciation. These symptoms sometimes manifested in alternating patterns of exacerbation and remission for decades.[2] For Peretz's protagonist, however, the prospect of consumption resonates as a moment of unseen possibilities. As he exclaims, "At least something should happen" (*abi zol epes geshen*). For him, a diagnosis of the disease signals an interruption in his mundane life and, perhaps, the start of something consequential.

Yet Peretz's would-be patient does not come to experience consumption in his own medical history. His offhand remark is cut short by a highly evocative daydream. Readers quickly learn that it is the protagonist's capacity to transform his childhood memories into allegorical psychodramas, rather than disease, that will fuel his creative energy. For many of Peretz's own peers, in contrast, consumption was not simply an abstract idea that one could invoke during moments of existential crisis or routine boredom. Rather, for the Yiddish and Hebrew writers whose biographies and texts occupy this study, tuberculosis was part of their lived reality. The Yiddish humorist Sholem Aleichem was diagnosed in 1908 and spent the next six years recuperating at health resorts in Italy, Germany, and Switzerland. For over a decade, the Hebrew poet Raḥel Bluvshtein suffered from the disease in places as distant as Baku and Tel Aviv. From the 1910s to 1930s, a cadre of Yiddish writers, including Yehoash, H. Leivick, and Shea Tenenbaum, sought treatment in Denver, Colorado. The modernist Hebrew writer David Vogel took "the cure," in turn, in the mountains of South Tyrol in the winters of 1925 and 1926.

At times, the disease incapacitated these writers and even prevented them from putting pen to paper. Yet the stories of their lives and work also demonstrate that tuberculosis provided a generative context for the development of their writing and the fashioning of their literary reputations. The words of Peretz's protagonist will soon read less as a desperate outburst than as the prescient and measured expression of a future author. Intentionally or otherwise, his words convey a strategic understanding of the role that tuberculosis played in the lives, careers, and texts of the modern Jewish writer. More than a bacterial infection or multivalent metaphor, tuberculosis served as the condition of possibility for the ailing writer's literary career. Keeping in mind the plea "abi zol epes geshen," we will see that *something did in fact happen* following a terminal diagnosis. Tuberculosis would come to function as a critical mediator in the creation, dissemination, and reception of modern Yiddish and Hebrew writing.[3] Addressing medical humanists and literary scholars alike, this study proposes a new analytical model for assessing the historical intersection of the infirmed body and the literary imagination. The cases of these modern Jewish writers offer a comparative paradigm for interpreting the association of illness and literary production across linguistic traditions. Indeed, constellating this series of disparate writers, texts, and geographies will reveal the counterintuitive role played by disease in the construction of a robust, transnational, and multilingual Jewish literary republic.

From Consumption to Tuberculosis

According to the World Health Organization's Stop TB Partnership, nearly 1.3 million people worldwide died from tuberculosis in 2012. The majority of these victims lived and perished in sub-Saharan Africa and South Asia.[4] An estimated 8.6 million people became infected by the disease in 2012 alone, and nearly 500,000 became infected with multidrug-resistant tuberculosis (MDR-TB) in 2013.[5] Rates of death and contagion, however, remain low in North America and Europe. Since the introduction of antibiotics in the mid-twentieth century, the number of infected Americans has dropped precipitously and stayed relatively stable. The result is that, save for the occasional media interest, tuberculosis does not receive extensive attention in American or European news outlets.[6] The disease has remained generally absent from the dominant cultural discourses of disease, infection, and chronic illness in these geographic contexts.

In contrast, when Peretz sat down to write his story in 1903, tuberculosis loomed large in the public health imagination as well as the lived reality of populations across the United States, the Russian Empire, and Europe. In Warsaw, where he wrote his short story, two publications outlining the sources and threats of tuberculosis had appeared only a few years earlier. The works specifically addressed Jewish readerships in both the language of a growing minority, Hebrew, and the language of the masses, Yiddish. The first, Y. Ḥ. Zagorodski's *Our Lives and Longevity* (*Ḥayenu ve-'orekh yamenu*), warned its readers in 1898 against the threat of consumption (*razon*).[7] The author cautioned his audience that the wasting disease spread through contact with the sick as well as by inhaling the air of a patient's room. Without mincing words, Zagorodski suggested that readers disinfect the clothing and personal belongings of a consumptive patient, refrain from drinking unboiled milk (to prevent contraction of bovine tuberculosis), and, if already coughing and feverish, seek respite in the high mountains or near the seacoast where fresh air was readily available.

Climatological therapies that advised patients to leave densely populated urban spaces or industrial centers were common in this period and soon became standard selling points of sanatoria and health clinics around the world.[8] Shortly after Zagorodski's text appeared, Tsukerman's Folksbibliotek published *Zayt gezund* by the physician M. Gotlieb.[9] The literal meaning of the title—"Be Healthy"—existed in an uncomfortable tension with the title's more colloquial meaning—"Good-bye." The work, a general introduction to various diseases, devoted the second of four volumes to the subject of *Tuberculosis (Consumption)*—in Yiddish, *Sukhote (shvindzukht)*. After opening the volume with several biblical quotations and couching his health agenda within a Jewish textual frame, Gotlieb echoed Zagorodski in urging his readers to seek out living conditions with good airflow. He further suggested that they make sure to drink clean water and take care to nourish themselves heartily if they wanted to keep the disease at bay.

Similar health pamphlets and texts were common throughout Europe at the turn of the century. Across the continent and throughout the Russian Empire, tuberculosis claimed high exposure and mortality rates. In the United States, from 1900 to 1910, it ranked as one of the top ten leading causes of death.[10] In Poland, as late as 1931, tuberculosis was measured as the leading cause of death nationwide.[11] As David Barnes has written, "It is possible that a near-totality of the population of many large European cities in the nineteenth century technically 'had' tuberculosis—that is, would have tested positive for exposure to the tubercle bacillus."[12] Global awareness of the disease only continued to grow after the German physician and scientist Robert Koch presented his research at the Physiological Society of Berlin in the spring of 1882. There, Koch attested to the discovery of the tubercle bacillus, *Mycobacterium tuberculosis*.[13] Introducing his work to a scientific community already sympathetic to the germ theory of disease, his findings spread quickly.[14] In 1909, the physician, writer, and advocate of Yiddish literature Gershn Levin published an article in the Warsaw daily *Haynt* titled "The Battle with the Consumption" (Der kamf mit der shvindzukht). Like many before him, Levin pointed to Koch's discovery as the key moment in the history of the disease. Levin emphasized just how important the work "of the great scholar Koch" truly was.[15] For the first time, tuberculosis had been rendered identifiable in the laboratory and, by extension, potentially treatable.

According to medical historians Jean and René Dubos, Koch's discovery also marked a semantic shift from a discourse of "consumption" to one of "tuberculosis." Prior to the discovery of the bacillus, diagnostic imprecision allowed a variety of so-called wasting diseases to be conflated as "consumption." Following the discovery, they explain, "certain types of nonpulmonary diseases [were] recognized as being caused by the tubercle bacilli," allowing a whole host of symptoms to be identified as "tuberculosis" that might have escaped such a diagnosis.[16] The importance of the shift for medical historians is further evident, for example, in such collections as *From Consumption to Tuberculosis: A Documentary History* by Barbara Gutmann Rosenkrantz, which includes a variety of statistical, scientific, and historical accounts of the trajectory of the disease from the 1860s to 1990s.

Nonetheless, the potential shift in naming practices following Koch's paper did not prevent physicians, patients, or writers from calling on the language of both "consumption" and "tuberculosis" to refer to the condition. This was true even when laboratory tests and, later, X-rays were made regular parts of the diagnostic process. Similarly, when Peretz's protagonist declares, "Let it be a consumption," he is not being willfully anachronistic. Rather, he draws on one of the many terms used in Yiddish to name a sickness that had only recently acquired a specifically bacterial identity. Alongside Peretz's *optserung*, which derives from the German word meaning "emaciation" (*Abzehrung*), Yiddish possesses multiple terms to evoke the dreaded *vayse pest* (white plague). Some of the terms are akin to "consumption," and others more directly translate the name "tuberculosis." Besides the Latinate *tuberkuloze*, one may refer to the disease in Yiddish using words of Germanic origin, such as *shvindzukht* (consumption), *di der* (alt., *di dar*; the withering), or, ironically, *di gute krenk* (the good disease); words of Slavic origin, such as *sukhote* (drying) or *tshakhotke* (wasting); or *katute*, a local term employed by patients at the Jewish Consumptives' Relief Society of Denver, Colorado, alongside *te-be*, a Yiddish version of the English acronym.

By 1900, Hebrew boasted a similarly rich range of terms to refer to the disease, including the Latinate *tuberkulozah*, the biblical term *shaḥefet* (cf.

Leviticus 26:16 and Deuteronomy 28:22), the Hebrew phrase *gniḥat dam* (moan of blood), and the descriptive *razon* (thinning) used by Zagorodski in *Our Lives and Longevity*. The tubercular Hebrew poet Raḥel Bluvshtein, known simply as Raḥel, also referred to the disease in her private correspondence by the more allusive expression *maḥalat ha-sofrim*, "the authors' disease."[17]

While 1882 may mark the biological recognition of the disease called tuberculosis, it certainly did not precipitate the complete dismissal of all other terms that remained at the Yiddish or Hebrew writer's disposal. Even writers who were diagnosed with pulmonary tuberculosis using the most advanced scientific methods of the twentieth century continued to draw on a wide range of vocabulary to define their own as well their subject's ailments.[18] Despite the medical profession's ability to define the illness more precisely, tuberculosis retained a myriad of associations. These connotations, in turn, were inflected by social, linguistic, and aesthetic considerations. Throughout this study, I refer to the illness in question using a variety of site-specific names, paying close attention to the writer's word choice and the connotations attending it. Relatedly, I restrict my inquiry to writers who specifically self-identified as tubercular or consumptive and who explicitly sought treatment for the disease. I leave the practice of retrospective diagnosis to medical historians and physicians.[19]

Tuberculosis, Beauty, and Romantic Genius

In addition to a rich and varied set of naming practices, the disease itself bore with it a tradition of interpretation that had long associated the illness with sexual attractiveness and refinement. Although it may seem surprising, a disease marked by bloody hemoptysis and emaciation was also considered a sign of beauty, delicacy, and creative potential. Already by the seventeenth century, consumption had been aestheticized as a manifestation of lovesickness across European belles lettres.[20] Melancholy gaunt lovers plagued by consumption—or *pthisis* as it was often called—filled the work of early-modern writers and poets alike. It was a depiction that also drew on and contributed to contemporary medical discourse on the subject.[21] By the eighteenth and nineteenth centuries, the illness had come to be seen as a mark of refinement, Christian spiritual grace, and even bourgeois luxury, as consumptive

Figure 1. Dante Gabriel Rossetti's *Beata Beatrix*, 1871–72. Source: The Art Institute of Chicago / Art Resource, NY. Reprinted with permission.

victims "took the cure" in port cities and mountain retreats around Europe. The grand health tour was so well documented that the critic Susan Sontag once noted with evident disdain that "the Romantics invented invalidism as a pretext for leisure."[22] The disease came additionally to be linked to ideals of beauty. The pale consumptive was modeled by such figures as the dying heroine of Alexandre Dumas's novel *La Dame aux camélias* (1848) and by portraits of Elizabeth Siddal, the consumptive muse of the poet and painter Dante Gabriel Rossetti.[23]

Both Dumas's heroine and Siddal came to exemplify the ailing female body, wasting away with genteel grace, burning eyes, and seductive red lips—all established tropes of European Romanticism. These female figures were deemed attractive in their suffering, and their wan, emaciated faces conveyed erotic allure. The figure of the pale tubercular beauty similarly appeared in fin de siècle German texts, such as Thomas Mann's novella *Tristan* (1903), in which the male hero finds the pallid visage of the consumptive heroine Gabriele Klöterjahn intoxicating.[24] By the mid-twentieth century, the elegant beauty associated with consumption had also morphed into a sign of sexual appetite, as tuberculosis was sourced as the cause of an increased sex drive.[25]

In addition to an illness of sensuality, sensitivity, and sexual allure, consumption became known as both the source and manifestation of creativity. The prevalence of wasting poets in the English tradition, most notably John Keats, only served to cement a reputation for the illness as one intimately connected to literary genius. As the Duboses summarize, "Throughout medical history there runs this suggestion—that the intellectually gifted are the most likely to contract the disease, and furthermore that the same fire which wastes the body in consumption also makes the mind shine with a brighter light."[26] The idea extended far beyond the borders of the British Empire, as Russian Romantic poets, such as the late nineteenth-century writer Semyon Nadson, became known not only for their elegant sentimental verse but for the symbiotic relationship between disease and cultural production. As Robert Dietrich Wessling has argued, "Nadson inscribed his life into a larger cultural context, employing a dualistic approach in a cultural idiom that fused the medical physiology of bodily illness with the literariness of the poet's suffering."[27] In short, the poet's aesthetics were understood to be inseparably linked to his physiological ailment.

This conflation between tuberculosis and literary creativity also flourished in the German sphere. As late as 1932, medical historian Erich Hugo Ebstein could still publish a collection of fifty-two sketches of consumptive figures. The collection, *Tuberkulose als Schicksal*, asserts the pivotal role played by *Tuberculosis as Destiny* in the lives of such famous men as Chopin, Goethe, Gorki, Keats, Klabund, Molière, Novalis, Paganini, Rousseau, Schiller, and Spinoza.[28] One might convincingly add to this list Thoreau, Chekhov, and, of course, Kafka. Less than a decade later, the American medical historian Lewis Moorman echoed Ebstein in his own work, *Tuberculosis and Genius* (1940), arguing that the feverish tubercular experience corresponds to an equally feverish burst of creativity. "Inescapable physical inactivity," wrote Moorman, "begets mental activity." That mental activity, in turn, was sparked as the tubercular patient suffered.[29] Across the globe and linguistic traditions, tuberculosis was commonly accepted as a mark of literary chosenness and creative potential, even as the disease proved physically harrowing and incurable.

Tuberculosis and Capitalism

For Romantic writers, the tubercular visage was deemed beautiful, alluring, and *interesting*. In what has now become almost legend, we are told of an occasion when the poet Lord Byron looked into the mirror and exclaimed, "How pale I look! I should like, I think, to die of a consumption." When Byron was asked why, he responded, "Because then the women would all say, 'See that poor Byron—how interesting he looks in dying!'"[30] His initial exclamation foreshadows those of Peretz's protagonist—"zol zayn an optserung." Yet these words, in contrast to those of Byron, are recognizably tinged with irony. The possibility of an ennobling illness is unavailable to the Yiddish protagonist who is poor, cold, and beginning to cough. The story as a whole works to undermine the Romantic impulse of the narrator. He may long to live a life of fairy-tale love, but his Jewish identity and material circumstances prevent him from yielding to those urges.

As an impoverished urban writer, Peretz's protagonist also would likely have been aware of the reputation of tuberculosis as a "social disease." Although the "perverted sentimentalism" of Romantic literary expression would continue well into the twentieth century, public health activists in Europe,

Russia, and the United States increasingly assessed the disease as an affliction of poverty and poor labor conditions.[31] Across Europe, tuberculosis was decried as an illness that was "inherent in the lifestyle of the working classes" and "determined by the dictates of industrial capitalism and wage labor." Unsanitary conditions and overcrowding only exacerbated contagion rates among the urban poor.[32] Similarly, in fin de siècle Moscow a scientific understanding of the causes of tuberculosis dovetailed with a social explanation. "Tuberculosis, as a social disease," writes the physician-historian Michael Zdenek David, "straddled the divisions among hygienists and bacteriologists because in the contemporary medical understanding, it was at once a bacterial disease and the result of poverty, poor social policy, and ignorance."[33]

For many Yiddish public health activists and writers, the idea of tuberculosis as a social disease also translated into a direct association of *di vayse pest* with the poor working conditions of the Jewish laborer. As Irving Howe later recalled, tuberculosis was known among Jews on the Lower East Side as "the tailors' disease."[34] Writing in Warsaw in 1925, Gershn Levin warned his Polish Jewish readership in words both sympathetic and authoritative to be aware of the relationship between a chosen vocation and a propensity for tuberculosis:

> There are many jobs that incline towards tuberculosis, those that are not conducted in the fresh air, in poorly ventilated apartments, in smoke, or in small rooms. That is why there is a lot of tuberculosis among printers, lithographers, waiters, painters, bookbinders, joiners, upholsterers, hat makers, bakers, and others similar. . . . I know it's not easy to change jobs, but if it's an issue of tuberculosis, one needs to figure it out.[35]

In this text, Levin calls on Jewish workers to advocate for themselves and to endeavor, to the best of their ability, to change their life circumstances. Of course, to do so, as Levin admits, would likely have been difficult if not impossible.

Other voices participating in the discussion were less instructive and far more strident. For example, the Yiddish novelist Sholem Asch describes one of the many Jewish types populating his New York saga *East River* (1946) as "the victim [*der korbn*] of the capitalist system."[36] It was an idea that had been reinforced in Yiddish writing for nearly fifty years, where coughing sweatshop laborers appeared ever more gaunt in publication after publication. We might consider, for example, the poem "A Teardrop on the Iron" by the so-called sweatshop poet Morris Rosenfeld. In the poem, Rosenfeld immortalizes the figure of the consumptive Yiddish laborer. The speaker is a typical garment worker. In the dank, dark space of the shop, he holds an iron in his hand and exclaims:

My heart is weak, I groan and cough;
my sick chest barely rises.
I groan and cough and press and think,
my eye grows moist, a tear falls,
the iron glows: my little tear
it seethes and seethes and does not boil away.

Mayn harts iz shvakh, ikh krekhts un hust;
es heybt zikh koym mayn kranke brust.
Ikh krekhts un hust un pres un kler,
mayn oyg vert faykht, es falt a trer,
der ayzn glit: dos trerl mayn
dos kokht un kokht un zidt nit ayn.[37]

The teardrop, presumably ephemeral but evidently persistent, remains the lone physical remnant of the worker otherwise consumed by his wasting disease. In the German collection of Rosenfeld's poems published around 1903, "A Teardrop on the Iron" appears several pages after a woodcut by E. M. Lilien of a pot-bellied vampiric capitalist sucking the life from an emaciated tubercular tailor slumped over his work.[38] Tuberculosis, as writers, artists, and health advocates contended, was the symptom of a global economic system that exploited workers, rendering them sickly, weak, and helpless.

Tuberculosis, Racial Difference, and Zionism

The specifically Jewish profile of the tubercular victim would also have been of concern to Peretz and his colleagues. During the first decades of the twentieth century, like syphilis and neurasthenia, tuberculosis was frequently coded as an illness with a particularly Jewish racialized visage. One might think here of the tubercular Leo Naphta, the Jewish-born Jesuit whose assumed racial background is evident in Thomas Mann's *The Magic Mountain* (1924) when Hans Castorp takes one look at the argumentative man's

Figure 2. Illustration by E. M. Lilien from Morris Rosenfeld's *Lieder des Ghetto* (Berlin: S. Calvary, 1903), 36. Source: The Leo Baeck Institute. Reprinted with permission.

nose. In Peretz's text, the protagonist's identity is similarly legible on his face. When he asks his Christian love interest how she had known that he was Jewish, she giggles and acknowledges his profile.

In *The Magic Mountain*, Naphta is only one tuberculosis sufferer among many. Yet he becomes the ailing voice that alternately advocates for authoritarianism, communism, illiteracy, and disease. According to cultural historian Sander Gilman, Naphta "represents the unhealthy Jewish presence in the world," in the landscape both of Mann's novel and in Europe more broadly.[39] According to Gilman's influential work, *Franz Kafka: The Jewish Patient*, the tubercular condition was a critical feature in the European project to pathologize the Jewish body, rendering it visible, legible, and categorizable. Kafka lived, writes Gilman, when "Jewish biological difference came to be understood as immutable and inscribed on the Jew's imagined body."[40] The Czech-Jewish modernist also wrote at a time when "a Jewish *fin de siècle* writer's modernity [was] inseparable from his allegedly diseased nature."[41] In Gilman's study, Kafka's entire corporeal being—from his lungs to his voice—becomes implicated in a discourse of the Jewish male body "predestined" to be effeminate, weak, and sickly.[42]

Paradigmatic for Gilman is, of course, Kafka's tuberculosis. Diagnosed in 1917, Kafka would spend his final years in various sanatoria around central Europe. Like the Hebrew writer David Vogel, whom we will meet in Chapter 4, Kafka also sought the cure in Meran, Austria (later, Merano, Italy), under the supervision of Dr. Josef Kohn. According to Gilman, the key to understanding Kafka's writings, including his fiction, diary entries, and correspondence, is by attending to this diagnosis. As *The Jewish Patient* contends, all the positive cultural associations of consumptive beauty—pallor, delicacy, and refinement—that had been so glamorized in the Romantic period were resignified on the tubercular Jewish male body as indicative of racial inferiority. The tubercular Jewish male was not genteel but weak, he was not delicate but emasculated, and he was not inflamed by the fever of tuberculosis as much as snuffed out by it. For Gilman, Kafka's tubercular diagnosis was above all overdetermined. Kafka, as *The Jewish Patient* maintains, was always already tubercular—physiologically, psychologically, and literarily. He could be nothing other than sick, and his texts should therefore be read as psychologically fraught elaborations on his inherently sickly state, specifically, and his racialized tubercular Jewish frailty, more generally.[43]

Gilman's argument is certainly strong, but to interpret the lives and works of these Yiddish and Hebrew writers as similarly overdetermined homogenizes the multiple symbolic systems in which these writers developed. It similarly glosses over competing connotations of the disease available to the Jewish writer. Yet, as Gilman and others convincingly demonstrate, many Jewish figures were concerned that the disease pointed to a racialized constitution that was inescapable. In the early twentieth century there is no dearth of voices—medical, scientific, political, or literary—that categorize the Jewish body in similarly reductive terms.[44] Scholars such as John Efron, Michael Gluzman, and Todd Presner have also investigated how this diminishment of the Jewish body (particularly the male Jewish body) was one background against which multiple Zionist efforts to "regenerate" the diasporic Jew were initiated.[45] "Jews," writes Presner, "participated in, extended, and variously adopted . . . strategies of 'biopower' for reforming the Jewish body and conceiving of the regeneration of the Jewish state."[46] In the words of the Zionist physician Max Nordau, the turn of the century was the time when a rejuvenation of Jewish strength was most necessary—when "muscular Judaism" was most required. For Nordau and other Zionist activists, a vision of Jewish national reconstruction would not include room for a glorification of tuberculosis.

If socialist and communist activists critiqued tuberculosis as a symbol of capitalist oppression, Zionist activists lambasted the illness as the manifestation of Jewish diasporic weakness. The dream of territorial Zionists of the *yishuv* (the Jewish settlement in Palestine during the British Mandate period) was to rebuild the physical Jewish body through working the land. What room could be made, then, to accommodate tuberculosis? A disease of indoor spaces, shortness of breath, and urban life? Tuberculosis was repeatedly diminished within Zionist cultural discourse. In 1927, for example, the Yiddish writers Sholem Asch (whose tubercular character was a "victim of the capitalist system") and Peretz Hirschbein visited Palestine.[47] Despite the protestations of many Hebrew activists, the Yiddish writers were invited to a reception in their honor at the Hebrew Writers' Union. The "Father of Hebrew Poetry," Ḥayim Naḥman Bialik, famously greeted the writers by describing the relationship between the two languages as a "marriage made in heaven," a complicated dynamic with explicitly gendered and sexual connotations.[48] Not all the Hebrew poets, however, were equally gracious. The modernist Hebrew poet Avraham Shlonsky lambasted the idea of Hebrew and Yiddish bilingualism:

> We see this calamity of bilingualism as we see tuberculosis, which gnaws at the lungs of the nation. We want Israeli breathing to be *completely Hebrew*, with two lungs. A Hebrew Land of Israel, working for the nation, loving its producers and its culture—this is the "Society of the War Against Tuberculosis."[49]

Hebrew cultural activism, according to Shlonsky, could rhetorically function in lieu of the Anti-Tuberculosis League. The Hebrew-language nationalist was the ultimate health activist. Most important for the purposes of the present discussion, tuberculosis was metaphorized as the illness of exile, as the language of diaspora, and as a disease that could be cured through Hebrew breathing—linguistically and physiologically.

Tuberculosis and Literature: A Question of Capital

When Peretz's protagonist announces, "Let it be a consumption," therefore, he invokes a multitude of positive and negative, political and aesthetic, ideological and biological connotations attending tuberculosis; it was a sign of beauty and genius, of industrial poverty, of racial distinction, and of Jewish-language politics. The symbolic range of the disease was also mobilized in work across modern Hebrew and Yiddish literature. Well into the twentieth century, characters coughed their way through various texts. A Romantic pallor characterizes the languishing sisters in Uri Nissan Gnessin's modernist Hebrew novella *Beside* (1913), gaunt ailing lovers similarly show themselves in Isaac Bashevis Singer's family saga *The Manor* (1953–55), and tubercular figures more dead than alive accompany corpses in Dvora Baron's Hebrew short story "At the End of the Summer" (ca. 1920).[50] A consumptive clown speaks loudly and clearly in Yisroel Rabon's Yiddish novella *The Street* (1928), and a tubercular patient lies ill in an integrated American hospital in Shlomo Damesek's Hebrew novel *My Fate* (1945).[51] And while nouveau riche Jews take the baths in the fictional Ukrainian village of Boyberik in

Sholem Aleichem's story "To the Hot Springs" (1903), an ailing father is sent to "the Davos of the American West"—Denver, Colorado—in the American film *Two Sisters* (1938).[52] From New York to Łódź, Vienna to Tel Aviv, the Ukrainian countryside to the American West, the ailing men and women of Yiddish and Hebrew literature and film occupy various roles as parents, patients, lovers, joke tellers, socialites, soldiers, and critics.

This study, however, moves beyond an exploration of the literary effect of these metaphors. I heed here the words of Susan Sontag, who famously writes in the opening pages of *Illness as Metaphor* that "my point is that illness is *not* a metaphor, and that the most truthful way of regarding illness—and the healthiest way of being ill—is one most purified of, most resistant to, metaphoric thinking."[53] According to Sontag, metaphors obscure the pain of the actual sufferer. They furthermore enable a hierarchy of diseases. Particularly egregious in Sontag's view is the manner in which cancer and AIDS patients have been symbolically diminished by the negative metaphoric frames structuring their illnesses.[54] This is in contrast to the metaphoric valence of beauty and refinement often—though, as we have seen, not always—assigned to tuberculosis.

Sontag's powerful work demands that a patient's suffering not be lost or forgotten in a symbolic system. Her insistence that critics look beyond the metaphor to perceive the patient in pain, aestheticized neither as beautiful nor as grotesque, is one starting point for the project at hand. The reality of tuberculosis in the Jewish writer's biography is of critical importance, and the biography of that writer must not be overlooked. At the same time, the cultural experience of illness, treatment, and support is also intimately connected to the metaphorics of illness, including those employed by the tubercular Jewish writers themselves. Accordingly, my work accounts for both the lived reality of tubercular Yiddish and Hebrew writers and the figurative language at their disposal. Reading archival sources alongside creative texts, considering both the biography of the writers and their literary output, and investigating the spaces of treatment as well as the figurative representations of those sites, I posit a new model for understanding the relationship between writing and disease—a relationship defined by what I call "tubercular capital."

The concept of "tubercular capital" that I describe derives most directly from the work of Pierre Bourdieu and his decades-long effort to understand the mechanisms of cultural capital. Bourdieu categorizes how, in various fields of production, different producers and players consecrate a work as possessing value. The value of that work of art takes into account the circumstances of its material production and those of its symbolic production. Not only is it important which materials the object comprises (e.g., gold, hours of labor) but also how prestige is bestowed on the object (e.g., who promotes the art, buys the art, names the art).[55]

One strength of Bourdieu's project for disciplines across the humanities and social sciences is that it identifies the value-driven superstructure that governs daily decision making and the ascription of high cultural value. The question this project concerns itself with is just how tuberculosis comes to feature in the production of value, both symbolic and economic, in the life and work of the ailing Jewish writer. How does a diagnosis grow or diminish an author's reputation? How might a public episode of coughing generate attention and fund-raising on behalf of the writer? And how would invoking the names of other tubercular Jewish figures or tuberculosis-themed texts structure genealogies of illness resonant with symbolic capital? While the Hebrew poet Raḥel certainly did not become wealthy as a result of her diagnosis, she generated literary capital through the public display of her ailing body, through the creation of her sickroom as a salon, and through the coded exploration of illness in her poetry. Posthumously, the symbolic value generated by her illness translated into what can only be described as the business of Raḥel tourism extant in Israel today.[56]

Of special concern will also be how various philanthropies, health institutions, editors, and audiences responded to the needs of tubercular writers, generating support networks that augmented both the finances of these figures and their literary exposure. How was tuberculosis mobilized to elicit the sympathetic support of a reading audience? How was the tubercular body figured in a manner that would raise funds as well as awareness of the plight of the ailing patient-writer? Was there a perceptible value in publicly acknowledging one's disease over and against the social stigma with which a contagious illness might otherwise be met? These questions would prove particularly important to the Yiddish writers of the Jewish Consumptives' Relief Society (JCRS) in Denver, Colorado. There, the Yiddish poet Yehoash would depart on a fund-raising tour while visibly ill to raise funds for the JCRS sanatorium as well as his fellow patient-writers. Yehoash's example is just one among others in this study that asserts the prominence of the physiological experience of a patient in determining a writer's reputation and legacy.

Alongside the literary-historical consequences of tuberculosis, this study also focuses attention on the appearance and affect of the disease in select texts by the ailing writers. How do the symptoms or environmental conditions of tuberculosis translate into the stylistic choices of the ailing author? Why is tuberculosis such a potent literary subject for the sick author? And how do tubercular authors fictionalize or aestheticize their own suffering? These questions prove vital when we consider what it means for a tubercular Sholem Aleichem to write a Yiddish text that, in his words, includes scenes that are "a bit pale, at times a bit short, and even at times a bit weak."[57] Similarly, when the Hebrew modernist David Vogel looks to tuberculosis as an intertextual key for engaging German modernism, we are prompted to reconsider the existence of tuberculosis as a vector of literary capital—one that is both internal and external to the textual record of the consumptive writer.

Attending to these tubercular topoi also draws us into the anxious world of the Jewish writer in the first decades of the twentieth century, where tubercular capital exposes a set of cultural anxieties germane to the Jewish writer across the Hebrew and Yiddish literary landscape. The differences between select writers' personal stories, creative output, and treatment histories are admittedly substantial and are discussed in detail. Yet these writers are united in experiencing tuberculosis as an illness of specific concern to their identities as modern Jewish writers. In addition to the range of symbolic possibilities attending tuberculosis, these writers demonstrate how the disease came to manage a concern for the stability of their chosen literary traditions. What would a diagnosis of tuberculosis mean, they each ask in turn, not simply for the patient but for Yiddish and Hebrew literature? How might the disease come to metaphorize the health and stability of a readership, literary market, or the flexibility of Hebrew and Yiddish as literary languages? The tubercular capital of the Yiddish and Hebrew writer was not only a question of personal concern to the authors and poets of this study. It also bore with it broad consequences for the construction and critique of Jewish literature well into the twentieth century.

The concept of "tubercular capital" urges readers to look beyond grand narratives of war and privation as the structuring agents of modern Jewish literature and cultural history. Instead, the concept redirects our attention to the role played by a "network" of medical professionals and institutions, including health officials, doctors, sanatoria, and hospitals, in determining the art and arc of modern Hebrew and Yiddish writing.[58] It further reveals how authors, readers, and literary critics became involved in and drew on oftentimes competing medico-cultural discourses circulating in their midst. Finally, "tubercular capital" serves as a methodological intervention into the study of literature and disease that will allow us to rethink and replot the relationship between writer and ailment, between literary reputation and medical institution, even between Romantic notions of feverish creativity and the historical conditions of cultural production. It does so by sidelining efforts to remove discussions about the author's body and physical self from close readings. Rather, it insists on reading the pathological experience of disease as professionally, financially, and literarily consequential. The following study thereby affirms the importance of the body in a writer's "self-fashioning" both within and by means of his or her literary output.[59] To be sure, I am not arguing that every text by a tubercular writer is an extended meditation on disease, nor, for that matter, am I saying that every text about tuberculosis is a reflection of an author's personal struggle with illness. Yet, as the examples of the Yiddish and Hebrew writers under discussion demonstrate, illness has the capacity to structure a literary conversation, to direct the career of an ailing writer, to reveal a set of cultural anxieties, and to condition a set of literary choices. To ignore the biographical within the literary output of these tubercular writers is at best to underestimate and at worst to efface the aesthetic potential of illness. Instead, this study insistently historicizes the work of these tubercular authors with recourse to the physiological experiences girding their creation and the pathological (sub)texts of their writing.

Modern Jewish Writing and the Literary Capital of Tuberculosis

Tuberculosis was more than a multivalent cultural symbol. It was a catalyst of literary opportunity. It was a biographical feature to be made public, performed, and mobilized. And it launched the careers and grew the reputations of those Yiddish and Hebrew writers who sought not to hide their contagious disease but to render it an integral part of their literary self-fashioning and creative oeuvre. It would further come to negotiate various anxieties surrounding the development of Yiddish and Hebrew as languages of cultural expression. We must, accordingly, recuperate tuberculosis as a critical variable in the history of modern Jewish writing.

Following this Introduction, we turn our attention in Chapter 1 to Sholem Aleichem, one of the three classic Yiddish writers. Today, Sholem Aleichem is perhaps most famous as the author whose work inspired the play and movie *Fiddler on the Roof.* Yet decades before Sheldon Harnick penned the earworm "If I Were a Rich Man," Sholem Aleichem was already the object of international attention—albeit far from rich himself. After being diagnosed with tuberculosis in 1908, a global campaign was initiated to help the destitute writer finance his travels to take the cure in Nervi, Italy. As a result of "the jubilee," as the fund-raising campaign was known, Sholem Aleichem's reputation ballooned, his assets stabilized, and he used his literature to develop a fictional persona whose health was made dependent on the reading practices of his audience. Analyzing news reports, promotional material, and Sholem Aleichem's personal correspondence makes it clear how tuberculosis came to mediate the relationship between author, reader, and publisher. This is especially important in the short story that Sholem Aleichem wrote to be read at jubilee celebrations around the world, "Shmuel Shmelkes and His Jubilee." The story offers its own fictionalized account of Sholem Aleichem's illness as well as an argument for tubercular capital.

Sholem Aleichem's personal history also begins to sketch out a concern for the nature of Jewish charitable giving that occupies each of the subsequent chapters. The tubercular Jewish writer often sought financial aid from a variety of sources and individuals. In other cases, the ailing writer specifically dismissed such charitable gestures. Yet how the question of money was mobilized, by whom and for whom, will be of immediate concern and literary consequence. To understand the nature of tubercular capital is to attend to the variety of financial and other forms of support offered conditionally or otherwise to the sick writer.

Chapter 2 leaves behind the Italian coast as well as the various German and Swiss health resorts where Sholem Aleichem spent years recovering.

Turning away from Europe, I look to Palestine, where the much-adored Hebrew poet known as Raḥel suffered from tuberculosis throughout the 1920s. With the financial and artistic support of her friends and editors, the poet transformed her sickroom into a veritable salon of literary exchange and creativity. Reading Raḥel's correspondence, poetry, and the memoiristic accounts published by her visitors, this chapter traces how Raḥel's Tel Aviv sickroom became the center of her public self-fashioning as an ailing female poet. Here I claim that we can productively read and interpret Raḥel's experience of illness through the imperial context of the gendered Victorian sickroom. I further argue that Raḥel's sickroom serves as the key for interpreting the link between her poetics of space, simplicity (*pashtut*), and the spread (*hitpashtut*) of disease. Tuberculosis provides the context for adjudicating not only the poet's public self-fashioning but also her aesthetic agenda and the topoi of tuberculosis and contagiousness that subtend her poetry.

Crossing the Atlantic, Chapter 3 investigates the literary scene of the JCRS, a sanatorium for indigent Jews in Colorado. There, a cohort of Yiddish tubercular writers would engage in a reciprocal relationship with the institution, becoming the public faces of the sanatorium and, in turn, being offered new venues to see their work published and translated. These writers include the lyric poet and Bible translator Yehoash, the epic poet and dramatist H. Leivick, and the prose stylist Shea Tenenbaum. If Sholem Aleichem and Raḥel were singular personalities, this chapter addresses the phenomenon of a tubercular Yiddish literary tradition. This tubercular literary genealogy was born out of and nurtured in the Denver hospital, and it would go on to be referenced by a variety of ailing writers beyond the walls of the institution.

From Colorado, Chapter 4 returns to central Europe and to another sanatorium for indigent Jews. Unlike the JCRS, this hospital built in the South Tyrolean town of Merano would not function as an ersatz writers' colony. Still, it would foster the creative energies of its literary clients. The Hebrew modernist David Vogel, for example, sought rest for his infected lungs in the winters of 1925 and 1926. His experiences influenced his first novella, *In the Sanatorium* (1927), which brought him into intertextual dialogue with the work of Arthur Schnitzler and Thomas Mann. Engaging these German-language texts, Vogel's Hebrew novella challenges precisely the possibility of such a Hebrew-German literary conversation. Vogel deploys illness as a hermeneutic key, conveying the impossibility of the Hebrew-German conversation through a series of interlingual puns, wordplays, and jokes concerning tuberculosis. In this chapter, rather than examine the literary and cultural concerns of the Jewish readership writ large, I focus my attention on Vogel's own perspective on the literary health of his chosen Hebrew milieu.

The Epilogue returns to Vogel as he makes his way from South Tyrol to France, where he would write a fictionalized chronicle of a painter who, like himself, would be imprisoned in internment camps following the outbreak of World War II. Once again, Vogel mobilizes the metaphors of tuberculosis to examine the limitations of Jewish life and creativity in a European context. Unlike *In the Sanatorium*, however, this final text would be written in Yiddish. The Epilogue to this study reads Vogel's late work alongside the writing of Aharon Appelfeld to investigate how tubercular capital has been mobilized in post-Holocaust Israeli literature. My reading of Appelfeld's work further considers the shifting metaphors of tuberculosis that arise in the wake of the introduction of antibiotic treatments in the 1950s. Appelfeld, in fact, is the only writer examined at length in this monograph who did not suffer from tuberculosis himself.

From a historical reconstruction of Sholem Aleichem's jubilee to a close reading of Vogel's first novella to a review of the tubercular topos across Appelfeld's oeuvre, this study demonstrates the heterogeneous reach of tubercular capital. Across the book, tuberculosis serves as both a historical context for the production of art and a multivalent literary theme and subject. As such, the case studies chosen in this book are by no means exhaustive or uniform. Indeed, there are numerous other ailing Jewish writers whose illness narratives are deserving of examination. Rather, the cases explored here serve to suggest the flexibility of tubercular capital to condition and reveal a number of different historical networks, literary systems, and aesthetic choices. Taken together, the chapters illustrate the diversity of methodological implications of tubercular capital, repeatedly prompting readers to reconsider and remap the relationship of illness and creative cultural production. Tubercular capital emerges across this manuscript as a dynamic hermeneutic tool that not only accommodates difference but is enriched by it.

The Paradox of Tubercular Capital

Before concluding this Introduction, it bears repeating that the intention of this research is not to validate notions of consumptive beauty or quiet death. Similarly, these four case studies in tubercular Jewish writing are not an extended exercise in retrospective schadenfreude, as the list of sick authors and poets seems to grow with each chapter. Tuberculosis, as indicated earlier, is nothing if not a devastating disease. During the lifetime of the majority of writers under discussion in this work, it was also medically incurable. The disease often precipitated pain, poverty, and the separation of family members. It cut short many lives and inflicted many with years of painful treatment. It similarly stigmatized patients who were no longer welcome to stay in their homes or among family for fear of contagion. In the case of the Yiddish author Daniel Charney, it even prevented him from entering New York alongside other would-be immigrants during his first attempt to enter the United States in 1925.[60]

Tuberculosis was and remains a disease that should neither be glorified nor underestimated. Rather than romanticize the illness, I examine the role played by tuberculosis in the life and writing of a host of Yiddish and Hebrew authors and poets. It is a role that, at times, resulted in positive outcomes. But it would be callous not to assert that patients likely would have preferred not to have fallen ill in the first place. While Peretz's protagonist perhaps unwittingly betrays a strategic understanding of tubercular capital when he asserts, "Let it be a consumption," he most probably did not want to experience tubercular symptoms firsthand. It would be similarly shortsighted not to hope that there might have been another way for literary opportunity to accrue to writers regardless of their physical condition.

The work of anthropologist Didier Fassin is particularly helpful in thinking through the politics and moral questions raised by this dilemma. In his recent investigations into the "politics of life," Fassin examines multiple cases in which disease is mobilized as a political resource, lending what he calls "biolegitimacy" to a suffering patient. For example, he presents the example of a Kenyan man who had lived for years in France and Germany illegally. He "finally received his documents," notes Fassin, "when he was discovered to be suffering from AIDS."[61] Fassin elsewhere writes of another AIDS patient living in South Africa whose diseased status functioned as a "social resource." "The disability grant he received from the state as a right because of his illness," writes Fassin, "gave him for the first time the opportunity to have a decent and independent existence."[62] These examples allow Fassin to analyze what meaning and value various governments assign to the lives of individuals under different circumstances. To that end, Fassin also investigates cases in which disease releases convicted criminals from serving a full sentence, such as those of Augusto Pinochet or Maurice Papon. He also examines the cases of various asylum seekers who "express despair when told that their case is not serious enough to be considered relevant with respect to the humanitarian clause."[63] For Fassin, the question of disease is not merely one of personal suffering but also one resonant with ethical implications for immigrants, patients, and government institutions.

Of course, Fassin concerns himself with patients who live decades after the Yiddish and Hebrew writers mentioned here sought treatment for acute pulmonary tuberculosis. Nevertheless, his work reminds us to be alert to the systems of power at play in the present literary-historical inquiry. The Yiddish and Hebrew writers under examination garnered support when they were in a most desperate state. They received help from philanthropies when they could no longer rely on their own resources for financial or medical support. The story this book tells may at times seem triumphant in its description of how a disease benefited a patient, how a readership rallied around an ailing writer, or how a stay at a sanatorium offered the patient-writer new literary vistas. Yet, at the same time, we must remember to keep in mind the troubling paradox of tubercular capital.

CHAPTER 1

IN THE HANDS OF EVERY READER

Sholem Aleichem's Tubercular Jubilee

A cough is your card; a hemorrhage a letter of credit.

—O. Henry[1]

On an April evening in 1914, an enthusiastic crowd welcomed the Yiddish writer Solomon Rabinovitsh to Warsaw's Elysium Theater. Today, Rabinovitsh is best remembered as the author whose work would inspire *Fiddler on the Roof.* At the time, he was known to a legion of fans as the comedic writer and satirist Sholem Aleichem—a Yiddish "Mr. How-Do-You-Do." Following a rousing public reading, the literary star was met with thunderous applause. His presence in Poland had been sorely missed. He had not stepped foot in the country in nearly six years, having spent over half a decade traveling across central and southern Europe seeking "the cure" for pulmonary tuberculosis. During that period, he rested and recuperated at health resorts on the Italian coast, at *Kurorte* across the German Black Forest, and at various sanatoria and hospitals throughout Switzerland. The performance that April reassured his audience that, despite the time away, he had not lost his way with words. It was just the opposite. His experience of illness seemed only to have augmented his talents. As the Yiddish writer I. L. Peretz remarked to his friend Gershn Levin, "The disease has been of good use to him; he has become more popular and he reads better" (*Di krankhayt iz im zeyer tsu nits gekumen; er iz gevorn populerer un er leyent beser*).[2]

Peretz's counterintuitive words would certainly have made an impression on Levin, who, while moonlighting as a Yiddish writer, made his living as a physician. He was well acquainted with the high rates of tuberculosis across Poland and in cities such as Warsaw. In the first decades of the twentieth century, tuberculosis was prevalent in Poland and would remain so well into the 1930s.[3] Levin himself would go on to produce pamphlets for the Jewish public health organization TOZ, joining a chorus of professional voices and community activists working to prevent the spread of tuberculosis.[4] Despite his best intentions, Levin could only implore patients to practice good hygiene and take cautions against a disease that rendered its victims pale, enfeebled, and coughing up blood. Rabinovitsh himself had been one such victim when he collapsed and began to spit up blood in the summer of 1908, following a public reading in the Belorussian town of Baranovitsh.[5]

Considering the debilitating symptoms of the disease as well as the years Rabinovitsh had spent in search of a cure, Peretz's words may seem all the more confounding if not discomfiting. Yet Peretz was not wrong. In fact, tuberculosis would be of decidedly "good use" to the author. Indeed, the disease set into motion a series of reader responses, public performances, and literary decisions that would garner the writer international renown and financial security. At the same time, public discussion of his disease revealed a host of cultural anxieties then motivating his Jewish literary support network. Of particular importance for the present study is an account of the 1908 celebrations held worldwide to mark the twenty-fifth anniversary of Rabinovitsh's entrance as "Sholem Aleichem" onto the Yiddish literary stage—what would come to be known as "The Jubilee." The celebrations that were organized and the public discussions that ensued proved integral in cementing the popular and critical legacies of the ailing literary persona. They further invited his readers to become active partners in his biological health and literary production. Rabinovitsh's reputation, finances, and literary choices in the final decade of his life would be tied to the tubercular capital of his fictional alter ego.

Baranovitsh, 1908

When Rabinovitsh arrived in Baranovitsh in the summer of 1908 ready to perform as Sholem Aleichem, he did so as a well-established writer. For nearly three decades, he had been catering to and challenging his readers with strident monologues, humorous short stories, and moralistic novels. He had also spent those years establishing a rapport with the audience that was mediated by his literary avatar. In 1883, Rabinovitsh had published the short story "The Elections" under the byline "Sholem Aleichem"—a Yiddish salutation that may be translated as "Peace be upon you" or, more colloquially, "How do you do?"[6] To the greeting "Sholem-aleichem," a Yiddish speaker responds, "Aleichem-sholem." Choosing this name had the clever effect of eliciting a figurative call and response between author and reader, establishing a relationship between the two parties that was direct and participatory. As Rabinovitsh's work gained in prominence, his legal surname faded into the background and the distance between author and pen name was functionally erased. Everywhere Rabinovitsh went, it was Sholem Aleichem who greeted his fans.

Unfortunately, Rabinovitsh did not keep good track of his finances. Although writing under a famous name, Rabinovitsh was in a desperate financial state. He had made a series of poor business decisions that saw him lose his wife's family's fortune on the Kiev stock exchange—not once, but twice; that saw him sell away the copyrights to his work; and that saw him make several regretful deals during a trip to America that had forced him back to Europe empty-handed. So, in the summer of 1908, Rabinovitsh set out as Sholem Aleichem on a reading tour of the Pale of Settlement.

Known for being an exceptional public reader, he likely hoped to attract large audiences and correspondingly large profits.[7] The archival record attests to the logic of such hopes. On launching this tour, local towns and literary societies across the Russian Empire as well as eastern and east-central Europe sent letters to Sholem Aleichem, eagerly inviting him to read for them. The patients of the Otwock Sanatorium in Poland, for example, begged him to visit.[8] Calling on the salvific power of literature, they added that his performance would surely cure their illness![9] According to newspaper reports, Sholem Aleichem was greeted with similar enthusiasm wherever he went: crowds thronged around his train at the depot;[10] his public readings quickly sold out;[11] and every night brought new performances in new places, with breaks few and far between.[12]

On July 26 [August 8], 1908, Rabinovitsh arrived in Baranovitsh.[13] Taking the stage, he read before a packed house. People in the audience had traveled from far and wide to attend the performance.[14] Some claimed that the audience reached nearly one thousand guests, even including a local non-Jewish nobleman.[15] One audience member, a townsman named Yankev Tsernikhov, later recalled that the reading was so successful that it had felt as if an earthquake had struck the theater.[16] Tsernikhov also recalled that although the writer had looked happy and full of life, he had occasionally coughed during the performance, held his chest, and looked rather pale.

Tsernikhov's observations were on point. Although the consummate performer, Sholem Aleichem could not hide his worsening symptoms. After the reading ended, Rabinovitsh returned to his hotel where he began to cough more violently. His temperature rose and he had his first episode of hemoptysis.[17] A local doctor arrived and managed to stop the hemorrhage. Soon, a committee of young Baranovitsh men and women formed to keep constant watch over their beloved literary icon; some swatted flies from his head, and others read to him for hours on end.[18] After several days, the author's condition still had not improved and a doctor from Vilna was summoned.[19] The diagnosis was pulmonary tuberculosis.[20] As was customary in the late nineteenth and early twentieth centuries, the patient was advised to recuperate in a warmer climate. Palestine was suggested and the coast of Italy ultimately chosen.[21] The warm, southern European temperatures and the fresh air of coastal living were thought to ease the patient's discomfort if not necessarily cure him. Under the byline Sholem Aleichem, the writer announced to the Yiddish press that the "doctors say that . . . I must go to 'where the citrons blossom.'"[22] As his readers understood, he was heading toward the region that produced the *esroygim* (modern Hebrew: *etrogim*), the yellow citron used for ritual purposes every fall during the Jewish holiday of *Sukkes*. But beyond the agricultural reference, he also echoed here the classic words from Goethe's *Wilhelm Meister's Apprenticeship* as Sholem Aleichem himself embarked on a journey of self-realization—one with the explicit goal of physical recuperation and healing.[23]

A Plan Is Hatched, 1908

But how was the nearly penniless author to pay for his own treatment? He had embarked on the reading tour precisely because he did not have the funds to support himself and his growing family. After some two months on the road, he still did not have the means to pay for an extended convalescence. Letters from this period underscore just how desperate his financial situation was. Even while lying ill in Baranovitsh, he wrote furiously to friends, plaintively begging for help to remedy his financial circumstances.[24]

Fortunately, like many of the tubercular Jewish writers examined in this study, Rabinovitsh was not without his supporters. His longtime friend Moshe Weizmann, a Geneva-based physician, proposed a solution.[25] Soon after hearing that the writer had fallen ill, Weizmann suggested celebrating the twenty-fifth anniversary of Sholem Aleichem's appearance on the Yiddish literary scene. Such a jubilee—in Yiddish, *yubiley*, *yoyvl*, or *yubileum*—would not have been foreign to Rabinovitsh's Jewish or east European audience. Fans and publicists alike trafficked in jubilees, eager for opportunities to boast of the importance of their favorite writers as well as eager to demonstrate the devotion of their readership. Public readings were organized, reflective articles were written, and writers were praised both in person and in print across the globe. Earlier jubilees, for example, had been organized to mark the birthdays of major writers, such as Sholem Aleichem's literary predecessor—Mendele Mocher Sforim (pen name of Sholem Yankev Abramovitsh).[26] In 1906, Sholem Aleichem himself had written to the Yiddish press to agitate for larger celebrations to mark Mendele's seventieth birthday and fifty years of his literary activity.[27] In 1908 and 1909, despite protests of the tsar, a jubilee celebration was also planned and celebrated in honor of Leo Tolstoy's eightieth birthday. It was an event celebrated by Yiddish and Hebrew writers from Vilna to New York.

Yet while the phenomenon of the jubilee was legible to the Jewish audience, Weizmann charged Sholem Aleichem's jubilee with an additional task. The jubilee would not simply celebrate the silver anniversary of Sholem Aleichem's literary activity but would double as a fund-raising event.[28] The formal date of the celebration was set for a Saturday that October known as the "Sabbath of Creation" (*Shabes breyshis*).[29] During the prayer services that Saturday, Jews around the world were set to read a portion from the Torah that included the opening chapters of Genesis (*Breyshis*). As would have been obvious to Sholem Aleichem's readers, *Shabes breyshis* was chosen for its rhetorical punch. As the message maintained, the life and health of Sholem Aleichem was just as important as the creation of the world.

Weizmann announced his plan in two public letters sent to Yiddish newspapers around the world.[30] The letters alert us to the stakes of the jubilee as well as to the ability of Sholem Aleichem to intervene on Rabinovitsh's behalf. Weizmann opens the first letter as follows:

> The 11th of October will be exactly twenty-five years since *Sh. N. Rabinovitsh (Sholem Aleichem)* appeared in Yiddish literature. I don't know whether Yiddish society is preparing to celebrate this jubilee. I know, though, that *Sholem Aleichem* is now seriously sick (in Baranovitsh) and he must travel to warmer lands to recuperate.
>
> *Dem 11-tn oktober hayor vert punkt finf un tsvantsik yor zayt* Sh. N. Rabinovits (Sholem-Aleykhem) *iz aroysgetreten in der yidisher literatur. Ikh veys nit, tsi di yidishe gezelshaft greyt zikh fayren dem dozikn yoyvel. Ikh veys ober, az itst ligt* Sholem-Aleykhem *ernst krank (in Baranovits), un er muz opforen in di varime lender zikh kuriren.*[31]

Weizmann serves his readers three points of fact: First, it is Sholem Aleichem's twenty-fifth anniversary as a Yiddish writer; second, he is sick; and third, he must seek care in warmer climates. He follows this list of facts with a description of the impoverished state of the writer's family. Lest he leave any doubt about his intentions, Weizmann concludes the letter with an extended paragraph demanding that material help be provided quickly and efficiently. In the second letter, Weizmann again reiterates the importance of Sholem Aleichem for the Jewish readership. He was a writer able "to reach the greatness of our pure, clear folk-humor [and] the depth of deepest tragedy of the true, Jewish laughter, which sparkles through tears."[32]

Weizmann's letters do more than repeat the by-now standard refrain that Sholem Aleichem was a writer who supported his readers as they laughed through their tears.[33] They also alert us to the tension between author and persona that subtends nearly all of the jubilee texts, no less the majority of Sholem Aleichem criticism. "The 11th of October," writes Weizmann, "will be exactly twenty-five years since Sh. N. Rabinovitsh (Sholem Aleichem) appeared in Yiddish literature. "Sholem Aleichem," he continues, "is now seriously sick."[34] As these two sentences demonstrate, Rabinovitsh's name cannot stand alone without its parenthetical aside. Regarding the power of an artist's name, Pierre Bourdieu writes:

> For the author, the critic, the art dealer, the publisher or the theatre manager, the only legitimate accumulation consists in making a *name* for oneself, a known recognized *name*, a capital of consecration implying a power to consecrate objects (with a trademark or signature) or persons (through publication, exhibition, etc.) and therefore to give value, and to appropriate the profits of this operation.[35]

As Weizmann's letter indicates, Rabinovitsh's name would not carry the same symbolic capital as his persona nor could it catalyze an international response among readers.

The difficulty of distinguishing between Rabinovitsh and Sholem Aleichem has, by now, been treated by multiple scholars. Like Mark Twain (Samuel Langhorne Clemens) and George Eliot (Mary Anne Evans), Sholem Aleichem appears to be the code by which Rabinovitsh became famous. Yet Rabinovitsh himself cautioned against such an elision. As Dan Miron has shown, it has been all too easy for the majority of readers and critics to deflate the distance between the historical author and the literary actor.[36] The figure of "Sholem Aleichem," as Miron argues, must be treated as a "presence." More than a "character-narrator," the figure occupies a variety of roles (narrator, author, character) in Rabinovitsh's oeuvre and in doing so unifies a diverse collection of texts by a single author. In Miron's words, Sholem Aleichem "was actually meant to be taken as a comically mysterious being with fantastic mobility, who is everywhere and nowhere in particular."[37]

Miron's canonical interpretation of Sholem Aleichem as a "presence" has not met without critique.[38] But Weizmann's letter and the rhetoric of the jubilee push the discussion in another direction. The question that remains is, what did the persona of Sholem Aleichem do *for* and *to* Rabinovitsh when the latter fell ill? In other words, who was sick? And how did tuberculosis renegotiate the relationship between the writer, his fictional alter ego, and the reading public? The persona-author debate, as it were, must be historicized—or, more accurately, pathologized.

After all, in the wake of Rabinovitsh's coughing fit in Baranovitsh, it would not have been far-fetched to assume that attention would be directed at the living, breathing, bleeding author himself. Yet Sholem Aleichem did not recede from view. As Weizmann's letters make clear, Sholem Aleichem was placed front and center. After his parenthetical aside "(Sholem Aleichem)," all references to Rabinovitsh fall away and Weizmann accords the persona all the biographical features and authorial functions that belong to Rabinovitsh. It is not *Rabinovitsh* but *Sholem Aleichem* who is sick and in need of support. As in many articles advertising or reporting on jubilee events, Rabinovitsh's name appears only to be replaced by Sholem Aleichem.[39] Every switch made from Rabinovitsh to Sholem Aleichem points back to the fact that Rabinovitsh's life has become dependent on the health of his literary figure and the ability of *Sholem Aleichem* to gain attention. Phrased differently, the physiological reality of Rabinovitsh becomes rooted in the disease of his persona. Accordingly, in the remainder of the chapter, I refer to the author as Sholem Aleichem rather than as Rabinovitsh. It is a move that historicizes the persona as a composite of biological experience, literary fiction, and audience response.

The Jubilee Goes Viral

For Yiddish and Hebrew readers, however, there was much more at stake in the health of Sholem Aleichem than merely his own physical well-being. At stake was the health of the entire Jewish reading public. Sholem Aleichem was not just *any* folk writer but, according to many, *the* greatest Yiddish *folksshrayber*. It was, in fact, an identity that Sholem Aleichem had been crafting for himself since the 1880s. New to the Yiddish publishing scene, the author took pains to establish himself as an arbiter of what constituted good and moral literature for the masses. In 1888, Sholem Aleichem had also assumed a paternalistic mantle to publicly excoriate the beloved Yiddish writer Shomer (pen name of Nokhem Meyer Shaykevitch).[40] That same year, he founded *Di yidishe folks-bibliotek*. Although the title bespoke a relationship with the masses, the address was aspirational.[41] The anthology sought to print high-quality Yiddish literature, the likes of which did not necessarily reflect the tastes of the uneducated Yiddish reader.

Yet, by 1908, the Yiddish reading audience had grown, daily Yiddish newspapers had appeared across eastern Europe, and Sholem Aleichem had become a widely serialized author. In short, the Yiddish writer had evolved from someone who sought to speak to the masses into a writer whom the masses agreed spoke for them. In response to Weizmann's call, dozens of writers—both amateur and professional—began to publish short pieces that articulated Sholem Aleichem's importance for the Jewish reading public. In the words of one supporter, Sholem Aleichem writes "*from* the *people*, *for* the people" (*fun* folk, *farn* folk).[42] According to a second, "Sholem Aleichem lives *with* us and *in* us."[43] And in the Bourdieusian words of a third, "[His] name alone is so Yiddish, so *heymish*."[44] Sholem Aleichem is repeatedly admired for being one of the few writers who reaches all levels of society, all classes, and people of all educational backgrounds. At a time of great upheaval in the history of Russian Jewry—in the wake of Bloody Sunday, during a period of mass migration of Russian Jewry to the United States, and on the heels of the Czernowitz language conference in which Hebrew and Yiddish were pitted against each other—Sholem Aleichem was recognized as a unifying force of global Jewish culture. As a fourth writer explained, "Sholem-Aleykhem is *ours*. He belongs to us with his lively language, with his Jewish humor, with his poverty and *with his sickness*."[45]

"With his sickness"—these three words are the hermeneutic key to the scores of articles that were published in the wake of Weizmann's call. These words alert us to the fact that the jubilee functioned not only as a celebration of Sholem Aleichem's literary activity and not only as a fund-raising event for the ailing author but as an occasion to harness the author's illness to a cultural agenda of self-censure. Sholem Aleichem's readers blamed themselves for the author's conditions, adding that it was now up to them to support him. Writing in the Warsaw daily *Haynt*, Gershn Levin demanded that every town form its own jubilee committee to collect money on the writer's behalf. To do so, he explained using language common to the jubilee, was to pay off a "holy debt" (*a heyliker khov*).[46]

This language of obligation and responsibility quickly slipped into a discourse of blame as the writer's disease came to signify an affront to national pride. At the turn of the twentieth century, many Russian-Jewish and Polish-Jewish reformers sought to "modernize" their communities through public health interventions. Efforts such as advocating for hygiene education and medical reform were public attempts to demonstrate a will toward modernization.[47] As historian Lisa Rae Epstein has argued, these activists were motivated "both by altruistic and self-serving goals to improve the health of Jews but also to improve their image and status within modern society, in order to render them worthy of acceptance as equals in the eyes of other peoples."[48] Large-scale medico-philanthropic efforts by Russian Jewry, such as the building of hospitals, were often initiated with the hope not simply of improving the health of the Jewish body politic but also of enhancing its public image.[49]

Sholem Aleichem's supporters were similarly aware of the communal and cultural-political stakes of supporting their author. Dovid Pinski, for example, used his position as the head of the Sholem Aleichem Jubilee Committee of New York City to rage against the "slave psychology" of the Jewish readership. He scolded readers of the communist *Arbeter* newspaper for not recognizing their great writers until tragedy struck. "Would [Sholem Aleichem] have been remembered," Pinski asks, "had he not become sick and did not need help?"[50] Here, Pinski invokes the phenomenon of tubercular capital with clear incredulousness. Echoing his words one month later, an anonymous author in Vilna's Hebrew *Hed ha-zeman* phrased the situation in equally blunt if frustrated terms: "In order to merit a jubilee . . . Sholem Aleichem had to become sick with a dangerous illness [*maḥalah mesukanah*]."[51] His colleague agreed, commenting that "the nation of Israel honors its writers with a different present: the disease of tuberculosis."[52]

Whether in New York or Vilna, many authors broached the jubilee from the same position of embarrassment. Sholem Aleichem, they acknowledged, had led a literary life in which the writer had relinquished himself of not only his creativity and talent but also his health and blood.[53] Making matters worse, as many writers noted, was that the situation made clear how the Jewish reading public differed from their Polish and Russian neighbors. Here, they differed from Polish readers, who honored their Nobel prize–winning author Henryk Sienkiewicz with accolades, praise, and, on the occasion of his silver jubilee, a large property.[54] And here, they differed wildly from Tolstoy's fans, who continued to rally around the Russian master even when banned from doing so by the tsar. Recall that just as Sholem Aleichem fell ill, Tolstoy was celebrating his eightieth birthday.[55] The Yiddish and Hebrew presses printed numerous briefs on Tolstoy's health along with countless articles on the jubilee, the art of the Russian master's writing, his ideology, and his importance for humanity at large.[56] These articles often appeared in the same editions as those announcing Sholem Aleichem's jubilee—sometimes even on the same page.[57]

Sholem Aleichem's admirers were also keenly aware that, like Sienkiewicz's readers, Tolstoy's fans had bestowed gifts on the already wealthy landowner. They offered him precisely the material recognition that Sholem Aleichem so desperately lacked and that Tolstoy, arguably, did not need.[58] It was a situation that was nothing if not scandalous.[59] However, according to many, it was a function of the culture of the Jewish readership. It was a result, simply put, of writing for Jews. The Yiddish writer Sh. Frug declared that after twenty-five years of welcoming readers to laugh, Sholem Aleichem had manifested the "true, authentically-Jewish red laughter [*royter gelekhter*]"—laughter expressed through a bloody hemorrhage.[60] "I am convinced," wrote Hillel Zeitlin in a Warsaw Yiddish daily, "that should geniuses the likes of Shakespeare or Goethe appear among us Jews, then they too would be spitting blood somewhere in Baranovitsh."[61]

The importance of this statement is not whether or not Zeitlin knew that Goethe had, in fact, fallen ill from consumption or that others would one day interpret the illness as coterminous with creativity.[62] The equation of genius and tuberculosis—a link that would have been readily available to Zeitlin's readers—is utterly absent from Zeitlin's admonition. Similarly, this was not the inspirational, ennobling consumption that had taken John Keats or Semyon Nadson from the world nor the disease that had left in its wake scores of languishing female beauties.[63] Rather, Zeitlin's words communicate a censorious message: Sholem Aleichem's tuberculosis was caused by his unsupportive and defective readers. His audience had reduced him, as well as others before him, into a pool of bloody laughter. Here is where tuberculosis draws a community of readers into the life of its leading author. Here is where the cultural understanding of disease is invoked to (re)train an audience in how best to read and relate to an author. And here is where tuberculosis comes to stand as the symbol of all that was wrong with the cultural practices, expectations, and relations of the Jewish literary community.

The Literary Health of Sholem Aleichem

To be clear, the actual cause of Sholem Aleichem's disease—the etiology of tuberculosis—was widely known by 1908 and would have been available to the Yiddish and Hebrew reader. Robert Koch had isolated the tubercle bacillus more than twenty years earlier in 1882.[64] Newspaper articles detailing innovations in the treatment of the disease even appeared in the same editions as announcements for Sholem Aleichem's jubilee.[65] Yet the cause of Sholem Aleichem's illness would not be described in organic terms alone. Rather, as we have seen, there emerges in the jubilee literature a discourse of blame where the fictionality of Sholem Aleichem merges with the medico-historical reality of Rabinovitsh and where the Jewish reader becomes the vector of disease. It was a discourse, moreover, in which Sholem Aleichem would take an active role. Never one to stay quiet, the persona became an instrumental force in the fund-raising efforts on the writer's behalf. And he mobilized his tubercular capital through the most immediate means available to him: creative writing. Shortly after arriving in Nervi, Italy, from Baranovitsh, he penned a short story titled "Shmuel Shmelkes and His Jubilee" (Shmuel Shmelkes un zayn yubileum).[66] In it, Sholem Aleichem directly addresses the contagious relationship of author, text, and reader.

This would not be the first time that the theme of illness, no less tuberculosis, had manifested in his work. As early as 1901, Sholem Aleichem published a short story, "In Boyberik," which was shortly followed by the 1903 sketch "To the Hot Springs." Both pieces describe the adventures of a bourgeois family that spends the summer in Boyberik, a summertime resort outside Kiev. Populated by a mix of social climbers and consumptives, the fictional town was, in fact, based on the Kiev suburb of Boiarka. A summer destination for the Rabinovitsh family, Boiarka had been home to a free sanatorium for destitute consumptives since 1899.[67] These early texts would also set the stage for later works, such as 1909's "From the Riviera" and the 1911 novel *Marienbad.* In the former, Sholem Aleichem narrates the experiences of patients recuperating on the Italian coast. Despite the exorbitant cost of treatment, the patients stay because they believe that the warm air will help soothe their coughs.[68] The latter chronicles the antics of bourgeois Polish-Jewish men and women who jump from one European spa to another in search of a variety of affairs, suitors, and romantic dalliances all while purporting to be taking the cure.[69]

Echoing Russian and European literary tropes of his era, tuberculosis

Figure 3. Sholem Aleichem on a return visit to Nervi, Italy, 1913. Source: Beth Shalom Aleichem Archive. Reprinted with permission.

and the cure in Sholem Aleichem's oeuvre would signify a variety of social and physiological ailments. It was a disease of the shtetl and of the bourgeois social climbers, of would-be urban transplants and of holidaying Jewry.[70] But "Shmuel Shmelkes" would approach the subject more obliquely. Little more than a thinly veiled allegory, the story recounts the troubles facing a Yiddish writer on the eve of his twenty-fifth anniversary of literary activity. Rabinovitsh wrote the story to serve as Sholem Aleichem's literary stand-in at jubilee celebrations, where it would be read aloud and reprinted widely.[71] The story would also be the first of Sholem Aleichem's texts to be translated into multiple languages simultaneously; the text was printed in its entirety in multiple Yiddish newspapers, distributed as a booklet in Hebrew translation, and excerpted in the London Jewish community's *Jewish Chronicle*.[72] The Russian-Jewish historian Simon Dubnow also made plans to have it translated into Russian, although the plans were never realized.[73] While this may seem incidental, this study will show that, for many tubercular writers a diagnosis catalyzed a variety of opportunities that would transmit their work—as well as their sickly visages—around the globe in multiple languages. Tuberculosis, to use Pascale Casanova's phrase, would allow for the *littérisation* of the Yiddish and Hebrew writers, ushering them into a "world republic of letters" via translation.[74]

"Shmuel Shmelkes," not surprisingly, was also praised by jubilee committees in multiple languages around the world.[75] But the short story was, admittedly, not Sholem Aleichem's most refined work. Yitsḥak Dov Berkowitz, Rabinovitsh's son-in-law, secretary, and literary executor, described the story as "almost like the cry of a wounded, sick man," noting that the "satire came from the exhausted hand of an overly sharp Sholem Aleichem, pathetic and tragic."[76] Sholem Aleichem himself wavered in his opinion of the story. In one letter he declared that "it came out better than I thought."[77] In another, he questioned "whether it had really come out weak."[78]

Sholem Aleichem was correct on both accounts: The story was weak, but it was also a great success. The rhetorical weakness of the story, in fact, should be interpreted as a calculated decision on behalf of the author to train his audience to collapse the distinction between writer and text. Sholem Aleichem announces the pedagogical agenda of his work in the introduction to the text. Later, he would go on to insist that this introduction accompany each publication, a gesture that would ensure that the text would be "*read properly*."[79] Titled "Apologies from the Author," the introduction offers readers some guiding remarks, signed "Sholem Aleichem, October 25, 1908, Nervi, Italy."[80] Lest they miss these geographic and temporal cues, Sholem Aleichem explains that he is writing these words while taking the cure in Italy. He is, admittedly, sick, and he asks his readers' forgiveness—hence the "Apologies" in the title—should any of "the scenes come out at times a bit pale, at times a bit short, and even at times a bit weak."[81] In short, Sholem Aleichem apologizes that his text has assumed the same tubercular affect that he himself now brandishes. In doing so, he instructs his readers to conflate his persona, his disease, and the text at hand. Reading here demands that the audience observe the biographical and the physiological within the literary.

Sholem Aleichem also quickly adds a moral clause to the introduction. "There is nothing in the world that is so bad," he writes, "that some good can't come of it" (*nisht af der velt aza shlekhts, vos zol nit aroyskumen derfun keyn toyve*). Just as leeches are of use to a sick person, bees make honey, and Spanish fleas are good for an ulcer, so too can all negative situations generate something positive. This is a lesson, he explains, that he learned while recuperating in Baranovitsh.[82] During that period, the doctors forbade him from speaking, reading, or writing. But, like the honey from a bee, Sholem Aleichem would go on to use this time to produce something sweet. He explains that he spent the time thinking and crafting stories and scenes in his head. As soon as he crossed the border into Italy, he put ink to paper. It is now his desire, he writes, to offer these works to his readers. As he maintains, "Sometimes a person can make some use of the greatest misfortune" (*A mol ken men funem grestn umglik oykh hobn a shtikl nutsn*).[83]

Years before Peretz would whisper to Levin, Sholem Aleichem was already aware of the potential usefulness of his disease and, by extension, of writing a text that would not be his best work. The story describes a day in the life of Shmuel, a devoted, talented, and underappreciated Yiddish writer, on the eve of his twenty-fifth year of literary activity. Readers learn early in the story that Shmuel is about to be evicted from his home in Sholem Aleichem's quintessential shtetl of Kasrilevke. He can no longer maintain the large apartment that he inherited from his father-in-law. Rather, he has been forced to sell the apartment to a local rich man. While on the way to his landlord's house to ask for a reprieve, Shmuel opens up the latest Yiddish newspaper to learn that his twenty-five years of literary activity are to be celebrated. He begins to daydream and imagines grandiose celebrations in his honor. Yet at the end of the story, his daydream ends abruptly. He returns to his house only to discover that he has been evicted. The final scene finds him impoverished, homeless, and helpless as the sun beats down on his sweating brow.

The allegory is certainly heavy-handed. Like the sweating, homeless Shmuel Shmelkes, an ailing Sholem Aleichem had been exiled from his cultural homeland of the Pale of Settlement. He had similarly been left to sweat and ache—albeit in the far more glamorous setting of the Italian coast. Also like Shmuel Shmelkes, Sholem Aleichem had not received sufficient material support from his readers, despite his devotion to them over the past twenty-five years. Finally, cementing the allegorical reading, Sholem Aleichem shares with Shmuel Shmelkes a whimsical name. In the story, "Mr. How-Do-You-Do" meets up with "Your Average Joe."[84] In other words, Shmuel Shmelkes is Sholem Aleichem by another name.

One might interject here that Shmuel Shmelkes is not a code name for Sholem Aleichem but for Solomon Rabinovitsh. As would have been obvious to Rabinovitsh's peers, the story has numerous autobiographical allusions. For example, like Rabinovitsh, Shmuel marries the daughter of a wealthy man and subsequently loses all his father-in-law's money. Yet Rabinovitsh persistently deflects from his own identity. Here is where the effect of the introduction to the story is felt most strongly. Sholem Aleichem has put his imprimatur on the text so that even a character whose profile mirrors Rabinovitsh's must be understood through Rabinovitsh's greatest literary mediator, Sholem Aleichem.

The text also consistently shares in the rhetoric of Sholem Aleichem's jubilee. The seventh section of the story is simply titled "Shmuel Shmelkes and Count Tolstoy."[85] When the section opens, we find Shmuel happily hopping along muddy streets basking in the news of his upcoming jubilee.[86] When he glances in the newspaper a second time, he notices that there, on the same page, is an announcement for the jubilee of Count Tolstoy. He wonders to himself: "How did he, the tiniest star, come to be next to the great, flaming sun that illuminates the whole world?"[87] Abruptly, his mood changes. No longer bewildered but rather insulted, he asks: Why not? Isn't he the same in his small town as Tolstoy is for the world at large? Why shouldn't his readers honor him in the same way that the "nations of the world [*umos haoylem*]" (i.e., non-Jews) do for their writers?[88] His questions directly echo those then being posed by the Yiddish and Hebrew press. Shmuel Shmelkes, in other words, becomes an advocate for the same type of Jewish communal self-criticism as those writers drumming up support for Sholem Aleichem. Both make the celebration of the jubilee an issue of cultural pride, poking the egos of their readers and prompting them to ask the same self-critical questions.

Sholem Aleichem himself understood the potential fund-raising power that Tolstoy's name carried. He had previously invoked the Russian master as a reference point for his own censure of the Jewish reading public when he began to publicly advocate for Mendele's jubilee celebrations in 1906. Writing from New York for Warsaw's *Der veg*, Sholem Aleichem had scolded his readers, noting that Mendele would have been considered a jewel had he written for "the nations of the world [*umos haoylem*]." But, as he wrote for Jews in a Jewish language, "he had not anyhow expected something like the Yasnaya Polyana of Count Tolstoy to come from his work."[89] There was to be no palatial estate for Mendele. Nor, Sholem Aleichem continues, could Mendele have expected to find a home in Odessa. Sholem Aleichem's words presage Shmuel Shmelkes's own question. In 1906, Sholem Aleichem had been only one of a few who asked such a question out loud and who endeavored to train the Jewish audience in an idealized set of active, responsive, and materially enriching reading practices. In 1908, Shmuel Shmelkes's remarks joined dozens of voices.

In the final scene, the link between story and historical context continues to leap out at the reader. Shmuel Shmelkes begins to daydream. He imagines himself the guest of honor at a grand dinner. Speeches begin, toasts are made, and he is publicly compared to Tolstoy! The wine flows freely as guests stand up and declare that they should buy Shmuel Shmelkes a business, an inn, or even a mansion. One guest then exclaims: "What does he need money for? Health—that is the most important!"[90] Money and health—these are the two values to be emphasized. Shmuel is then abruptly brought back to his own pathetic reality.

The story here exceeds its function as entertaining fiction. Rather, it serves as a blunt reminder of the funds and cure of which Sholem Aleichem was in desperate need. Here, we might also recall the message of the introduction: even the worst of situations can generate positive outcomes. Shmuel Shmelkes, evicted and destitute, is left with only an imaginary jubilee celebration. The task for this story's readers, I suggest, is to actualize that celebration and to ensure that the finances and health of Rabinovitsh's persona are the primary concern. The text is the ultimate indication of Rabinovitsh's dependence on the fictional mode to effect real-life change. Using the same rhetoric of the jubilee, the story stands as a warning to readers lest they render their beloved author homeless and destitute like Shmuel Shmelkes and lest they leave Sholem Aleichem in a weakened authorial position.

Read more aggressively, the ending of the story stands as a threat. Recall that Sholem Aleichem apologized if "Shmuel Shmelkes" might seem "at times a bit pale, at times a bit short, and even at times a bit weak." Admittedly, the ending of this story lacks the writer's signature twist or clever change in perspective. The story as a whole seems to meander, lacking the oxymoronically tight verbosity recognizable in Sholem Aleichem's best work. Rather, at the end of the tale, Sholem Aleichem leaves it in his readers' hands to help the writer get back to his best writing—to allow for the physical recuperation that would enable literary excellence. Reading, according to the text, is not a passive act but participatory and necessarily responsive. The question is whether his readers will respond with the same nonresponse of the audience in Shmuel Shmelkes's fictional world. And just as the distance between Rabinovitsh and his persona are collapsed throughout the jubilee, here too is the space between text, reader, and Sholem Aleichem completely evacuated. The readers have been tasked with curing Sholem Aleichem—they have been asked by jubilee committees to raise funds to improve the material circumstances of the author, and they have been asked by the author's own aesthetically wanting text to intervene.

The Jubilee's Success

From today's perspective, it may seem that "Shmuel Shmelkes" had a decidedly finite effect. The short story does not feature in any English-language collection of Sholem Aleichem's work, nor has it found a critical audience. Yet the commercial and cultural impact of the text at the time of its original publication cannot be understated. In the text, Shmuel Shmelkes dreams of a jubilee celebration where attendants will respond to the needs of the author, keeping him healthy and well funded. This was a dream echoed by Sholem Aleichem himself. In a letter sent from Nervi in the fall of 1908, Sholem Aleichem explained to his editor that, in order to regain his health and continue to write, he needed "light, sun, and good food. And for these three things," he added, "one needs money, money, and money." Unfortunately, as he wrote, "at this point I have bad luck [*a gut oyg*], grief [*agmes-nefesh*], and a whole lot of nothing [*nekhtikn tog*]."[91]

This letter stands in stark contrast to one written shortly after to Gershn Levin. This second letter boasts the curious statement: "No more money needs to be sent to me here."[92] Sholem Aleichem goes on to explain that, over the past month, he had received hundreds of rubles from readers around the globe. He had also become acquainted with a potential patron from the Caucasus named Sh. Sharira.[93] Finally, he had learned that societies were being organized in honor of his jubilee from London to Kiev, Warsaw to Odessa, and throughout America. In his vast body of correspondence, this letter stands out for its genuinely positive outlook. There is no undertone of pain or resentment. Rather, it projects an image of a sick but energized author, excited at the immediate response of his audience.

Far from an unnoticeable ripple, the jubilee efforts fictionalized in "Shmuel Shmelkes" generated an international response. Writers around the world met their so-called holy duty by rallying around Sholem Aleichem. Between October 1908 and February 1909, events were planned, committees were established, and money was raised in the Pale of Settlement (Bialistok, Łódź, Odessa, Vilna, Warsaw) and in the urban centers of the Russian Empire (Kiev, St. Petersburg), western Europe (London, Geneva), South Africa, South America (Buenos Aires), the Middle East (Jerusalem; Alexandria, Egypt), and North America (Toronto, New York, Philadelphia, Jersey City, Denver). Money was collected on Sholem Aleichem's behalf from Vilna to Irkutsk, from South Bend, Indiana, to Waco, Texas.[94]

These committees and programs included the major public faces of Jewish communal and literary life. We might look to the New York scene as a model. There, the Yiddish dramaturge Dovid Pinski organized a fund-raising evening for the sick author's jubilee on December 28, 1908, in the Thalia

Theater. That evening, Pinski read "Shmuel Shmelkes" aloud.[95] He was followed by speeches from the Yiddish socialist and linguist Chaim Zhitlowsky and the prominent Reform rabbi Judah Leon Magnes. They were followed by a performance by the Yiddish actor David Kessler.[96] Alongside Pinski, Joseph Marcus was the treasurer of the New York jubilee committee. As president of the Public Bank, he received the donations on behalf of the author.[97] Contributions also arrived from such figures as Philip Krantz (editor), Solomon Schechter (rabbi and president of the Jewish Theological Seminary of America), and Getzl (George) Selikovitch (professor of Semitics).[98]

Outside New York, similarly impressive lists of local celebrities populated the committees, participated in celebrations, and donated funds in towns and cities worldwide. Author of *The Melting Pot*, the British-Jewish writer Israel Zangwill sent a note to be read at the celebration in London.[99] I. L. Peretz attended a Warsaw evening in honor of Sholem Aleichem's jubilee, where a special song—"Long Live Sholem Aleichem!" (S'zol lebn Sholem-Aleykhem!)—had been written for the occasion.[100] In Odessa, Hebrew writers, including Mendele, Bialik, Borochov, Levinski, Lilienblum, Ravnitsky, and Ussishkin, wrote a public letter announcing their desire that "the laughter of Sholem Aleichem remain among the Houses of Israel for many years."[101] It was a who's who of Jewish cultural actors and agents rallying across the globe on behalf of Sholem Aleichem.

Sholem Aleichem's jubilee was undeniably grand. His tuberculosis became an international concern, and the response to it a global Jewish literary phenomenon, engaging writers and readers across the political spectrum. During a period when Jewish particularist politics were brewing, when competing visions of national unity vied for support, and at a time when thousands of Jewish migrants were wending their way across Europe and the Atlantic Ocean, Sholem Aleichem emerged as a cause célèbre, and his health became a rallying point for a transnational Jewish response. One politically motivated writer who had taken the opportunity to criticize Sholem Aleichem as a bourgeois Zionist penned a follow-up article in which he apologized, writing that "Sholem Aleichem is now sick and that is where all criticism stops. With his literary work, at any rate, Sholem Aleichem has earned [our] help in this critical moment. He has earned it and we are obliged to provide it."[102]

In spite of several disappointing turnouts, the efforts of the jubilee committees resulted in an overwhelmingly successful fund-raising effort.[103] While in Nervi, Sholem Aleichem was stunned by the influx of donations from small towns and large cities from across the world. With the help of these funds, he was able to remain in Italy to begin his recuperative process. Even more significantly, these funds allowed him to buy back the copyrights to his works, which he had sold to publishers at various desperate points in his career. When he fell ill, he was at the mercy of notoriously dubious publishers and perpetually bankrupt Yiddish editors. In the months leading up to his tubercular hemorrhage in Baranovitsh, he wrote multiple letters to publishers and editors who he claimed owed him money based on contracts that had been signed and promises never fulfilled. He would later colorfully claim that certain publishers treated him worse than the proverbial publishers of Sodom.[104] It was no coincidence, according to a friend, that Sholem Aleichem had begun to cough blood shortly after a particularly nasty disagreement with one Warsaw newspaperman.[105] Just as Shelley had claimed that a series of bad reviews had led to Keats's consumptive end, so too was *Unzer lebn*'s Saul Hochberg accused of inducing Sholem Aleichem's tubercular fit.[106]

In the wake of Sholem Aleichem's departure to Italy, the Warsaw jubilee committee also took it upon itself to rectify Sholem Aleichem's relations with these publishers, including Hochberg.[107] A committee dedicated to buying back Sholem Aleichem's copyrights was formed.[108] Their stated goal to buy back the rights—to buy back "the fruit of the pen"—became a refrain in jubilee-related articles.[109] For Sholem Aleichem, it was an effort he would call "redeeming the captives [*pidyon shevuim*]."[110] And soon after the committee was formed, contributions began arriving and were publicly acknowledged in the pages of the local press.[111] One hundred rubles from the editors of the Zionist daily *Haynt* and two rubles from the director of the Warsaw theatrical group HaZamir received equal attention.[112] After months of acrimonious negotiations, the committee called in Olga Rabinovitsh, the writer's wife, for additional assistance.[113] By the summer of 1909, the copyrights had been successfully reacquired from four major publishers: Hochberg (publisher of *Unzer lebn*), Ben-Avigdor (pseudonym of A. L. Shalkovich and head of the Tushiyah publishing house), Magnus Krinski (publisher of the *Bikher far ale* series), and Yankev Lidski (head of the Warsaw-based Farlag Progres). As

Lidski had been the first to sell back his rights, he was given permission by Sholem Aleichem to become the Yiddish writer's official publisher.[114] He would go on to publish the high-quality three-volume American jubilee edition of Sholem Aleichem's collected writings. It was precisely such a jubilee edition that had been Sholem Aleichem's dream for many years.[115] Most significantly, the combination of general donations and the resumption of rights to his work allowed Sholem Aleichem once again to support himself and his family with his writing alone.[116] Until the outbreak of World War I, Sholem Aleichem and his family would live relatively comfortably (albeit peripatetically), as he continued to profit from his exclusive contract with Lidski.[117]

Beyond the financial benefits that accrued to the Yiddish author, the jubilee would also inaugurate a new phase in his literary reception. For beyond demonstrating Sholem Aleichem's appeal to readers, the jubilee also witnessed the first formal stage in highbrow criticism of his work.[118] The Yiddish critic Bal-Makhshoves delineated a paradigm of the author's literary "types" that remains a key for scholars working today. Sh. Niger declared Sholem Aleichem to be a "happy pessimist"—a title that has also stuck. Finally, the Yiddish critic Bal-Dimyen declared the writer to be the "democrat" among the literary greats Mendele and Chekhov.[119] After twenty-five years, the international jubilee offered Rabinovitsh's persona the chance not only to be publicly lauded but also maturely critiqued.

Conclusion: Ailing from beyond the Grave

In a letter to Gershn Levin written shortly after his diagnosis, Sholem Aleichem wrote: "I am missing two things that are deeply close to me and without which Sholem Aleichem cannot be Sholem Aleichem: (1) health, (2) my soul [*neshome*]."[120] The latter, he defines as "my children, my work, which must be mine, not someone else's." And when the copyrights were finally returned to him, Sholem Aleichem wrote to Levin to thank him for giving him back his "free, redeemed soul [*fraye, oysgeleyzte neshome*]."[121]

But what of his health? The question this chapter has explored is how health—or, more precisely, a lack of health—made it possible for "Sholem Aleichem to be Sholem Aleichem." His disease catalyzed an international fund-raising effort, allowed him to resume ownership of his copyrights, saw his work translated into multiple languages, and elicited a critical response far more extensive than had previously been granted to him. It further ingratiated him to his reading public, creating a link between author and reader that was mutually effective. In Rabinovitsh's bioliterary network, illness was the paradoxical condition of possibility for the continued existence of his literary persona and literary career.

It may come as little surprise, therefore, that Rabinovitsh was not so quick to abandon the sick visage that had garnered so much sympathy. On May 13, 1916, the Yiddish author passed away in New York City. At his funeral, more than one hundred thousand mourners lined the street as his casket processed through the city on its way to Mount Carmel Cemetery in Queens.[122] There, a headstone was soon erected bearing the name "Sholem Aleichem" on one side and "Rabinovitsh" on the other. Underneath "Sholem Aleichem," there appeared an extended poetic epitaph in which the writer described himself as a "simple Jew" (*a yid, a posheter*) who wrote for his audience despite the many obstacles he faced.[123] The last stanza of the epitaph reads:

And as the audience was
laughing, applauding and enjoying itself,
he had been ill, as only God knows,
in secret, so no one would see.

Un davke demolt ven der oylem hot
gelakht, geklatsht un fleg zikh freyen,
hot er gekrenkt, dos veys nor got,
besod, az keyner zol nit zen.[124]

There is an obvious historical tension in these last lines. Sholem Aleichem's disease was a decidedly public affair. Since 1908, tuberculosis had functioned as a metaphorical calling card for the author, as his avid supporters used it to raise funds on his behalf. And throughout the years 1909 and 1910, the progression of his disease was repeatedly featured in the Yiddish and Hebrew press.[125] Sholem Aleichem's suffering was the stuff of current events, and it continued to direct his public image, his profitability, and his relationship to his readers throughout his illness.

This final stanza further appears to ironize the secrecy of his disease. After all, it publicly announces the private experience of Sholem Aleichem's illness, and it does so engraved in stone. Even if it is true that he had suffered far from the eyes of his readers, he had also moved his sickness directly into their line of sight in perpetuity. In fact, the reference to his illness had replaced an earlier version of the line that read, "that he had cried [*hot er geveynt*], as God only knows."[126] The original line had been more Gogolian. But in the revised epitaph of 1916, Gogol's aphorism was modified. Sholem Aleichem moved from tears to illness. His readers now laugh through his disease. Laughter through tuberculosis. As Frug would write, *royte gelekhter*. In short, his sickness was to be part of the posthumous self-fashioning that Sholem Aleichem would continue to project even after his death.

Rather than forget the events of the jubilee, the gravestone announces that Sholem Aleichem understood its lessons quite well. Even after his death, the literary figure would continue to compel his graveside visitors to consider whether or not they had ignored his suffering during his lifetime. He would continue to manipulate his audience's guilt to cement a connection between author and reader. Like "Shmuel Shmelkes," the epitaph would invoke feelings in the viewer of shame, responsibility, and admiration. Like the activists of the jubilee, Sholem Aleichem's headstone would continue to publicize the writer's illness, agitating for an engaged reader to intervene in the legacy of the writer. Tubercular capital, as it were, mobilized from beyond the grave.

Despite his graveside epitaph, Sholem Aleichem would not long be remembered on account of his disease or the global reaction it catalyzed. Rather, since the 1960s, the figure of an ailing literary jokester has been overshadowed by the afterlife of his most famous text, *Tevye the Dairyman*—or, as it was later repackaged with Chagallian flair, *Fiddler on the Roof*. Sholem Aleichem's name and work would come to function as shorthand for an imagined Jewish past in the proverbial "old country."[127] The English versions, both the musical and film, would also modify several key features of Sholem Aleichem's work to accommodate an American audience. For example, in the American versions, Tevye no longer lives in a village but in an iconic shtetl populated by a variety of folksy Jews. Similarly, a Yiddish narrative critiquing intermarriage becomes an opportunity for a lesson in American ecumenism. It is Tevye's non-Jewish son-in-law who on stage and screen accuses his father-in-law of intolerant behavior. In all of the versions, Tevye's eldest daughter also marries a tailor named Motl in a romance that rejects the normative matchmaking procedures. In the English version, however, Motl remains a healthy, hardworking, and loyal husband. In the Yiddish, of course, he dies early on from consumption.

Sholem Aleichem's personal history of illness would not define his posthumous literary legacy. Even traces of his disease in his most famous literary work would be erased. Accordingly, the goal of this chapter is to recuperate Sholem Aleichem's disease as a consequential if forgotten variable in his public and literary self-fashioning. In contrast, for the subject of the following chapter, the Hebrew poet Raḥel, a posthumous legacy would prove just the opposite. It is, in fact, nearly impossible to discuss Raḥel's life and work without mentioning at some point that she suffered from tuberculosis and ultimately died from the illness outside Tel Aviv in 1931. Unlike that of Sholem Aleichem, Raḥel's literary legacy has been overdetermined by an attention to her experience of illness. The aesthetics of disease have even marked her published work—most often, diminutive collections accompanied by simple line drawings of the supine poet against a white background.

But Raḥel was also responsible for recognizing and endorsing the cultural capital attending her disease. Unlike Sholem Aleichem, she would not engage the disease primarily to monetize her illness. Rather, she would call on tuberculosis as a source of literary capital—as both the subject and context for her writing. Specifically, as a turn to her early Russian poetry introduces, it was Raḥel's personal and poetic experience of the sickroom that would direct the path of her career and her literary style.

CHAPTER 2

IN A SICKROOM OF HER OWN

Raḥel Bluvshtein's Tubercular Poetry

A sick-chamber may often furnish the worth of volumes.

—Jane Austen[1]

In 1916, while thousands gathered in New York City to pay their respects to the great Sholem Aleichem, a Russian-Jewish poet was beginning to find her voice far away on the coast of the Black Sea. She had entered a sanatorium there after what can only be described as a life lived in transit. Born Raia Bluvshtein in the Russian city of Saratov in 1890, she was afflicted early on by various lung infections.[2] As a young girl, she was sent to Crimea to recuperate, to relax, and, as was commonly prescribed, to drink kumis.[3] While there, according to family legend, Bluvshtein also wrote her first poem.[4] In 1909, she moved to Ottoman Palestine and, by the fall of the following year, had begun to work as a farmhand. In 1911, she accompanied her teacher Ḥanah Maizel to the newly established agricultural school for women in the Galilee. Two years later, Raia—now the Hebraicized Raḥel—traveled to Toulouse to study agronomy.[5] Yet she was soon forced to move again. With the outbreak of World War I, she was unable to remain in France as a Russian subject. Instead, she returned to eastern Europe, where she spent the war years volunteering in a Ukrainian-Jewish orphanage and seeking treatment for acute pulmonary tuberculosis along the Black Sea.

Just as Sholem Aleichem would turn to his pen to narrate his own experiences taking the cure on the Italian coast, so too did Bluvshtein begin to seriously distill her life into poetry in the port city of Sukhum.[6] "I live high up in a sanatorium," begins one such text.[7] The poem introduces components of a topos—the sickroom—that she would come to mobilize repeatedly in her later work. From a high vantage, she looks down onto an unnamed city, spending long boring days whimsically catching strings of melodies from the distant ocean. The lights of the enchanted city flare up, summoning her to a life of urban splendor. Yet she is unable, no less unwilling, to leave the sanatorium. As the final stanza reads:

I will go to my narrow room
I will close the shutters more tightly . . .
Oh, disperse heavenly forces,
evil spells of the evening lights![8]

The speaker here returns to her small room. She shuts herself off from the world outside her window. Most significantly, she retreats into a narrow and cramped space and moves to close the shutters, further restricting herself within an already claustrophobic environment. At the end of the poem, readers are left to wonder what will happen next. On the one hand, it seems likely that the speaker will remain in her narrow room frustrated by her inability to leave. On the other hand, the poem hints that there might be something potentially productive in her act of retreat. The closed room offers the speaker a sense of safety or power. After all, the speaker makes her demand on the "heavenly forces" only after having declared her intention to go back into the room. Only after stating a plan to enter this confined space does she explode into apostrophic lyrical command.

This amateur poem models several features that would become hallmarks of Bluvshtein's later Hebrew writing. The lyrical intimacy of the text, its short length, and its clear yet evocative images bespeak the poet's future allegiance to the acmeist poetics of compact form and expressive simplicity—in Hebrew, *pashtut*. In this accessible poem, the distance between the first-person speaker and the poet is also intriguingly close. Yet this poem is seldom read by scholars of Bluvshtein's work as a model of her poetic *pashtut*, as the critical reception of her work has focused almost exclusively on her Hebrew writing.[9] Although it was not yet clear in 1916, the tubercular poet would go on to become one of the most popular and beloved Hebrew writers of Zionist culture in the twentieth century, most often referred to by her first name alone. "Raḥel's" poetry would be set to music, her writings would be read during national holidays, and her grave would become a site of "civil pilgrimage."[10]

And like Sholem Aleichem's own fame in 1908, much of Raḥel's renown would result from her public experience of tuberculosis. After returning to British Mandate Palestine in 1919, Raḥel moved to Kibbutz Degania by the banks of the Sea of Galilee. However, the young agricultural community was unable to support the ailing poet, lacking basic resources such as electricity or a sufficient infirmary.[11] As a result, Raḥel lived out the final decade of her life in a series of apartments and rooms in Jerusalem and Tel Aviv. Her subsequent Hebrew poetry was later assessed as the product of a would-be pioneer (*ḥalutsah*) who was torn from her beloved land.[12] Unable to sacrifice herself either by fighting or farming, Raḥel became the ultimate symbol of sacrifice. After all, as Ḥamutal Tsamir has argued, she had sacrificed her ability to sacrifice herself. And her disease was the root cause.[13]

Many of the recent critical efforts to interpret Raḥel's life and poetry have worked to escape this interpretive paradigm, which reads her biography and Zionist legacy in tandem with her poetry. Such biographical readings, they claim, ignore Raḥel's modernist innovations, her insistence on using a vernacular register, and her ability to champion a poetics of simplicity during an era of increasingly bombastic and allusion-heavy Palestinian Hebrew writing.[14] My appreciation of Raḥel's work as artful and potentially iconoclastic is indebted to these scholarly interventions. Yet the Russian poem with which this chapter opened compels us to ask the question anew, as it once again alerts us to the imbrication of the physiological body and literary expression. This early work does so by announcing a spatial and poetological thematic that would come to be central in Raḥel's later work: the narrow sickroom. To that end, this chapter examines how the site of this confined space—a room of pain and illness—came to manage Raḥel's metaphoric range and condition her experiments with writing. It was in the sickroom where the poet would direct her public self-fashioning and perform her literary illness. There, she also would locate herself in a cultural context of illness that reached from the Russia of her youth to the Palestine of her adult years, allowing her to harness Romantic possibilities to the needs and concerns of Hebrew territorial nationalism. There, she would narrate both the tensions and connections between her experience of tuberculosis and her commitment to the Zionist project, between the spread of disease and the colonial work of Jewish settlement in Palestine. And there, Raḥel would craft a poetic agenda over and against the willfully masculine, antidiasporic, and insistently healthy vision of Zionist Hebrew writing in Palestine. In short, unlike Sholem Aleichem, Raḥel did not mobilize her illness primarily for financial gain, even if business opportunities did accrue to her. Rather, she capitalized on the spaces of her illness to anchor her literary oeuvre, cement her posthumous reputation, and explore the semantic ramifications of her stylistic *pashtut*.

The Victorian Sickroom

When Sholem Aleichem began to cough up blood in Baranovitsh, he received what was by then a common prescription: Go to Italy. John Keats had been given similar advice nearly a century earlier, and two decades later, the ailing Hebrew poet David Vogel would make the journey southward from Vienna. Throughout the nineteenth and twentieth centuries, those suffering from lung ailments had traveled to Italy in the hopes that the fresh air and warmer climate, whether coastal, inland, or mountainous, would soothe their chests. Patients, including Sholem Aleichem, were also advised to seek treatment at a growing network of sanatoria and hospitals scattered across central Europe—and he did so, in Badenweiler, St. Blasien, Lausanne, Lucerne, Lugano, and Montreux. In the first decades of the twentieth century, health tourism was a booming industry in southern and central Europe. For tubercular patients in Palestine, the European health resorts also may have seemed like the best option. As late as 1935, there were only three sanatoria extant in Palestine—Mekor Ḥaim in Jerusalem, the tuberculosis division at the hospital of Tsefat, and a sanatorium at Gedera—and between them, only ninety beds available.[15] For tuberculosis patients such as Raḥel, the space of recuperation that was most readily available was not a large regimented sanatorium but a succession of sickrooms in a series of apartments.

The notion of the sickroom has long borne with it a gendered connotation. Traveling to take the cure, as American historian Sheila Rothman has shown, "was primarily the province of men."[16] In contrast, women often pursued their curative regimes at home. To that end, the notion of the constructive sickroom that I draw on emerges not only from Raḥel's lived experience of disease in British Mandate Palestine but also from the lived experience and literary representation of "invalid" women in Anglo-American literary and medical discourse of the nineteenth and early twentieth centuries.[17] The sickroom, as Miriam Bailin has noted, would come to signify a domestic space where fictional and real-life women could experience an "alternative society."[18] For Victorian middle-class women, this meant an opportunity to indulge in personal reflection and the pursuit of projects outside those defined by motherly or wifely duties. In the case of Florence Nightingale, for example, life in the sickroom "permitted the inversion of the sentence imposed by her gender and class by permitting her to sequester and immobilize herself while laboring prodigiously on projects of national and imperial importance."[19] In other words, "her invalidism paradoxically enabled a life of almost uninterrupted exertion" and attention to matters of grave social import.[20] This description of Nightingale's "imperial" work echoes the interpretive tradition surrounding Raḥel, which has often suggested that Raḥel did the work of labor Zionism through her poetry. As we will see, the bridges between her literary output and her vision of colonial expansion were constructed in the confines of the sickroom and under the poetic sign of illness.

Writing about the cultural history of invalidism, Maria Frawley also adds that "confinement could be experienced as liberating" for a select group of the ailing.[21] Much of Frawley's evidence comes from the bestselling memoir *Life in the Sick-Room* (1844) by the English sociologist Harriet Martineau. Martineau experienced her own sickroom both as a prison cell and as a place of privilege from which to gaze out onto the world and "vindicate the supremacy of mind over body."[22] The sickroom functioned as a heterotopic space in which women could redirect their experience of illness from one of restricted movement to one of expansive opportunities.[23]

There is no evidence that Raḥel knew the work of those British and American women whose life stories form the backdrop of these analyses. Yet writing under the guise of the female invalid in the sickroom was an experience notably available to the Hebrew woman writer in Palestine. Raḥel's colleague, the prose writer Dvora Baron, spent more than thirty years in a self-imposed isolation in her room, cared for by a fiercely devoted daughter and visited by a select group of Hebrew writers and cultural activists.[24] Decades later, the psychologist Amia Leiblich would write an experimental biography of Baron, in which she imagined herself having twenty-four conversations with Baron in her room. Their discussions would range over a number of topics, including Baron's own experience of invalidism (or what Leiblich, trained in psychoanalysis, suggests echoes the symptoms of hysteria) in parallel with that of Florence Nightingale.[25]

For Raḥel, however, the space of the sickroom remains uninterrogated as a site of literary, ideological, or biographical importance. To that end, I propose the ostensibly anachronistic spatial-experiential frame of the Victorian sickroom to reassess how tubercular capital was mobilized in Raḥel's life and career, by her supporters and by the poet herself. As a woman in the *yishuv* (the Jewish settlement in British Mandate Palestine), there were few avenues open to Raḥel to locate herself in a position of power.[26] Neither a mother (like Baron) nor a laborer, she occupied neither the archetypical role of birthing "the new nation" nor of working the land with her own two hands. But, like Nightingale and Martineau, she was positioned and positioned herself squarely in the sickroom. From there, she asserted her authority over her readers by involving the poetic exploration of colonial settlement with the literary investigation of disease.[27]

It was in spaces of health confinement—especially her final two rooms in Tel Aviv—where Raḥel would write, entertain, and fashion her legacy. When Sholem Aleichem fell ill, announcements of his condition flooded the Yiddish and Hebrew press across the globe. The discourse of his disease was expansive, far-reaching, and insisted on spreading the news of the Yiddish author's cough throughout the world. Tubercular capital was mobilized by and on behalf of Raḥel, in contrast, not by looking abroad but by localizing attention to her immediate surroundings, by bringing those readers physically and literarily into the room with the poet herself—a poetic room she had already begun to construct in 1916 and would continue to refine throughout her career.

The Romantic Sickroom

Raḥel's room was also a space in which she was rarely alone either metaphorically or physically. For Raḥel's interlocutors, her experiences as a tubercular poet placed her within a long tradition of writing and ailing. In 1931, one month after her death, the so-called father of Hebrew literature, Ḥayim Naḥman Bialik, eulogized the recently departed poet.[28] He declared her passing to have been a great loss for Hebrew literature in Palestine. After all, she had belonged to a group of Hebrew writers who had all died in the prime of their youth, including Uri Nissan Gnessin, who succumbed in 1913 to heart disease, as well as Raḥel's Romantic consumptive predecessors Mikhal Yosef Lebensohn (known as "Mikhal"; 1828–52) and Mordecai Zevi Mane (1859–86).[29]

It was also a group populated by writers who had all been mortally afflicted with chest ailments.[30] All had also come of age in a Russian literary context in which illness and literary creativity were considered mutually effective. Like their Victorian counterparts, consumptive male poets of the nineteenth-century Russian Empire understood the literary process as an inspired by-product of their illness.[31] If consumptive women were depicted as languishing beauties, men were afforded the privilege of consumptive genius. The representative figure for this link was the Russian poet Semyon Nadson (1862–87), for whom disease dominated his self-perception, writing, and posthumous legacy.[32] In one of his more famous poems, "He Died from Consumption, He Died Alone," Nadson draws us into a sickroom suffused by the Romantic glow of an imminent, delicate death.[33] The consumptive subject lays his feverish head on a pillow and passes away. Shortly thereafter, the heat that had consumed his body silently disperses to become the stuff of poetic verse.[34]

Investing consumption with creative potential was a poetic conceit that Raḥel's male colleagues, Mikhal and Mane, also explored in their Hebrew work. In one of Mane's most famous poems, "Alone in My Dwelling Place" (Badad bi-me'oni), the speaker's cough resounds in his sickroom as the source of his creative inspiration.[35] At first, the speaker appears by himself far from the tumult of the city. He tries to read a book, but his blood races and he erupts into brutal coughs. He cannot sleep, he cannot read, and he resigns himself to remain as quiet as possible. Read quickly, the poem seems to suggest that the disease prevents the speaker from engaging in literature. Yet Mane's language presents a complication that bespeaks his allegiance to the Russian Romantic tradition. The speaker sits down, opens a book, and exclaims, "But the breath [*nishmat*] erupts from my mouth with the sounds of thunder / and my limbs [*vitsuri*] move without rest." Mane employs a curious term for limbs, *yitsuri*, which shares its root (*y.ts.r.*) with the Hebrew words for "inclination" (*yester*) and "creation" (*yetsirah*). In Mane's poem, it is precisely when a coughing fit appears to preclude the speaker's engagement with literature that careful readers will observe the physiological source of inspiration.

This was a poetic conceit that was not foreign to Raḥel's oeuvre. Already in her earliest Russian work, Raḥel had linked pathology, creativity, and architecture. A decade later, in 1926, she echoed the sentiment in a short poem that she wrote in her apartment on Ha-yarkon Street in Tel Aviv. The poem, "My New Room" (Ḥadri he-ḥadash), reads in full:

Hooray, for my new room, which faces the sea,
raised twenty cubits above the sidewalk!
Winds from four directions,
with night—a festival of lights,
loneliness blessed.

So join with me, injuries small and large,
to make weary the exhausted.
I will shut my ears, hide my eyes:
My heart is reconciled to the disruptor.

Hedad, ḥadri he-ḥadash, ha-tsofeh pnei yam,
ha-nisa be-ʿesrim ama me-ʿal la-midrekhet!
Ruḥot me-arba ruḥot,
im laylah—ḥag-negohot,
bedidut mevorekhet.

Kishru na alay, efo, pegaʿim ketanim im gedolim
lehal'ot ha-yageʿa.
Et ozni mikem e'etom, et eynay aʿalim:
Libi mefuyas le-mafreʿa.[36]

Raḥel places her speaker at a high remove from the world below. "Hedad, ḥadri he-ḥadash," she exclaims, opening the poem by praising her surroundings. The reader might quite rightly expect a simple poetic exercise of praise for the speaker's interior space. Yet illness attaches itself to this deceptively harmless first line. The sentiment may be positive, but the alliterative repetition of the breathy *h* and guttural *ḥ* choke the poem's speaker, as if causing her to cough and gasp for breath. Writing about the dependence of Proust's literary style on his asthma, Walter Benjamin concludes that "a physiology of *style* would take us into the innermost core of [his] creativeness."[37] Here, Raḥel's tuberculosis phonically brings us into the space of the sickroom. There, like Mane's subject, the speaker appears alone. And as the length of the final lines of both the first and second stanza suggests, she is in an increasingly small space. At the same time, she is at the center of four crosswinds, she has a lovely view of the water, the world around her sparkles, and loneliness is "blessed" in the quiet of the windy heights.

In that high room, moreover, the speaker's loneliness does not seem to last very long. In the first line of the second stanza, the speaker invites "injuries small and large" into the room with her. Put otherwise, this is not a poem about a languishing female consumptive beauty but, like that of her male counterparts, a poem in which the speaker mobilizes pain and injury in the name of poetic practice. The space of Raḥel's sickroom becomes populated by pain, and the speaker shuts herself inside. And like the sanatorium room she had earlier poeticized in Russian, the Hebrew space becomes one of conscious protest. For more than inviting injuries into the room, the speaker commands that they connect to her, attach to her, and even work to tire her out. Yet she will shut her eyes and ears. The *pega'im* will not disrupt her. Her *lev*—her heart, her chest—will remain calm. There, in that sickroom, the speaker will demonstrate her power and her ability to remain above the fray. Rather than break down, she will transform that pain into poetry and exclaim, "Hedad, ḥadri he-ḥadash."

The Zionist Sickroom

For Raḥel, however, to transform tubercular pain into poetry was not a neutral act. In an undated letter from the 1920s, she writes to her friend and colleague Menaḥem Poznanski to express her discomfort with assuming the cultural capital of her disease. First, she tells Poznanski that she is unhappy with her current status as an invalid. As she explains, she is stuck in a world where her visitors give her special treatment and seem only to ask, "How are you doing?" She then goes on to reflect that tuberculosis is "a distinguished disease [*maḥalah meyuḥeset*]." After all, it has "earned the reputation [*shem*] as 'the authors' disease' [*maḥalat ha-sofrim*]. And yet," she cautions Poznanski, "don't think that because of this that I would imagine joining them."[38]

Thematically, Raḥel may have found poetic inspiration and literary allies in the Romantic space of the sickroom. However, it was not a tradition in which she felt fully comfortable. After all, it was a tradition far removed from her Palestinian home. Recall here Bialik's eulogy, when he placed Raḥel in a room of male poets, all of whom were afflicted by chest ailments and, notably, all of whom died far from Palestine: Gnessin in Warsaw, Mikhal in Vilna, and Mane in the town of Radoshkovitsh.[39] During World War I, Raḥel had similarly experienced her illness in an eastern European setting, suffering while working in an orphanage in the Ukrainian city of Berdyansk.[40] But, unlike her predecessors, she had then settled in the *yishuv*, where she would have encountered a radically different cultural understanding of tuberculosis—one that directly insisted that the disease prevented her from Zionist labor.

Although the Romantic image of the feverishly creative writer persisted among certain segments of the cultural elite in the *yishuv*, that image was countered by the dominant perception of tuberculosis as a diasporic illness. When Raḥel's Zionist colleagues narrate her biography, for example, it is rare that her illness is not specifically mentioned as having first manifested in Russia and as having been brought back with her to Palestine in 1919. Historically accurate or not, her interlocutors insist that tuberculosis was not the result of life in the *yishuv* but of her life and suffering in Russia. The process of the negation of exile demanded that, over and against eastern Europe, Palestine be seen as a site of health and physical renewal, where the "New Jew" could walk and work the land with vigor.[41]

At the turn of the century, Palestine was even said to be a location that would heal the Jew—not just the Jewish body politic but the body of the Jewish patient. As early as 1886, the Hebrew weekly *Ha-magid* (the *Preacher*) proposed Palestine as a new health destination for those with chest diseases. According to the article, Palestine should be considered a Jewish substitute for the already established health resorts in Italy, Madeira, and Algeria.[42] The idea even appealed to Raḥel's predecessor Mane, who wrote of his desire to go to the healing Land of Israel rather than Alexandria or Cairo, as his doctor had recommended.[43]

Yet like Sholem Aleichem twenty years later, Mane would not make the journey to Palestine. Such a journey also likely would not have lived up to either the Hebrew poet or the Yiddish writer's expectations. The availability of treatment for tuberculosis in Palestine was decidedly slim. The Anti-Tuberculosis League of Palestine did not become active until the early 1920s, when it immediately set an agenda of opening dispensaries, increasing the number of available hospital beds, raising money on behalf of Jewish tuberculosis victims, and organizing local branches. For decades, the league's plaintive cry went unanswered, and the number of patients consistently overwhelmed the number of available hospital beds.[44] Later, a frustrated contributor to the *Palestine Post* decried the lack of available care for tuberculosis patients. Riffing on a Zionist adage, he lamented that "we Jews come here to build Palestine, to redeem and rebuild the land and to repopulate the country yet calmly let the best building material decay."[45] Just like Sholem Aleichem's supporters, the anonymous writer censured the Jewish public en masse as communally responsible for the terrible plight of its sick members.

Compounding these institutional and medical obstacles, the tubercular patient in Palestine also faced a hostile cultural landscape, which continually marked the illness as a disease of the diaspora. In 1919, the same year that Raḥel returned to Palestine, a report was issued by the Department of Immigration and Colonization of the Zionist Organization in which the author blamed the increase in the number of tubercular cases in Palestine on the recent Russian-Jewish immigrants.[46] If the dream of labor Zionism was to rebuild the physical Jewish body by working the land, then what was one to make of a disease like tuberculosis—a blight of urban life?[47] And how were labor Zionists to handle such a disease in the idealized fields and valleys of Palestine? Tuberculosis was not troped as a Romantic disease of the *yishuv* but rather as an existential threat to national-cultural health.[48] Perhaps no one articulated this concern better than Raḥel's colleague Avraham Shlonsky—the Hebrew "poet paver" (*paytan solel*) who combined his national duty of building a literary canon with his duty as a laborer building the physical infrastructure of Zionist society.[49] Shlonsky, resistant to all things diasporic, lambasted the idea of Hebrew and Yiddish bilingualism:

> We see this calamity of bilingualism as we see tuberculosis, which gnaws at the lungs of the nation. We want Israeli breathing to be *completely Hebrew*, with two lungs. A Hebrew Land of Israel, working for the nation, loving its producers and its culture—this is the "Society of the War Against Tuberculosis."[50]

Hebrew cultural activism, according to Shlonsky, could rhetorically function in lieu of the Anti-Tuberculosis League. In other words, the Hebrew language nationalist was the ultimate health activist. Shlonsky's formulation also takes a clear swipe at the oft-cited anecdote of Mendele Mocher Sforim. The classic Yiddish and Hebrew writer Mendele had reflected that Hebrew-Yiddish bilingualism was as natural to Jewish writing as breathing through both nostrils.[51] Here, Shlonsky disagrees with Mendele's eastern European adage. For Shlonsky, Yiddish represents the diasporic language of confinement and disease in contrast to the thriving and healthy-lunged language of the Zionist laborer.

If there was a disease that acquired mythic status among labor Zionists, it was not tuberculosis but malaria.[52] "The poetics of malaria," writes Eric Zakim, "describe how illness becomes the intermediate bridge between a sick land and a sick people."[53] The cure for malaria was also rhetorically worse than the disease, as it took the would-be pioneer away from his beloved land and "denie[d] the very goal of self-identification with the land."[54] Such a dynamic resonates in canonical works like Yosef Ḥayim Brenner's 1914 novel, *Breakdown and Bereavement* (*Shekhol ve-kishalon*), where the protagonist must retreat to the "shtetl-like confines of Jerusalem" after contracting malaria while working on a farm.[55] In this light, tuberculosis would fail doubly as a Zionist disease. It was perceived as having been contracted far from the rural landscape of Palestine, and its treatment kept its victims at a further remove.

In short, for Raḥel, tuberculosis bore the reputation of a disease that was anathema to the Zionist project. Following Tsamir, the only sacrifice Raḥel could make for the *yishuv* was to die. Although certainly the ultimate sacrifice, it would have been accomplished without the heroism of the fighter dying in battle, the farmworker dying from malaria, or the would-be mother dying in childbirth. It would be accomplished, moreover, at a remove from the idealized setting of Zionist fieldwork. Unlike for her Victorian counterparts, the urban sickroom was not a recognized space of imperial sacrifice or productivity. It was also not the anticipated site of poetic inspiration in a Palestinian Hebrew literary conversation increasingly saturated by agricultural vistas.

It is here we might turn back to Raḥel's work "My New Room." In a letter to her sister, Raḥel first described the room in which she wrote this poem—a sparsely furnished space—as quite pleasant. But by the end of the letter, she had changed her mind, declaring the room to be desolate and unsatisfying.[56] This trajectory offers an instructive lens for reading the poem itself. As the eponymous opening line indicates, Raḥel was aware of something positive in her new setting. Yet, as the Hebrew suggests, the situation comes with a cost. "Hedad, ḥadri he-ḥadash, ha-tsofe pnei yam" is a cumbersome line, one that a speaker coughs out rather than sings. With this line, Raḥel places herself in an ambivalent position, as a hesitant advocate for and an active resister of the coarticulation of literary expression and disease. Put otherwise, Raḥel is acutely aware of both the cultural capital (Romanticism) and cultural debt (Zionism) attending her illness.

Raḥel's Sickroom

A fuller assessment of Raḥel's archival record underscores that she both resisted the reputation of an ailing author and nurtured it. At the same time that she dismissed those who claimed she wrote with *dam libi*, "the blood of my heart/chest," she also announced herself in a lineage of tubercular writers that included such Russian greats as Chekhov.[57] She further drew on the medical aphorisms of Sholem Aleichem—citing him in both Hebrew and Yiddish to remind herself that "doctors prescribe laughter!"[58] She also repeatedly, if obliquely, connected her writing process to her experience of illness. For example, on a visit to Raḥel's apartment in Tel Aviv, one of the poet's admirers, Rivkah Davidit, encountered the poet in a particularly tempestuous mood. During the visit, Raḥel asked Davidit whether she would prefer "that I were healthy but my poems would not exist at all [*ve-shiray lo yihiyu be-nimtsa klal*], or that I would be as I am and my poems exist?" Davidit looked at the ailing Raḥel, listened to her terrible cough, and responded that she would prefer Raḥel to be healthy. The insulted poet immediately responded, "Then you must not love my poetry!"[59]

Raḥel was clearly capable of acknowledging a link between her disease and her writing. After all, it is implied that were her health to improve, her poetry would cease; similarly, had she not fallen ill, her poetry might never have existed. Raḥel, in fact, only began to actively publish her Hebrew poetry after she was publicly suffering from tuberculosis. For critics like Dan Miron, this anecdote exemplifies Raḥel's sharp and aggressive nature.[60] Yet the circumstances of the anecdote point us in other directions. They compel us to reconsider how tuberculosis mediated Raḥel's creative process, without resorting to Romantic explanations of literary genius and also without denying the social stigma that attended her disease. Raḥel's writing would not directly address tuberculosis as a subject as much as poeticize the space in which she found herself and in which this conversation with Davidit occurred—the sickroom.

Investigating the history of the Victorian female invalid, Diane Price Herndl has argued that "representing oneself as an invalid [put] into play a whole structure of care, attention, responsibility and privilege."[61] In certain cases, this allowed the invalid to become a venerable hostess with multiple attendants in her own sickroom. In other cases, it allowed the invalid to become the center of a sickroom salon, as she entertained visitors in the privacy of her own room. It was a gathering where the formerly off-limits space of a woman's bedroom became the site of social engagement. Such would be the case for Raḥel's various sickrooms, where the singular poet took center stage, playing the coughing host to her admiring visitors.[62]

In fact, that Raḥel received visitors at all may seem curious. Unlike her colleague Dvora Baron, Raḥel was suffering from a disease that was already known to be highly contagious. After a brief stay with her brother and sister-in-law, for example, Raḥel left, afraid that she would infect her young niece.[63] Notoriously, she had also been asked to leave Kibbutz Degania out of the fear that the toddlers in her care would contract tuberculosis. Yet Raḥel's communicable disease did not dissuade many of her friends and admirers from visiting her for short periods of time. Nor did it prevent her from conducting business there. Living close to the office of *Davar*, the labor Zionist newspaper that would make her a household name, Raḥel often met with the paper's editors in her room and effectively turned it into an ersatz office. It was there that Zalman Shazar, her former lover and *Davar* editor, flipped through Raḥel's notebook to find poems to publish and to provide the impoverished patient with a modest payment.[64] It was also there that she was approached by the toy salesman Re'uven Goldberg, who hired her to versify an illustrated children's book he wished to publish.[65] Raḥel's sickroom served double duty as both a space to recuperate and a space to conduct business.

The room itself also became the measure by which her supporters demonstrated their loyalties. Finding a room on her behalf, in fact, was one of the few activities she allowed her colleagues to do. When *Davar* editor Moshe Beilinson visited Raḥel in her room on Ha-yarkon Street, he was immediately dissatisfied. In his professional opinion as a physician, the apartment was untenable for the tubercular patient because it lacked an indoor toilet.[66] Mobilizing Raḥel's tubercular capital, he and the editors of *Davar* took it upon themselves to find their new star poet a more suitable abode. They found more appropriate lodgings in the attic apartment of Lipman Levenzon at 5 Bogroshov, which boasted a room facing the sea and offered access to the open-air roof. There, Raḥel thrived artistically if not physically. She even helped Levenzon's wife, Rika, translate several operas into Hebrew.[67] For Sholem Aleichem, the experience of recuperation was always at a remove from his editors and collaborators. For Raḥel, her sickroom—so close to the urban center of labor Zionism—allowed her to participate in the nascent Hebrew literary projects around her and to do so from the relative comfort of her private room.

Beyond entertaining her closest colleagues, Raḥel used the sickroom to present herself to an increasingly admiring public. The poet's retreat into the sickroom did not correspond to a withdrawal from society but the opposite. It was there that she acted as host to such venerable literary guests as Gnessin and none other than Bialik himself.[68] It was also there that she met with young and aspiring writers. Avraham Broides, for example, recalls visiting Raḥel in Tel Aviv shortly after reading her poetry for the first time. The discussion during his visit touched on a wide variety of subjects, including the nature of love and contemporary literature.[69] The Hebrew poet Levi Ben-Amitai also recalls visiting Raḥel in the city several times.[70] During these occasions, they spoke about poetry, in general, and Raḥel's often caustic reviews of other writers' works, in particular. Raḥel also read Ben-Amitai some of her unpublished poems from her personal journal. Raḥel's sickroom became a space of poetic experimentation, where she would test out her own works in progress in front of her visitors as well as recite poetry in Hebrew and Russian.[71] Among these poems were those of Anna Akhmatova, Raḥel's acmeist predecessor, whose work she would translate and who had also suffered from tuberculosis in her youth.[72]

There are so many memoiristic accounts of visits to Raḥel's sickroom that a paradigm emerges: Friends/admirers/aspiring writers visit Raḥel in her rented room. They find Raḥel alone next to a bouquet of flowers or branches. They notice the ocean visible through the window—a conceit that would prove generative in her poetry. They take note of the sparsely furnished room, save a bed, rocking chair, and small table on which only a single book—the Hebrew Bible—can be found. They look at her dark brown hair, fiery blue eyes, and tall stature (noticeable even when she is lying down). And they comment on her pale face and weak body, the latter covered only by a simple white linen dress. The poet appears to blend into the background, with only her piercing eyes and long brown hair offering any break in the white vista.

But Raḥel was not to be remembered as a pale consumptive beauty, like the iconic invalid who inspired the canvases of Dante Gabriel Rossetti. For, like Florence Nightingale and Harriet Martineau before her, Raḥel experienced the sickroom as the space in which she could dominate and determine her posthumous legacy. It was a space where her ostensible infirmity and feminine invalid delicacy would be sharply contrasted by her behavior. After all, the paradigm of the sickroom visit rarely ends with the visitor taking final notice of the plain poet in her plain room. Rather, belying the simplicity of her pose and unadorned surroundings—what we might call her performance of *pashtut*—Raḥel would subsequently engage her visitor in a lively conversation about poetry. Sometimes, she would begin heated conversations about her own work or contemporary culture in the *yishuv*. She would then challenge visitors to explain their opinions and then, sometimes, interrupt their discussion with an insuppressible cough. The interruption worked not only to remind visitors of the gravity of the situation but also to give Raḥel the upper hand in the conversation; confronted by the contagious cough, guests no doubt worried about the poet's health as well as their own. Sometimes, these conversations would even occur while Raḥel was bedridden. Perhaps counterintuitively, her opinions registered as all the more powerful, all the more strident, as she announced them with force from the supine position.[73] The gendered politics of these visits also are highlighted in these moments, as the often-male visitor sits by Raḥel's bedside, completely enamored by her frailty and then overwhelmed by the pitch of her opinions. Contemporary scholars may find biographical interpretations of Raḥel's poetry as limiting, but the more one examines the history of Raḥel's sickroom, the more one begins to see that some of her first critical performances were executed under the sign of illness, in the space of a sickroom, and in front of sympathetic readers who were well aware of her disease.

The Poetic Sickroom

More than a place of business, more than a salon, and more than a place to direct her public image, the sickroom would also be encoded as a space of poetic possibility—specifically, one that was creatively expansive if physically restrictive. Recall here once more the Russian poem with which this chapter opened. The first line of the final stanza finds the speaker retreating into her room. "I will go to my narrow room," she explains, before closing the shutters and commanding that the heavenly forces disperse. The poet assumes an emboldened pose, commanding the ineffable and willing away distractions. Yet she does so only after entering into her narrow abode.

This retreat into the confined space of illness reverberates across Raḥel's Hebrew oeuvre, in which the topos of the narrow room repeats. We might begin with one of Raḥel's latest and, perhaps, most famous poems—the 1930 text, "I Knew Only to Tell about Myself" (Rak al atsmi le-saper yad'ati).[74] The poem opens:

I knew only to tell about myself.
My world is narrow like the world of an ant,
I also bore my burden like her
too large and heavy for my weak shoulder.

Rak al atsmi lesaper yadati.
Tsar olami ke-olam nemalah,
gam masa'i amasti kamoha
rav ve-khaved miktefi ha-dalah.

Written in March 1930 in Tel Aviv, it is one of Raḥel's most oft-quoted poems. As in her earlier Russian work, this later poem also bears witness to a series of distant lights that both draw and taunt the speaker. In tightly rhymed poetic verse, it similarly describes the narrow spatial context in which the speaker finds herself. "I knew only to tell about myself," the speaker humbly begins the poem, before observing her surroundings. "My world," she writes, "is narrow [*tsar*] like the world of an ant." The simple statement, however, belies the industriousness of the speaker's entomological counterpart. The speaker may have shrunk herself down to the size of an ant, but the remainder of the poem traces the ant's movement to a place on high—not a sanatorium but a treetop. All the while, she is burdened by a heavy load. The difficulty of the act is made all the more evident by a second meaning of *tsar*. In the nominal form, the term translates to "trouble" or "distress." Raḥel's poem offers a vision of the speaker's world as restricted, painful, and all the while dominated by the productive labor of the intrepid ant.

Naomi Brenner has argued that this poem's reference to the ant should be read in conversation with Raḥel's review of Maeterlinck's *The Life of the Ant*. Raḥel, argues Brenner, lauded Maeterlinck's image of the ant as "part of a well-organized *meshek le'umi*, a national economy."[75] As the Hebrew ant is gendered feminine (*nemalah*), Brenner reads Raḥel's analysis of Maeterlinck's text as an allegory of women's contributions to Zionist society and the external forces that hinder them.

Yet the allusion also functions on a level supplemental to the call of Zionist labor. Consider Raḥel's summary of Maeterlinck's description of the physical infrastructure of the ant colony. "In general," writes Raḥel, "the ant colony extends into the earth to a depth of thirty to forty cm.," where "days and nights pass filled with agricultural labor, food preparation, reciprocal feeding." When an ant returns to the colony exhausted, Raḥel continues, her friends rush to her, brush the dust from her body, and lead her to her small bedchamber (*kiton*) where she is allowed to rest.[76] The ant's world may be narrow and her bedchamber confined, but it is in this world and in that tiny room—*kiton* derived from the root *k.t.n.*, meaning "small"—that ants care for those in need while they recuperate. The *kiton*, in other words, is the sickroom, and it is at the heart of the Zionist economic network. It is not only the place to which the exhausted Zionist laborer returns but also the place where the tubercular poet recuperates. When Raḥel's poetic speaker exclaims that "my world is narrow [*tsar*] like the world of ant," she describes the world of her sickroom, where she can assert her poetic voice and where she can do so while being the object of attention and care, visited and admired by friends and colleagues. There, like the female ant, she can take center stage in the space of her convalescence, and she can do so all while insisting on the centrality of illness in a territorial project insistent on the health of its subjects.

Admittedly, the *kiton* is a singular space. But that singularity once again allows the speaker to confirm Zionist ideological norms while at the same time disrupting them, placing illness at the center of the colonial project as well as expounding on the poetic possibilities of a condition of illness. After all, it is only in the narrow room of pain that the speaker begins to narrate her life—to "tell about [herself]" for public consumption. And this is also true elsewhere in Raḥel's oeuvre. We might consider here one of Raḥel's lesser-known works from 1926/1927, "I Don't Complain" (Eni kovlah)," in which she also reflects on the individualized experience of the narrow room:

I don't complain! In a narrow room
the longing for space is sweetened;
in days of grief, in the cold fall
there is crimson and there is gold.

I don't complain! A poem flows
from a heart wounded in the act of loving,
and the desert sand—like the green of the field
from the peak, from Mount Nevo.

Eni kovlah! Be-ḥeder tsar
timtak kol kakh ergat merḥav;
Lime tugah, la-stav ha-kar
yesh argaman ve-yesh zahav.

Eni kovlah! Nove'a shir
Mi-petsa-lev be-ohavo,
ve-ḥol midbar—ke-yerek-nir
me-rosh pisgah, me-Har Nevo.[77]

The rhymed poem opens with an explanation, as if in response to the question that Raḥel hates so much: "How are you doing?" The assumed answer to that question would, it seems, be met with a complaint. But "I don't complain!" exclaims the speaker. Rather, the cramped and narrow room (*ḥeder tsar*) that would be expected to elicit displeasure in the speaker becomes the location in which her emotions become sweeter, more acute, and more powerful. The speaker has located herself in a confined space of distress, in a narrow room of pain, in my reading, in a sickroom.

The opening exclamation—marked by the rare exclamation point in Raḥel's oeuvre—is also one of the few instances in her poetry where the speaker is clearly identifiable as female. "Eni kovlah," she declares, conjugating the verb in the singular, feminine first-person. Like the ant in the colony, the female subject in the poem is now located in narrow quarters, demanding that we attend both to the space of the poetic action and to the gendered identity of the speaker. And, just as in the ant colony, there are elements of value and beauty even in grim situations. Referencing the colors of crimson and gold, she poeticizes what might be rendered as the clichéd aphorism in which every cloud has a silver lining. Recall here Sholem Aleichem's introduction to "Shmuel Shmelkes" where he writes that "there is nothing in the world that is so bad that some good can't come of it." For Sholem Aleichem, this includes leeches that help the sick and bees that make honey.[78] For Raḥel, this has previously included the ant colony and now expands to include the narrow room of pain where the female speaker will begin to express herself.

In the second stanza, the difficult situation acquires creative potency. A wounded *lev* becomes the source of poetry. In "My New Room" Raḥel "had reconciled" her heart "to the disruptor." Here, in contrast, poetry flows precisely from her afflicted and ailing *lev*—her heart, her chest, perhaps her lung. Famously, Elaine Scarry has argued that pain destroys language. "Whatever pain achieves," writes Scarry, "it achieves in part through its unsharability, and it ensures this unsharability through its resistance to language."[79] For Scarry, the power of pain is that it brings "about an immediate reversion to a state anterior to language." But, as Raḥel shows, while pain may stifle speech, it may also become the inspiration for written expression. Here, the speaker's wounded chest becomes the source of poetry, and pain stands as an uncomfortable catalyst for her literary output.[80]

After linking the wound with the word, Raḥel's speaker then looks out from Mount Nevo onto desert sand. For Raḥel, Mount Nevo was a location resonant with rhetorical meaning, as indicated by the title of her third collection, *Nevo*. The mountain references the biblical peak from which Moses would see the Promised Land but would not be allowed to enter.[81] But here Moses has been replaced by the female speaker. Here, Mount Nevo addresses the view from Raḥel's sickroom, from which she could see the sandy Mediterranean coast and ocean beyond. Placed in the final position of the final line, Mount Nevo seems almost to tower over the preceding poem, asserting its grandeur over what might otherwise be described as an insistently modest text in which the speaker does not wish to complain.

From this vantage on high, Raḥel's speaker also perceives desert sand as a verdant pasture (*yerek-nir*). The poem easily lends itself to a reading in which the speaker looks longingly out onto the beach and imagines a fertile land she cannot work. And such an interpretation would certainly be in line with those produced by so many of Raḥel's most sympathetic readers, who understood her poetry as performing "a project of national importance" in a manner that echoes Florence Nightingale's own efforts. In this line of interpretation, Raḥel's poetry would be the Zionist offering she submits in lieu of physical labor.

But the network of allusions, substitutions, and wordplay pushes us into a conversation about poetological subtexts and the gender politics of Hebrew writing. For Raḥel to expel her poetry onto the land, she must compare herself to Moses. The comparison aggrandizes the specifically female speaker by rendering her male. Her labor, by extension, appears as the masculine physical labor of Zionist settlement. She must transform herself into a man, the poem asserts, for her to do the work of labor Zionism. But that transformation is not neutral or, as the poem's symbolic system suggests, necessarily successful. After all, the speaker transforms herself into a failure. Like Moses, Raḥel will be physically unable to actualize her imperialist impulse.

This situation most likely vexed Raḥel, and the opening line of the poem—"I don't complain"—begins to ring hollow. The phrase *yerek-nir*, however, appears to offer both Raḥel and her readers a poetological solution. When unvocalized, the Hebrew word *nir* (*nun-yud-resh*) may also signify *niyar*—not a field but paper. This secondary interpretation is reinforced by the shared end position of *shir* (poem) in line 5 and *nun-yud-resh* (paper) in line 7. Raḥel appears to substitute her poetry for her inability to work the land. Like her Victorian counterparts, Raḥel performs the work of imperial labor from her sickroom.

Matters, however, become complicated when we consider a secondary meaning that attends the term *yerek*. Ostensibly a word referring to the green vegetation on the field below, the term also shares its root with that of the ailing poet's sputum, *yerikah*. It further phonically signals the poet's own physical emaciation—a body made empty (*reik*) by the devastating disease. The labor that the speaker provides is now seen to be not just literary but also pathological. Here, the poem fights against the Zionist impulses of the poet, as the speaker inseminates the land with disease. On the one hand, she surpasses Moses, who could only gaze upon the land. On the other hand, she does so by seeding the land with the stuff of her illness. She thus offers an alternative to an idealized vision of Hebrew writing as male, strong, and vivifying. Rather, she harnesses the Romantic and diasporic possibilities of tuberculosis to send forth her poetry onto the Hebrew literary landscape of the *yishuv*. In short, she has infected the land and left her mark using a biological weapon, writing herself into the canon through the inconvenient truth of illness.[82]

Wendy Zierler has argued that, by isolating herself, Dvora Baron was able to produce work primarily set in eastern Europe that artfully commented on the flaws of Zionist literary orthodoxies and political aspirations with which she was confronted in Palestine and, subsequently, Israel.[83] As evidenced in "I Don't Complain," the sickroom similarly offers Raḥel the possibility of critique. To be sure, it is unlikely that Raḥel would have volitionally sought to debilitate the Zionist project; any attempt to read her as anything other than a Zionist writer falls decidedly flat. Yet here, the colonial project appears poetically and botanically corrupting. An experience of disease may have provided the spatial conditions for her poetic project, chosen motifs, and even her poetic perspective, but it also reveals itself to be a contaminant. Her poetry, like the colonized land, has been implanted with the germ of an incurable illness. The consequences for the Zionist project, no less Zionist poetics, may be terminal. With this choice, moreover, the poem appears to offer a countermode to Shlonsky's vision of Hebrew culture. Instead, Raḥel's work imagines poetic output that is contagious, expansionist, and explicitly the product of female intervention.

From behind the Window

In light of my reading of "I Don't Complain," the question remains: With what type of literary expression has Raḥel flooded the land? Is the poem simply a nationalist offering of a poet to her people? Is it a work of self-castigation? Or is it a more complicated exposition of disease, rage, and vengeance couched in a lyrical poem? Is it, by extension, an ambivalent commentary on the source of poetic expression or the pathological corruption of the colonialist project? Such similarly complicated explorations of disease, writing, and the space of confinement reappear across Raḥel's writing. The tension is further encompassed by a second architectural motif that punctuates her oeuvre: the window.

The motif of the window draws our attention to the liminal space between the confined sickroom and the world beyond. If in her earliest sanatorium poetry, Raḥel announced her intention to "close the shutters more tightly," in her later poetry she came to embrace her position next to the window. As it did for her Victorian counterparts, the position by the window would function as "a place of visionary perspective."[84] As scholars have shown, the presence of a window in the sickroom was extremely important for the Victorian patient. Confined to a narrow space, the patient often invested the act of looking out the window with great rhetorical power. Harriet Martineau, for example, preferred a view of the sea. The waters that were "perpetually shifting" gave her a sense of the motion of life outside the sickroom. Yet, as she warned her readers, "there must not be too much sea."[85] Only with moderation would the sense of vastness not overwhelm the confined patient. Martineau's memoirs are filled with similar anecdotes about how she managed to psychologically escape her housebound life not by physically leaving but by looking through the window at the sea.[86]

Raḥel's experiences suggest the same. Her visitors repeatedly comment on the importance of the view from her apartment's window, and the poet herself would repeatedly find inspiration through the windowpane, as in the poem "Pear Tree."[87] Inspired by the tree visible from her room, the poet describes an unnamed male subject who watches as a pear tree blooms into a wreath of flowers outside his window (*mul ḥalono*). This wreath, a symbol of spring, also prevents the subject from dwelling on a flower that had perished the previous fall. As the speaker explains, the figure cannot remain glum when there is a "giant wreath of flowers right outside his window [*zer peraḥim anaki lemo ḥalono mamash*]." The proximity of the wreath is emphasized—it is *mamash* outside the window—as if to indicate that the window

Figure 4. Illustration by Aba Fenichel. Source: *Shirat Raḥel* (Tel Aviv: Davar, 1972), 157.

is not a projection of an imaginary space but a mediator of real-life and real-time experience.

Across Raḥel's oeuvre, the window itself repeatedly occasions reflection and the act of poetry. It also becomes a metaphor for the insights that accrue to the poet in pain. We must consider here one final poem, written in July 1926. Here Raḥel thematizes together both the window and her narrow space of confinement. The poem reads in full:

Not a relative—but so very close,
not a stranger—but so very far,

and embarrassed wonder pours forth
from tender touch.

Will you remember? The walls closed
and above the strange crowd
there was woven from threads of looks
a bridge—a letter.

If you have caused pain—blessed is the pain,
pain has clear windows.
My way is on the side paths
and my heart is calm.

Lo go'el—ve-karov kol kakh,
lo nokhri—ve-khol kakh raḥok,
u-temihah nevokhah yitsok
ha-maga ha-rakh.

Ha-tizkor? Sagru ha-kirot
u-me'al le-hamon ha-zar
mi-kure mabatim nishzar
gesher—ot.

Im hikh'avta—barukh ha-ke'ev,
yesh la-ke'ev ḥalonot tsaḥim.
Netivi be-tside derakhim
ve-libi shalev.[88]

The poem addresses an unnamed male counterpart with whom the speaker has a fraught but close relationship. He is introduced through a series of litotes—he is neither a redeemer (*go'el*) nor a relative (alt., *go'el*), and his distance and relationship to the reader are equally suspect (*karov* as relative / *karov* as close). The first stanza suggests that perhaps the speaker and this man were lovers, between whom a "tender touch" elicited "embarrassed wonder." Yet the delicateness of that "touch" and the simplicity of that exchange is called into question when we consider the pathological connotation of *maga*—contact. It was precisely *maga* with a tubercular victim that was to be avoided.[89] It was also the tuberculosis patient who, across the European Romantic tradition, bore with it the connotation of seductive beauty and sexual allure.[90] So too, here, the ostensibly ominous threat of contagion and contamination also bears with it an overt sign of affection. Once again, the rhetoric of illness is coded as both positive and negative, generative and destructive, and engaged with European and Russian antecedents while transplanting them into a Hebrew, Zionist idiom.

The dual valence of disease as well as the pathological connotation of *maga* gains further currency as we move to the second stanza. The tone switches from a reflective mode concerning the relation of the speaker with the man to a direct address. "Will you remember?" asks the speaker, who proceeds to narrate an experience, whereby walls closed in and a space of confinement on high emerges. The space on high recalls here the titular location of Raḥel's early Russian poem "I Live High Up in a Sanatorium." There, the speaker retreats of her own volition into a narrow room. In the later Hebrew poem, the speaker has no choice. The walls do not close themselves; rather, an unknown set of forces causes the walls to close in on the speaker (*sagru ha-kirot*). Yet this space of confinement is not without opportunity, as it manifests as a place of literary possibility. From the enclosed room on high, looks are woven together into a bridge of letters, the building blocks of words. *Ot*, which I have here rendered as "letter," may also refer to a sign. The speaker's looks are braided together into a discursive bridge that connects the room on high to the world below, the poet in her garret to her reader on the ground and outside the walls. The possibility of confinement does not elicit a poetic command, as it did in "I Live High Up in a Sanatorium"; rather, it begins a process in which the gaze becomes another set of poetic expressions.

The importance of the visual mechanism is further emphasized in the third stanza. The speaker turns her attention once again to the unnamed male object who has caused her pain. Specifically, the pain he has caused is identified as the proprietor of "clear windows." Here, the speaker blesses pain, for it enables clarity and allows the speaker to see through the window. At the end of the poem, the speaker declares that "my heart is calm." Once again, the process of writing is placed in conversation with the speaker's chest. The question for her readers then becomes, if her *lev* is now calm, will more poetry come forth? That the poem ends directly after the statement may indicate a negative answer. Does this imply that a precondition of poetry is the body in pain? Will poetry, as "I Don't Complain" posits, pour forth only from a wounded *lev*? And, considering the Zionist ideological context of her writing, is this a poem that acknowledges the limited cultural capital attending tuberculosis in the time and place of Raḥel's experience of illness?

Conclusion: Pathological *Pashtut*

Navigating between the previous texts generates more questions than answers. Nevertheless, by reading these poems together and investigating Raḥel's poetic fascination with the window and confined spaces, we are able to rearticulate the relationship between her writing and her disease. That relationship is not merely one of posthumous back-narration but also of immanent literary concern to Raḥel as a poet who sat, wrote, and socialized in the sickroom. For more than a metaphorical space, Raḥel's sickroom was also a very real physical dwelling. Between its four walls and window, the sickroom was the physical space where she demonstrated her literary magnetism, where she wooed her guests, where she recited poetry, and where she placed herself at the center of a network of readers, writers, and editors. These admirers and friends went in and out of her urban abode, engaging her in conversations about literature, helping her garner financial support, and cementing her posthumous reputation as a pale figure in a sparse room. Although she never achieved the complete financial security so lauded by Virginia Woolf in that "room of her own," she planted the seed of her tubercular capital in the sickroom, and it would grow into what might now be called the "Raḥel industry" of contemporary Israeli tourism and publishing.[91]

It was a room, moreover, in which Raḥel negotiated her relationship within the Zionist project as an ailing writer. Repeatedly, we see that the space of the sickroom would nurture a poetic and poetological conversation between her experience of illness, her impulses as a writer, her subtle reflections on her identity as a woman artist, and her ideological commitments. The result is a complicated poetic field, seeded by both spit and politics. It is one where Raḥel continuously charges her poetry with the work of labor Zionism while, at the same time, reflecting on its infected source. It is a source that stands as a pathological and poetic point of origin at distinct odds with Zionist cultural ideals.

It is here that we might consider one final consequence of the sickroom motif as an interpretive lens into the biography and writing of Raḥel. The tight spaces of her home, I suggest, further function as shorthand for the architecture of her own acmeist work. At times, this work translates the conditions of her dwelling place into the framing of her poetry: her lines are consistently short; her tone, restrained; and her subjects—the room, the land, unrequited love—consistently bounded. Yet, as we have noted, the so-called simplicity (*pashtut*) of her work belies an often complicated engagement of phonic and lexical codes, of aggrandizing biblical allusions, and of subtle references to the pathological conditions of her writing. In fact, Raḥel's chosen mode also bears with it the coarticulation of style and symptom. *Pashtut*, after all, shares its root (*p.sh.t.*) with the verb *le-hitpashet* (to spread, to be disseminated) as well as the verbal noun *hitpashtut* (spreading, dissemination). Both of these forms were already in use among physicians and public health advocates during Raḥel's lifetime. In 1927, Dr. Avigdor Mandelberg of the Palestine Anti-Tuberculosis League wrote an article for *Davar*, the same weekly paper that would make Raḥel a household name. In it, he warned of the high potential for the spread (*hitpashtut*) of tuberculosis in Palestine, specifically among Zionist laborers. He called on his readers to support the efforts of the recently established Anti-Tuberculosis League, both ideologically and monetarily.[92] In the same year that Mandelberg advocated on behalf of the tubercular patients, Raḥel publicly agitated for a new mode in poetry. In 1927, Raḥel championed *pashtut* as the "literary sign of the times [*ot ha-zeman*]" in what has been taken to be her unofficial literary manifesto.[93] The subject of Raḥel's *pashtut* has long intrigued scholars, who correctly argue that her poetry is neither simple nor superficial. Yet they overlook here the semantic range of the aesthetic choice—the pathological potential energizing her poetry. Disease, and the sickroom that framed it, would become the conditions of possibility for Raḥel's poetry, writing practices, and posthumous legacy. Tubercular capital, as it were, mobilized to define and complicate one writer's intervention in the project of Zionist poetics.

For both Sholem Aleichem and Raḥel Bluvshtein, the tubercular experience offered an entrance into a literary conversation with a host of consumptive literary predecessors. Yet in their immediate context, the disease marked these two writers out as decidedly singular. Neither writer found himself or herself taking the cure alongside fellow literary travelers afflicted by the so-called authors' disease.[94] When Ḥayim Naḥman Bialik placed Raḥel in a literary line following Mane and Mikhal, he did so only after she had already passed away. Raḥel, in fact, is the sole tubercular figure of the modern Hebrew canon who took the cure in Palestine. While the space of her sickroom was decidedly, if not surprisingly, social, her visitors did not share her experience of illness. They could not speak of tubercular pain firsthand.

For the group of writers explored in the following chapter, it was precisely a shared experience of illness and space of recuperation that proved to be of paramount creative importance. If the sickroom was the key medico-experiential space of Raḥel's recuperation, the many rooms of Denver's Jewish Consumptives' Relief Society would provide the content, context, and support for an ailing group of Yiddish writers. There, a cohort of writers would engage in a mutually beneficial relationship with a health-care institution, fashioning their literary identities and crafting their legacies under the sign of the sanatorium.

❨ CHAPTER 3 ❩

IN THE KINGDOM OF FEVER

The Writers of the Jewish Consumptives' Relief Society

> Nevertheless for publicity purposes, we may mention en pas[s]ant that it seems the JCRS is a fountain of poetry.
>
> **—Dr. Charles Spivak**[1]

Nearly two decades after her death, Raḥel Bluvshtein's poetry and tubercular history caught the attention of the Yiddish writer Shea Tenenbaum. Based in New York, Tenenbaum had recently published a review of Raḥel's work in the Buenos Aires weekly *Di naye tsayt*. Reading her work in Yiddish translation, Tenenbaum had been immediately impressed by Raḥel's simple style and gentle tone.[2] He also expressed particular sympathy for the suffering she had endured as a result of her disease. It was her suffering, he also noted, that placed her within a long line of patient-poets, including her consumptive Russian predecessor Semyon Nadson. For Tenenbaum, this was a literary genealogy with which he was intimately familiar. Like Raḥel, Tenenbaum had suffered from tuberculosis for many years. In 1936, he entered the JCRS, a sanatorium for indigent Jews in Denver, Colorado. While there, he would narrate himself into a tubercular tradition parallel to that of Raḥel—in his case, one that that would run to and through the JCRS.

While Sholem Aleichem sought relief on the Italian coast and Raḥel retreated to her sickroom in Palestine, the poets of the JCRS recuperated at what might be described as an ersatz writers' retreat in the shadow of the Rocky Mountains. When the future Bible translator Yehoash left behind his East Coast work in a glass factory, he found an eager literary collaborator in the JCRS director Dr. Charles Spivak; together, they would author a dictionary containing "all the Hebrew and Chaldaic elements of the Yiddish language"—all the Yiddish words of Hebraic and Aramaic origin.[3] When the aspiring Yiddish poet Lune Mattes left a suffocating cigar factory in Chicago to enter the JCRS in 1918, he found himself handed pencil and paper and shown to a library filled with Yiddish, English, Russian, and German works of world literature.[4] And when the established Yiddish poet H. Leivick entered the sanatorium in 1932, he found that he had ample time to devote to writing—time he had sorely lacked while working as a wallpaper hanger in New York City. During his two stints in the JCRS, Leivick composed dozens of poems, wrote hundreds of letters, and edited multiple journals. He also published what would become perhaps the most famous example of JCRS poetry, "The Ballad of Denver Sanatorium."[5] The writers who entered or connected with the JCRS encountered an institution that would foster their professional careers, offering them new publishing venues, new opportunities to be translated, and new forums in which to craft their literary and public identities. In what Leivick called "the kingdom of fever," the JCRS emerged as a generative space of literary opportunity.[6]

The story this chapter tells is one in which a health institution came to function, in the words of Charles Spivak, as a "fountain of poetry." We will see precisely how the JCRS supported such creative potential. The JCRS relied on a group of writers to advertise the mission of the sanatorium and, in turn, provided those writers with a national platform. The JCRS also generated such symbiotic relationships with tubercular and nontubercular writers alike. Most important, it offered several of its writers the chance to see their work translated and to break into the English-language market. The JCRS also provided its writers with a literary tradition in which to situate their own literary careers as the chroniclers, advertisers, and inheritors of the JCRS's cultural legacy. Tubercular capital, accordingly, was both acquired and expended by JCRS writers who worked to bolster their own careers while supporting the institution that would make those careers possible.[7]

The JCRS and Its Field Solicitors

At the turn of the twentieth century, tuberculosis was the second leading

Figure 5. Interior view of the JCRS Library, ca. 1940s. Source: The Beck Archives, Special Collections, Center for Judaic Studies and University Libraries, University of Denver. Reprinted with permission.

cause of death in the United States.[8] For many ailing Americans, Colorado was seen as the ideal health destination. In the years before antibiotics, pulmonary patients had flocked to the Rocky Mountain region in search of what was considered Colorado's restorative mountain air.[9] Resorts and hospitals attracted a diverse group of patients, from the African American writer Paul Laurence Dunbar to the socialite Constance Pulitzer.[10] As one health seeker recalled, "What magic there was in that name—Colorado! To my mind it was truly Eldorado!"[11] Years later, Rabbi Zvi Hirsch Masliansky, a national director of the JCRS, would similarly declare Colorado to be the "Eden of the West."[12]

For many Jewish patients, Masliansky's statement resonated strongly. By 1903, the Denver Jewish community was facing a mounting problem. Every day, tubercular Jews arrived in the western city lacking the resources to pay for treatment, shelter, or even burial.[13] They arrived from across the country, most often from the urban centers of New York, Philadelphia, and Chicago. There, they frequently lived in overcrowded tenements and worked in poorly ventilated sweatshops. Such patients were commonly known in Yiddish circles as "victims of the capitalist system," having worked until they were too sick to continue yet too poor to seek help.

It was a situation with which the founders of the JCRS were very familiar. Soon after ground was broken on the JCRS in 1904, the institution established itself as the sanatorium that specifically catered to indigent Jewish patients. Led by the Russian-Jewish immigrant Charles Spivak, the JCRS welcomed those considered most in need of help.[14] Whereas the National Jewish Hospital of Denver denied entry to patients with late-stage tuberculosis, the JCRS welcomed them.[15]

As Spivak was well aware, many of the most desperate and poorest patients were also Yiddish speakers. As a result, when Spivak set out to fund-raise on behalf of the JCRS, he enlisted help not only from the English-speaking Jewish middle class but also from those closest to the Yiddish-speaking community: its writers. These writers, like those who had written appeals on behalf of Sholem Aleichem, voiced their support across party lines. By 1906, calls to support the JCRS had appeared in the communist-anarchist *Fraye arbayter shtime*, the socialist *Forverts*, and the Orthodox *Yidishes tageblat*.[16] The beloved "sweatshop poet" Morris Rosenfeld also wrote a stirring appeal in *Der teglikher herald* of Chicago. "In years past," he wrote, "old Jews would go to the Land of Israel to die. Now the best of our Jewish youth go to Denver."[17] In Rosenfeld's language, Denver had become an ironized Promised Land.

In addition to newspaper appeals, the JCRS enlisted a cohort of writers to take the message of the JCRS on the road. The most prominent among these field solicitors was Yehoash, perhaps best known on account of his magisterial Yiddish translation of the Hebrew Bible.[18] Né Yehoash-Solomon Bloomgarden, the then-aspiring poet had immigrated to America from Lithuania in 1890. After arriving, he had bounced around from job to job, trying his hand as a Hebrew tutor, tailor, peddler, and bookkeeper in a glass factory. The choking dust of the factory proved deleterious to his health and exacerbated his tubercular condition.[19] On June 16, 1899, nearly a decade after landing in New York, he arrived in Denver "more dead than alive."[20] He found temporary shelter in a farmhouse, surrounded by snow-capped mountains that he would go on to poeticize in such works as "Sunset in Colorado" and "Amid the Colorado Mountains."[21] In the latter, a fiery sun sets over the mountains.[22] After a tumultuous storm, the landscape regroups, and the calmness of the gold and purple twilight resumes its tranquil reign. The energy in the poem soars to great heights as the storm passes over the range.

During the decade or so that Yehoash spent in Denver, his career would similarly climb peak after peak, and he would leave Colorado with a glowing reputation. Before Yehoash had arrived in America, he had already begun to make a name for himself in the Warsaw literary scene, where he had published a Yiddish translation of Lord Byron's poem "The Gazelle."[23] In New York, he turned his attention to Hebrew writing with little success. While in Denver, he returned to Yiddish and began to publish regularly in the New York newspapers. He also oversaw the publication of his first volume of poetry. Finally, he became involved with the JCRS. Although never formally an in-house patient, he was actively invested in the JCRS's success.[24] In January 1904, he was named to the JCRS Printing Committee, and in 1906, he became the chair of the Committee on Press and Propaganda.[25] In that role, he oversaw the publication of the in-house journal, the *Sanatorium*. He also served as the official editor of the *Sanatorium*'s Yiddish-language supplement.

Alongside this editorial work, Yehoash also became involved with the fund-raising arm of the JCRS. In the summer of 1908, Yehoash became a JCRS field solicitor, embarking on a cross-country fund-raising and reading tour. Distinguishing himself among his fellow agents, Yehoash assumed the role while visibly ill.[26] Audience members who attended his readings recalled the poet's willingness to sacrifice his own well-being for the JCRS. "Yehoash is a sick man and his physicians told him he must remain in Colorado if life was dear to him," wrote one reporter for the *St. Louis Star*. "But he knew that the institution which had saved many a man needs funds. . . . He, therefore, disregarded the advice of his physician and of his friends and went East. He has reaped financial success. Not for himself, but for the institution on whose behalf he went."[27] A reporter in Philadelphia similarly lauded Yehoash as "brave almost to foolishness, for he is risking his health for the sake of the cause so dear to him."[28] Here, we find echoes of Yehoash as Molière, but with

Figure 6. Dr. Charles Spivak in the office of the JCRS with a photograph of Yehoash on his desk, ca. 1910. Source: The Beck Archives, Special Collections, Center for Judaic Studies and University Libraries, University of Denver. Reprinted with permission.

a twist: Yehoash appears to sacrifice his health not for art but for his fellow sufferers of tuberculosis.[29]

The reporter's description of Yehoash's success, however, is only partially accurate. True, his tour had proven economically profitable for the JCRS. "The renown and esteem which the classes and the masses have shown for their beloved poet, Yehoash," wrote Charles Spivak, "helped to replenish the coffers of the Society to the extent of $10,000."[30] But the financial success of the tour also translated into a shift in Yehoash's own symbolic capital. While on tour, Yehoash recited poetry at benefits throughout the Midwest and Northeast, leaving in his wake a network of promotional reviews. Large crowds also attended his many performances, which themselves were publicized heavily in Yiddish papers. Newspaper advertisements and event tickets further displayed his name in a large font, graphically communicating his growing stature.[31] As described by one JCRS physician, Yehoash was frequently greeted with hero worship.[32] His fellow JCRS field agent Jacob Marinoff wrote proudly to Yehoash's wife to report on his success. "When Bloom got up on the stage," wrote Marinoff referring to Yehoash by his nickname, "every one [*sic*] in the vast audience rose to their feet and cheered, cheered, cheered. . . . The Theatre shakes, the stage cracks, and bloom [*sic*], deeply moved, bowes [*sic*] again, and bears up like a heroe [*sic*]."[33] Written with quick strokes, the letter evinces the excitement of Yehoash's performance. But Marinoff's words are also a signal to historians of tubercular literary complexes, offering a glimpse into Yehoash's performance as that of both a field agent on assignment and a poet on a publicity tour.

That a writer would lend his name and literature to a charity evening was not uncommon during this period. Just as Yehoash's tour passed through New York, the Yiddish writers Leon Kobrin and Jacob Gordin were slated to perform at benefits for Sholem Aleichem, who was then taking the cure in Italy. Advertisements for a benefit to assist Sholem Aleichem even appeared on the same page as advertisements encouraging readers to buy tickets for a JCRS evening where Yehoash would be appearing.[34] Scholars of nineteenth-century literature and medicine may also recall Charles Dickens's first public reading held in 1858 on behalf of London's Hospital for Sick Children. Dickens was already a beloved author, and that evening marked what Malcolm Andrews has shown to be the "launching [of] his professional career as a [public] Reader." Dickens, demonstrates Andrews, would go on to secure a handsome income through his public readings around England.[35]

By 1858, Dickens had an active readership and was capable of filling performance venues across Britain. Similarly, Sholem Aleichem was already a beloved Yiddish writer, and his illness generated a global fund-raising response. In contrast, Yehoash's national fund-raising campaign corresponded to the poet's *first* poetry tour. It was his *first* chance to read from his *first* volume of poetry, which had only appeared in 1907. Just as we find advertisements identifying Yehoash as a famous and beloved poet, we also find material that introduces him as a writer who is presumably unknown. A reporter in the Chicago *Jewish Courier*, for example, acknowledges that his readers might not be as familiar with this poet as they are with other writers.

After all, his poor health had pulled him to Denver, far from the hubs of Yiddish cultural life and potential readers.[36]

Going to Denver, however, would also bring Yehoash into contact with the JCRS, which subsequently funded his cross-country promotional trip. To be clear, Yehoash was not an unknown figure in the Yiddish literary world. He was, necessarily, famous enough to be the headlining act of a fund-raising tour. Nevertheless, the tour afforded Yehoash national exposure and publicity that had heretofore been unavailable to him. For the first time, we find poems in his honor, his poetry set to music, and his legacy publicly acknowledged.[37] There emerges an entire network of Yehoash reception literature that is contingent on his participation in the JCRS evenings. The mission of the JCRS further dovetails here with Yehoash's own process of cementing his legacy, winning over readers, and capitalizing on his public experience of illness. Perhaps this is best exemplified by the words of Judge Julian Mack. In May 1909, Mack had introduced Yehoash at a JCRS benefit in Chicago. He explained to the audience how best to help their tubercular brethren, by encouraging them to become "members and contributors to the Jewish Consumptives' Relief Society, but *above all* tonight," he added, "we must not forget the tribute to the Yiddish language and literature . . . and to the profound and beautiful verses of Yehoash."[38] *Above all*, they should not forget that the benefit was not only for the JCRS but also a symbolic and economic tribute to Yiddish literature and its representative—Yehoash.

The JCRS as Agent of Translation

Yehoash was not the only writer whose reputation grew as a result of his involvement with the JCRS. Other writers followed suit not by going on tour or by traveling to Denver but by contributing to the JCRS's in-house magazine, the *Sanatorium*. Publications like the *Sanatorium*, as Ernest Gilman has shown, were a common feature of sanatorium life in America. According to some physicians, writing could be palliative and patients were encouraged to flex their literary skills. "In the absence of any magic bullet," Gilman explains, "writing, as a means of alleviating fear and boosting morale, served along with diet, bed rest, and sunlight as a means of detoxifying the tubercular body."[39] This message was not lost on the pages of the *Sanatorium*. In May 1907, the journal introduced a column titled "Cough Drops," which devoted itself to the humorous side of JCRS life.[40] In later years, the JCRS also funded patient journals, such as *Tales of the Tents* (1914–18), *Hatikvah* (1923–32), and the *Cure-ier* (1950–60), which printed texts by JCRS "guests" regardless of quality.[41] "Think you have no writing ability?" asked the editors in April 1926. "Make an attempt. . . . 'Unload' by writing for *Hatikvah*."[42]

In the early years of the JCRS, however, the *Sanatorium* was more discerning in its literary tastes. Unlike future patient journals, the *Sanatorium* charged itself with the task of raising money and attracting donors. When it first appeared in 1907, its editors stated that "we want this magazine to be an open forum for the expression of views as to the best means and methods for increasing interest and raising funds for our cause."[43] By the second edition, the magazine was paying for itself. Five hundred subscriptions had already been sold![44] By 1909, the journal had a circulation of more than twelve thousand and claimed that seventy-five thousand readers perused its pages.[45] The magazine emerged as a productive advertisement for the JCRS that would go on to be praised by Jews and non-Jews, in Yiddish and English, for its aesthetic standards and material quality.[46] It also published a variety of texts, including articles about the JCRS as well as accounts of new treatments. Never far from its fund-raising goal, the journal also printed the records of both large and small donations—including one of fifty cents by Harry Yudkoff of Bayonne, New Jersey, and one of five dollars by S. Post of New York City, otherwise known as the great-grandfathers of the present author.[47]

Recognizing that its project required the broadest support base, the JCRS also knew it had to attract both Yiddish and English speakers. The result was that the *Sanatorium* became a bilingual publication. At the turn of the twentieth century, this was not a widespread phenomenon.[48] The Yiddish literary tradition in America had been gaining momentum since the 1880s, as immigration increased and new readers and writers arrived in the United States; however, the crossover appeal of Yiddish literature remained negligible, and support for translations was generally uncommon.[49] Yet from its inaugural edition in January 1907, the *Sanatorium* published material in both English and Yiddish, and, as mentioned earlier, an official Yiddish supplement was formally inaugurated under Yehoash's editorship that September.[50] The English section was certainly dominant and usually longer than the Yiddish component. The magazine also did not always print the same material in both languages. Nevertheless, the *Sanatorium* became an occasion for English-Yiddish translation and experimentation that offered Yiddish writers the chance to cross linguistic boundaries.

The editors even solicited Yiddish writers to contribute to the journal by specifically highlighting the magazine's bilingual nature. In April 1908, Yehoash invited the famous playwright Jacob Gordin to submit material to the *Sanatorium*. Appealing to Gordin as a fellow "Russian Jew," Yehoash explained that the sanatorium published a "bi-monthly journal *in Yiddish and English* together." He then added that "it doesn't matter how small the submission, your prestige as a world-famous dramaturge will indirectly help our holy work."[51] Yehoash's request is calculated: First, he appeals to fraternal sentiments; then, he specifically identifies the *Sanatorium* as a bilingual publication; and, finally, he requests a submission that speaks to the symbolic capital that Gordin's donation would engender. In short, Yehoash framed his appeal in the name of philanthropy. Gordin, in turn, responded enthusiastically, and his reply letter was printed in the journal that July.[52] In his letter, he praised the JCRS and committed to writing more for the journal. Unfortunately, the pledge would not bear fruit before his death in 1909 from esophageal cancer.[53] This, however, did not stop the editors from capitalizing on Gordin's reputation and repeating in both Yiddish and English that the famous playwright had written for their publication.[54] After Gordin's death, the journal also published an English translation of his letter under a note honoring the writer's commitment to the JCRS.[55]

Unlike Gordin, the Yiddish playwright Leon Kobrin lived to see his work translated into English in the *Sanatorium*.[56] In 1908, the journal published Kobrin's one-act play, *The Rescue* (*Di retung*), in both Yiddish and English. The drama tells the story of Morris Gutman, a desperate man suffering from tuberculosis. The play's message on behalf of the JCRS is blunt: Donate money or else the wife of the aptly named Gutman (good man) will be forced to prostitute herself to raise the money to send her husband to Colorado. Never missing an opportunity to capitalize on the prestige of the journal's contributors, the editors emphasized that Kobrin's text had been "specially written for 'The Sanatorium' by the well-known Yiddish litterateur and playwright."[57]

Kobrin was indeed a beloved figure of Yiddish drama at the turn of the century. He was also an active translator, rendering the work of Turgenev, Chekhov, and Zola into Yiddish. He further maintained an authorial persona that constantly referenced his own wide reading habits. For example, his Yiddish play *The Blind Musician, or, the Jewish Othello* premiered in New York in 1903. The play is loosely based on the Shakespearean drama, taking its title both from *Othello* and Vladimir Korolenko's Russian novel *The Blind Musician* (1886). As Joel Berkowitz has demonstrated, Kobrin's production drew little inspiration from either text besides the titular allusions. The importance of the play as a Shakespearean adaptation, however, rests in Kobrin's decision to reset *Othello* in New York.[58] To that end, as Shmuel Niger notes, Kobrin's play deployed an Americanized Yiddish idiom. Reading Kobrin with Niger as his guide, Berkowitz considers the language used by Kobrin's characters, who pepper their speech with Yiddish Americanisms such as "never mind" and "don't be fresh."[59] Such Americanisms are also in evidence in *Di retung*, where one character enters from *nekst-dor* (next door) and another visits a *poyn-shap* (pawn shop).

Despite such diction, Kobrin did not cross over into English until *The Rescue*. There, his Americanisms are of course undetectable. Instead, what stand out are the Yiddish or Hebrew phrases that are glossed in footnotes. The English reader of Kobrin's text appears not to be expected to understand that "Blessed be the true judge" is a translation of the Hebrew phrase recited upon hearing the news that someone has died; the phrase remains undefined in the Yiddish text, where such verbal practices would be recognizable as part of everyday discourse. Similarly, the English text italicizes the *arbe kanfes* that Morris wears and footnotes the ritual garb as a "small prayer shawl . . . worn constantly by pious Jews."[60] Evidenced in this explanation is the broad range of potential donors whom the JCRS hoped to attract, ranging from recent Yiddish immigrants (who would have read *Di retung* in the original) to more assimilated English speakers at a cultural remove from Jewish custom.

Most important, the needs of the JCRS translated into Kobrin's opportunity to cross linguistic boundaries. With his textual submission to the *Sanatorium*, he became legible to an English readership, and he did so with a heavy-handed and moralistic tale about an ailing consumptive in need of funds to travel to Colorado. Here, a translation complex begins to emerge, linking institution, writer, and translated story in a literary-philanthropic network. This network would go on to crisscross the country, as Kobrin's text landed in the hands of English and Yiddish donor-readers alike.

Finally, the *Sanatorium* also worked to bring not only Yiddish texts to an English audience but also English texts to a Yiddish audience. In 1908, the JCRS journal printed a translation into Yiddish of Morris Winchevsky's English short story, "Cranky Old Ike."[61] Known primarily as a socialist Yiddish poet, Winchevsky also wrote prose for the British socialist press. "Cranky Old Ike" first appeared in the London monthly the *British Socialist*.[62] Like Kobrin's play, Winchevsky's story lent itself to a fund-raising cause. Its hero is named "Cranky Old Ike," which is rendered into Yiddish as "*der alter krenk Ayk*." Intriguingly, the English term "crank" is not translated but, rather, transliterated, rendering the title character sick (*krenk*) rather than curmudgeonly. Ike/*Ayk*'s sickly nickname announces that illness is at the center of this story.

The text also informs its readers that Ike's family died in a typhoid epidemic in Russia. He subsequently immigrated to America, where he began to work in a factory. At this point, the story narrates Ike's shift from an apathetic laborer to a socialist ideologue. The transformation specifically occurs after Ike hears the speech of a socialist politician who "showed that the unsanitary conditions prevailing in the dwellings of the poor render them a sure prey to every contagious disease."[63] In the Yiddish translation, "prey" is rendered as *korbn*, a polysemous word meaning both "sacrifice" and "victim." As described earlier, those suffering from tuberculosis were often troped in Yiddish as *victims* (*korbones*) of the capitalist system or of the proletarian disease. The socialist in Winchevsky's English text trying to gain political constituents becomes the anti-tuberculosis Yiddish activist fund-raising on behalf of the JCRS and its patient-*korbones*. If the reader of the *Sanatorium* wondered why this story had been chosen, the answer is now clear. The socialist politician's message is the same as that of the field solicitors of the JCRS: poor urban Jews are living in conditions that predispose them to diseases such as tuberculosis, and something must be done. Time and time again, the *Sanatorium* fostered a translingual and translational conversation with the agenda of the JCRS never too far out of reach.

Yehoash: Between English and Yiddish

For Gordin, Kobrin, and Winchevsky, the *Sanatorium* provided a space to cross language boundaries. For Yehoash, it became the venue for working out his identity as a bilingual writer—between Yiddish and English. Yehoash's history as a translator into Yiddish is well known. Along with the Bible, he rendered the work of Byron, Heine, and sections of the Koran into Yiddish. Less known, however, is that Yehoash began to try his hand at writing poetry in English in Denver. Drawing on the connections of his colleague Jacob Marinoff, Yehoash managed to publish his first English poems in the Zionist monthly the *Maccabaean*. These first poems were accompanied by a biographical note introducing Yehoash to the readers as a poet who had relocated to Denver on account of a pulmonary infection.[64] His entrance into English poetry would thereby be marked with reference to his disease. The poems themselves would also point obliquely to his state of illness. The first, "Phantom of Death," describes a dying soul that ". . . like the drowning man will cling / To waning life with lingering breath." The latter, "At Quarantine," describes a ship that is refused permission to dock due to illness on board—an experience that would have been familiar to tubercular Jewish immigrants.[65] Daniel Charney was perhaps the most famous Yiddish writer who had been refused entrance to America because of his ailing lungs. Chronicling the experience in the Yiddish daily *Der tog*, he reported that he had undergone each medical examination in quarantine like "a mute beast before the slaughterer."[66] After all, at the time he was unable to speak English and could not communicate with the immigration officers.

Recourse to English was painfully unavailable to Charney. It was not, however, unavailable to Yehoash, and the *Sanatorium* became the venue for him to test out his American voice and to engage the Anglo-American literary tradition—both in English and Yiddish. Consider his 1908 contribution to the journal: a jocular Yiddish poem signed in English by one pseudonymous "Lung-Fellow." Lest readers miss the allusion to his American referent, the byline is presented in Roman letters on a page otherwise devoid of English text. The poem, "A literat-kandidat," narrates the symbiotic relationship between writing and being sick. The relationship is modeled by the eponymous subject who is both a *literat* (man of letters) and *kandidat* (patient eligible for treatment). The impoverished patient-writer fears for his life, as the final quatrain reads:

There's just *one* plus, and it's big enough,
for us to now consider,
how nice and sweet, the coupling is,
of *writing* and *being sick* . . .

Eyn *mayle bloyz, genug iz groys,*
haynt ken men zikh shoyn denken,
vi sheyn un zis, der ziveg iz,
fun shrayberay *un* krenken . . .

These lines offer a wry commentary on the condition of the ailing writer who finds himself the companion of an endlessly suggestive subject: his disease.

Two years after the publication of this poem, Yehoash published his magisterial translation of Henry Wadsworth Longfellow's epic, *The Song of Hiawatha.*[67] The translation has received increased scholarly attention, as it employs the figural landscape of Native America as a site of Jewish American identity formation.[68] "What better choice for entry," notes Alan Trachtenberg, "into the alien world within which Jews found themselves on the streets of New York, a ruthlessly modern world that still dreamed itself innocent by imagining origins in an imaginary Indian past."[69] Ernest Gilman has added that taking up residence in Colorado would also have placed Yehoash in a new landscape of the American West and potentially "in contact with Native Americans for the first time."[70] Gilman also carefully analyzes the excisions Yehoash made to the text, such as removing certain Christological references that might have precluded a message of universal brotherhood from governing the moral agenda of the poem.[71]

Attention to this translation, however, has not yet considered the earlier instantiation of Yehoash's pulmonary persona. Might we find in Lung-Fellow not just playfulness but a serious claim to an American tradition inspired in and by the sanatorium? Expressed through infected lungs? And occupying a zone that rests between an English byline and a Yiddish poem? Here, the Yiddish poet makes a name for himself not as Yehoash but as *Lung-Fellow*, as the embodied poetic alter ego of a classic American writer. The more one examines the pages of the *Sanatorium*, the more one finds Yehoash continuing to work out his identity as a poet of the Anglo-American tradition, between English and Yiddish, with tuberculosis as his subject, and while advancing the JCRS mission. The premier issue of the *Sanatorium* also includes one such piece of functional creative literature, "The Dying Consumptive," a Yiddish poem by Yehoash. The poem comprises four quatrains and introduces the titular *shterbender konsomptiv* in typically Romantic terms:

His face grows thinner, paler,
his limbs, more tightly contracted,
yet his voice grows ever softer,
and his eyes ever more beautiful.

Zayn ponim vert als darer, bleykher,
di glider eynger ayngetsoygn,
dokh vert zayn shtime tomid veykher,
un tomid shener zayne oygn.

In these lines, Yehoash sketches a refined tubercular subject who is pale, gentle, and thin. He grows ever more lovely as he approaches death, to which he succumbs by the poem's closing. Keats hovers closely as the poetic interlocutor for this aestheticized invalid. In his 1819 "Ode to a Nightingale," Keats writes of a world "where youth grows pale, and spectre-thin, and dies."[72] Keats's brother had died of consumption shortly before the ode's composition. The life course of Yehoash's poetic subject would be similar to that of Keats's brother and the Romantic consumptive poetic subject he inspired.

Yehoash also published this poem in a journal explicitly aimed at attracting attention and donors. A few pages before Yehoash's text, we find a direct appeal titled "A Plea for the Consumptive" written by the local clergyman, Rabbi C. Hillel Kauver. Kauver's text further garners sympathy by describing patients with tuberculosis as "victims of the tragic, economic conditions of the East."[73] Yehoash, in contrast, presents the consumptive figure through the soft glow of a Romantic death scene. Yehoash's literary mode reads here as an alternative fund-raising technique that highlights the nobility of the tubercular-in-need rather than his desperation. Throughout this first edition of the journal, even in Kauver's article, we see a tension in the depiction of those ill as helpless but brave, sickly but determined, physically incapacitated but mentally alert. Yehoash's poem reminds potential donors of these dualisms, harnessing the Romantic tropes of consumptive beauty to the fund-raising goals of the JCRS. In short, his work elicits sympathy for the patient by depicting him as gracefully languishing and by positioning Yehoash-as-poet as the cultural arbiter of the Romantic.

Lest readers of the *Sanatorium* think, however, that Yehoash has simply fashioned himself into an ailing Yiddish Keats (predating his stint as a tubercular Lung-Fellow), we might turn to an English-language poem, "The White Plague," that Yehoash published in the following issue of the journal. The text differs both in style and language from "The Dying Consumptive":
Humanity is changing color as it goes

Its onward march—so are the miseries and woes;
Of yore the fatal war-scourge was the terror red
That like a bloody blade hung o'er the nation's head,
Black epidemics swept and thinned the human race,
Turning whole continents in one huge burial-place;
Now Fate, unsated still, is on our heels once more,
But not in robes of night or crimson garb of yore—
This greatest of all human sufferings, we call
White Plague, though blackest, fiercest of them all,
All silently it gathers in its harvest dread.
And killing inch-wise long parades its living dead.[74]

The poem compels readers to action not by depicting the person infected by tuberculosis as a capitalist victim or as a refined invalid but by presenting the disease as a relentless foe. Here, the ennobling metaphoric field of Romantic consumption has been replaced by what Susan Sontag has identified as the stigmatizing complex in which the description of illness is embedded in a metaphorics of warfare.[75] The victim is presented not only in a personal battle but confronted by an imperialist threat. "The White Plague" appears as uninterrogated Manifest Destiny gone awry. The poem's physical placement in the *Sanatorium* reinforces this message, as the text appears above a report titled "The Greatest Death Rate." The report announces the dire mortality statistics for those afflicted by pulmonary tuberculosis.[76] If the readers did not already sense the threat of "The White Plague," the subsequent article communicates it fully.

More than conveying the terror of the disease, the poem sheds light on

Yehoash's developing English-language poetic voice. Absent entirely is Yehoash the elegant Yiddish poet. Rather, his skills appear amateurish. The figurative field is heavy-handed (black, red, white); the meter is forced; the sixth line turns on an awkward preposition; and the lofty diction is repetitive to no clear rhetorical end ("yore" in lines 3 and 8). The poem reads as the product of a poet not yet comfortable or fluent in English. Compared to his Yiddish poetry, which boasts precise meter and full rhymes, "The White Plague" stands as a clunky exercise published for the benefit of the JCRS at the expense of poetic grace.

The poem had, in fact, appeared two years earlier in the *Colorado Medical Journal*, following an article about the dedication of new tents at the JCRS.[77] But if the poem were not Yehoash's finest, why republish it? Here, again, the publication context proves critical. In addition to "The White Plague," the March 1907 journal published only one other poem: "A Climate Worshipper," by the Denver-based cowboy poet, James Barton Adams.[78] The text is a paean to climatological therapy. The speaker describes his family's health as follows:

Sca'cely looked like human bein's, more like skeletons we were,
Wife a-hackin' with consumption, that was ketchin' hold o' her,
An' the younguns both a-coughin', me a-worryin' till—well,
Got discouraged till I wasn't wuth a pinch o' salt in hell![79]

The family moves from Arkansas to a mountainous region, presumably Colorado, and sets up a ranch. The new climate proves palliative, and the speaker's family soon feels well again. Written in the dialect of a rancher, purposefully riddled with misspellings, and freely making use of a low linguistic register, Adams's bawdy poem stands in contrast to the staid and now evidently polished effort of "The White Plague." Yehoash's poem is insistently grammatically correct; the diction is sophisticated; no accent is perceptible, nor any regional or ethnic locution. Yehoash's technique, albeit flawed, allows him to "pass" as an English writer of a high register.[80] His assessment of tuberculosis may no longer be Romantic, but his style bespeaks his own high literary aspirations brought into stark relief in the network of textual relations of the *Sanatorium*. Yehoash's literary profile now comes into focus, between Yiddish and English, on the pages of the *Sanatorium*, through the thematic prism of tuberculosis, and with the agenda of the JCRS lingering nearby.

The JCRS as a Literary Tradition

The final lines of "The White Plague" also read as a prescient assessment of Yehoash's time as a field solicitor. While on tour for the JCRS, he was admired in his tubercular state as an *umshterblekhn* poet who produced *umshterblekhe* poetry.[81] He and his writing were declared *undying,* immortal. Yehoash, accordingly, became one such tubercular on parade, on the border between life and death, and on the mission that became his first reading tour. Yehoash's legacy—both poetic and propagandistic—would also remain prominent in the institutional memory of the JCRS. In 1918, an aspiring Yiddish poet named Lune Mattes entered the JCRS. Five years later, he published his first poetry volume, *Open Portals* (*Ofene toyren*). Taking on the self-proclaimed roll as a "publicity man," Charles Spivak wrote to newspapers and poets alike to advertise Mattes's work. In one letter to the modernist Yiddish poet Zishe Landau, he recounted the miraculous literary ascent of Mattes in the JCRS from a near illiterate to an elegant stylist, adding:

> It is not out of place to mention the fact that one of our founders of the JCRS is a poet and to my mind perhaps the greatest Yiddish poet in the world. I refer to the fact that Mr. Yehoash wrote his first volume of poems while a resident of Denver. . . . Of course we have to say lehavdil when we mention these two poets, nevertheless for publicity purposes we may mention en pas[s]ant that it seems the JCRS is a fountain of poetry.[82]

To promote Mattes, Spivak invoked the literary lineage of the JCRS and Yehoash, albeit with the requisite *lehavdil.* Without the same caveat, Mattes himself would go on to poeticize his connection to Yehoash in his 1928 poem "Crown of His Grace" (Kroyn fun zayn genod). Dedicated to Yehoash, the poem describes an illuminated figure who beckons Mattes's poetic subject with "a gesture from his hand and a call."[83] The poem in its entirety reads as Mattes's response.

In fact, Mattes was only one among a cohort of JCRS poets who began to position themselves within a legacy of JCRS writing.[84] Chief among them was Shea Tenenbaum, the writer who at the outset of this chapter placed Raḥel's poetry in a corresponding tradition of patient-poets. When Tenenbaum entered the JCRS in 1936, he announced his arrival in Denver as a poetic homecoming. "We are finally in Denver," he wrote for a New York weekly. "Here is where those magnificent poets sought the cure and to rest: David Edelshtat, Yehoash, L. Mattes and—here's to many more years—our dear H. Leivick."[85]

Alongside Yehoash and Mattes, Tenenbaum placed himself in a lineage alongside the poet David Edelshtat, a buttonhole maker–turned–communist anarchist who died from consumption in Denver in 1892.[86] He also situated himself alongside H. Leivick, perhaps the most famous JCRS poet. By the time H. Leivick arrived in Denver in 1932 for the first of his three stays, he had already published multiple volumes of poetry, multiple dramas in verse, and the first edition of his collected works. His work has also been translated into Hebrew, and his Yiddish drama in verse, *The Golem*, was then being performed in English in Los Angeles.[87] Leivick was famous enough in the Yiddish literary world that his trip west warranted comment in all the major North American Yiddish papers.[88] His third stint at the JCRS even garnered the attention of Denver's local English-language *Post*.[89] After he left the institution, Leivick was invited to fund-raisers on behalf of the sanatorium and was called on by JCRS administrators to help other patients publish their work.[90]

For Tenenbaum, Leivick would also prove a powerful—if, at times, unsympathetic—literary interlocutor. Born in 1910 near Lublin, Tenenbaum lived a rather peripatetic lifestyle, including an extended stay at a Belgian sanatorium as well as at various homes across the United States.[91] To say that he was a prolific writer would be an understatement. He wrote multiple memoirs as well as scores of articles and poetic reflections he called "miniatures." Admittedly, the quality of his writing is inconsistent. While living in Oklahoma in the 1930s, Tenenbaum submitted work to be published in multiple American journals only to be met with frequent rejection.[92] He also corresponded with Leivick, who was then recuperating at the JCRS. At the time, Leivick was involved in editing the anthology *Zamlbikher*, to which Tenenbaum submitted his writing. He received feedback from Leivick that his style was bombastic, hysteric, and artificial. Despite the criticism, Tenenbaum continued to send Leivick his work throughout the latter's time at the JCRS.[93] He would also continue to correspond with Leivick after he, too, arrived at the JCRS and the established poet had left.

Indeed, Tenenbaum repeatedly linked his career to his literary predecessor. He did so in two ways: First, he began to explore the same poetic motifs that had occupied Leivick. Second, he fashioned himself as Leivick's literary inheritor. To do the first, Tenenbaum began to draw on the same topoi that Leivick had employed while at the JCRS. He began to make heavy use of the image of the Coloradan sunset. In an article written for the Romanian Yiddish paper *Tshernovitser bleter*, titled "H. Leivick—the Person," Tenenbaum describes sitting alone in a white room in the JCRS. There he reads Leivick's poetry and looks out the window to "see the same landscape that Leivick saw two years ago." Tenenbaum writes: "Yesterday I saw a sunset, red and flaming, and I was reminded of Leivick's poem where he sees in the sunset the Creator himself, opening the red wounds of humanity to suffer with them."[94] The scene offers us a glimpse into Tenenbaum's highly impressionable literary process. He refers here to Leivick's poem of 1930, "Clouds behind the Forest." It is a complicated, extended poetic exploration of birth, love, imprisonment, poetry, and the relationship between the human and the divine.[95] For Tenenbaum, what is most important is the final section in which a sunset is described as a scene of divine eros, where human violence and God's mercy meet and create new life. In Leivick's poem, the speaker remains lying on the ground, bloody, as if having been born a second time, and cries out, "Creator—Creator!—." We find echoes of this scene in Tenenbaum's own text, "Spring in Denver." Written during his stay at the JCRS, the vignette reproduces Leivick's fraught scene of love and death at sunset.[96] More a series of evocative poetic images than a linear narrative, the text describes the sunset against a feverish sky, which is so bright it is as if there were not merely a single sun but thousands of sun-women on the cusp of death. Similarly, a piece by Tenenbaum titled "Tuberculosis" opens with an image of sunset. It focuses on the rays of a sun, which bleed as they pierce broken windowpanes.[97] There a pale, tubercular woman lies next to a child in an atmosphere saturated by the glow of death and melancholic music.

It is decidedly possible that Tenenbaum may have broached the subject of the fiery, Coloradan sunset of his own volition, as it was a common theme among poets of the region, including Yehoash. However, throughout his time in Denver, Tenenbaum would repeatedly turn to the poetry of H. Leivick and insist on his connection to the literary great—a connection that was literary, personal, and experiential. Of particular importance would not just be various nature scenes but one specific poem by Leivick and perhaps the most famous example of JCRS writing, "The Ballad of Denver Sanatorium," later published in his ironically titled collection, *Lider fun gan eyden* (Poems from Eden).[98] The ballad, a staggering 112 quatrains, dramatizes the life and death of a tubercular patient named Nathan Newman.

Newman, as we learn, is the roommate of Leivick's first-person speaker. They do more than share a room; Newman's own life experiences mimic or complement Leivick's own. Born in a Russian shtetl, the poem explains, Newman was declared too young to be exiled to Siberia. He was similarly too young be bound by the "prison chains [*tfise-keytn*]" as Leivick would be as a young man on account of his Bundist activities.[99] Yet, as the poem asserts, Newman was old enough to contract tuberculosis. Now, in "Spivak House," he lies bound to his bed. Ernest Gilman explains that "backdating Newman's illness to his childhood," the ballad "elides political exile and tubercular wandering, Siberia and the sanatorium."[100] In doing so, Leivick collapses the temporal and biographical distinctions between imprisonment and disease, between the experience of Siberian prison camps and being chained to a sickbed.

As both Newman's roommate and double, Leivick is also witness to a parade of ailing Jewish figures who enter and exit their room and their dreams. These figures include the poet Heine, the philosopher Spinoza, and David Edelshtat—the latter two, of course, having also died from consumption.[101] Edelshtat's presence is particularly important as, in one major scene, a disembodied hand appears in "The Ballad" to write the first stanza of his most famous poem, "My Will and Testament," on the hospital wall. The poem, which would later appear on Edelshtat's Denver gravestone, calls on the working class to raise the flag of revolution. As the opening stanza reads:

O, good friends! When I die,
carry to my grave our flag of red—,
the flag of red with colors bright,
flecked with the blood of the working man!

O gute fraynt! Ven ikh vel shtarbn,
trogt tsu mayn keyver unzer fon—
di fraye fon mit di royte farbn,
bashpritst mit blut fun arbetsman![102]

In "The Ballad," Newman proceeds to make Edelshtat's poem his own. He declaims, "O, good friends, when I die / also carry to *my* grave [*tsu* mayn *keyver*] the flag of red—."[103] Newman, however, is stopped mid-verse as a tubercular hemorrhage erupts from his throat, somatizing Edelshtat's blood-splattered flag. The relationship between disease and writing is rendered most fraught in these lines as Newman's poetry becomes physically and literarily expressed in his own blood. With this act of writing-ailing, Newman also continues Edelshtat's legacy, making his own tubercular contribution to Jewish literary history. Leivick, in turn, picks up the mantle. Toward the end of "The Ballad," the speaker visits Newman's grave, which is in the same row as Edelshtat's. He looks up to see the tubercular forebearer's gravestone, on which the poem "My Will and Testament" has been etched. For the second time, the poem records the opening stanza in full. This time, however, Newman's rewriting is absent. Rather, the speaker recites Edelshtat's verse and then, in the penultimate stanza of "The Ballad," leaves the cemetery and returns to the "the kingdom of fever [*kenigraykh fun fiber*]."[104] One final stanza follows before the poem closes. Edelshtat is dead. So is Newman. But, as the poem implies, the tradition of tubercular writing in the kingdom of the JCRS continues—and it is Leivick who carries it forth.

This charge would subsequently be picked up by Shea Tenenbaum. When he reviewed Leivick's *Poems from Eden*, he could not refrain from mentioning that he had found himself in the same sanatorium where Leivick had written his poems.[105] Time and time again, Tenenbaum refuses to assume a position of critical distance from the text. As we learn from a private letter that he sent to Leivick, "The Ballad" was one of the texts that he loved to read "over and over again."[106] He further saw himself as Leivick's acolyte who sought to position himself as the poet's heir and as heir to the tradition of JCRS poets. While recuperating, Tenenbaum wrote to Leivick to inform his literary elder that he wished to write a series of articles about life in the JCRS. In the letter, he tells Leivick that he wants "to name it after a phrase from 'The Ballad.'" The phrase was *In kenigraykh fun fiber*. For Tenenbaum, the kingdom of fever to which Leivick's speaker retreats in the penultimate stanza of "The Ballad" was the definitional title of the JCRS and its literary landscape.[107]

Although Tenenbaum's volume devoted to his experiences at the JCRS was never published, he still assumed the task of chronicling its literary history.[108] In an article titled "Artists in Spivak Sanatorium," he constructs a pantheon of artistic greats who were affiliated with the sanatorium, including Leivick, Yehoash, and Mattes. Elsewhere, Tenenbaum speaks of "The Ballad" and imagines Leivick standing on Edelshtat's grave. He wonders whether Leivick would feel "dependent on the hero above whom he was standing."[109] In another memoiristic piece, Tenenbaum recalls sneaking out of the JCRS at night to visit Edelshtat's grave.[110] In the cemetery, he recites the poem engraved on Edelshtat's gravestone, "The Will"—the same poem that Leivick's Newman would recite. As Tenenbaum reads aloud, the poem "glows and burns in [his] blood like fire."[111] Then, he prophesies that soon Yehoash and H. Leivick will arrive, make a pilgrimage to Edelshtat's grave, tread on its holy ground, and read the gravestone inscription like a prayer.

The short piece inverts the generational progression of the Denver poets, as Tenenbaum places himself between Edelshtat's grave and a future arrival of Yehoash and Leivick. He also does so by reciting the poem written by Edelshtat and rewritten by Leivick. Tenenbaum's article now reads less as a confused temporal pastiche than as a volitional statement announcing the shared medico-literary history of the JCRS writers. Throughout his time in Denver, Tenenbaum repeatedly sought to identify, narrate, and situate himself in a literary genealogy of tubercular Yiddish voices. In this final act, he places himself squarely in the *kenigraykh fun fiber*, in a poetic trajectory that would condition and encompass his creative output. Far from the East Coast and eastern Europe, Tenenbaum draws his readers into the literary world of the JCRS—one that was supported by writers, one that was maintained by its writers, and one that was passed down by its writers to the next generation of patient-poets.

Conclusion: The Tubercular Network beyond the JCRS

Following the tubercular trail to and through the JCRS, there has emerged a picture of the Denver sanatorium as not only an institution for the treatment of tuberculosis but as an occasion for literary experimentation and the working out of literary identities. For Yehoash, affiliation with the JCRS offered him multiple public venues to augment his reputation and, at the same time, assist in fulfilling the mission of the JCRS. It also offered him an editorial platform, from which he could refine his poetic relationship to the

Anglo-American tradition through the thematic prism of tuberculosis. For his colleagues, such as Leon Kobrin, the JCRS provided the space to support philanthropic goals while crossing linguistic boundaries and reaching new audiences. For Leivick and Tenenbaum, it was the recognition of just such a tubercular literary tradition that was at stake. In the JCRS, Leivick brought himself into conversation with David Edelshtat and elected himself as the next tubercular flag bearer. Tenenbaum picked up that same flag and wrote himself, as well as Leivick, Yehoash, Mattes, and Edelshtat into the *kenigraykh fun fiber*.

This *kenigraykh* would also extend beyond the immediate environs of the JCRS. The literary vitality sustained by the JCRS never precluded communication with the world beyond the sanatorium. As editor, Yehoash actively solicited Yiddish writers back east to submit material. In turn, the *Sanatorium* was sent to subscribers and local JCRS support groups across the country. When Tenenbaum wrote his chronicle of the artists of the JCRS, his text appeared both in Chicago's *Yidisher kuryer* and in Warsaw's *Literarishe bleter*. His personal reflections of "H. Leivick—The Man" appeared in Czernowitz.[112]

The extension of the *kenigraykh* beyond the confines of the JCRS or Denver is best exemplified in the literary output of Daniel Charney. Having been denied entry to the United States on account of his tuberculosis, Charney spent most the 1930s moving between various sanatoria and hospitals throughout central Europe. While recuperating, he began a series of memoirs exploring his experience of disease. In 1935, Charney sent one such memoir, *Up the Mountain: Pages of a Life* (*Bargaroyf: Bletlekh fun a lebn*), to Leivick, who was then recuperating at the JCRS. The collection narrates Charney's experiences as a child and nascent socialist activist. Much of the first half concerns disease; his father died of tuberculosis, and Charney himself soon showed evidence of the disease as well as a host of other viruses and infections. Leivick wrote to Charney to thank him, explaining that he had read the text "in one breath [*in eyn otem*]," an expression that no doubt gains significance considering Leivick's tubercular state. He also suggested that Charney check out his own work, specifically recommending his "Ballad."[113]

Charney did just that. Four years after his second, and this time successful, attempt to enter America, Charney's tuberculosis had worsened. He was forced to leave his new home in New York City for the Catskills, where he entered the Workmen's Circle Sanatorium (WCS) in Liberty, New York. Like its Denver counterpart, the WCS became a space where writers socialized and developed their literary voices, although the institutional support offered the Yiddish writer in Liberty was far less developed than at the JCRS. During his stay in the WCS, Charney met his fellow tubercular poet Mani Leib.[114] He also occupied himself with reading and took particular pride in the in-house library. There, to his delight, he found his own volumes alongside those of tubercular writers like Chekhov and Maxim Gorky as well as the works of another tubercular Jewish trifecta: Sholem Aleichem, Yehoash, and Edelshtat. Charney would write that the works of these three "hover in the sanatorium library and inspire [me] to live on and create."[115] In Charney's hands, the tubercular literary tradition extended from Nervi to Denver and on to Liberty.

Charney also wrote prolifically at the WCS, chronicling his experiences as a tubercular immigrant whose hometown and family in Europe had been decimated. It was from this position that Charney wrote to Leivick in a letter dated March 1, 1946. He sent the letter one month before Leivick was to leave for war-torn Europe as a cultural representative of the Jewish World Congress. Charney tells Leivick that he hopes they can meet up once Leivick returns from Europe, where he will likely see those of Charney's friends who have survived. The purpose of the letter, though, is business. Charney explains that he has been keeping *bizi* by writing articles. In one of them, he would like to describe the "Leivick Room," likely referring here to the room that Leivick occupied during his short stay at the WCS in 1937. He asks that Leivick send him "The Ballad of Denver Sanatorium," from which he would like to quote. Four days later, Charney received the book *Poems from Eden*. In his thank-you note, Charney quotes extensively from the poem "February in Liberty."[116] Written while Leivick recovered in Liberty, the text uses many of the same motifs as Leivick's "Ballad," such as the burning sunset and the feverish hospital roommate. It even places its speaker in a *kenigraykh*, this time of silence rather than fever. We see here the JCRS literary network and tradition expanding, not only as its poets travel but also as its writers and readership extend beyond the Coloradan borders.

Charney would continue to engage Leivick's tubercular work, sometimes explicitly, sometimes elliptically.[117] For example, he would preface a subsequent memoiristic collection, *On the Threshold of the Other World* (*Oyfn shvel fun yener velt*) with a citation from Leivick's own memoiristic work, *Among the Survivors* (*Mit der sheyres hapleyte*). Leivick wrote the text during and after his trip to a displaced persons camp. The epigraph Charney chose reads:

> Consumption does her destructive work quietly, gradually, as if with silk fingers, spinning thin, delicate webs. . . . Consumption wraps herself in a mystical-philosophical canopy and carries death in her hands, as cake is carried to a holiday dance. Very few groans are heard in a tuberculosis sanatorium. And if so, the groans are inner, ashamed.
>
> *Shvindzukht tut ir tseshterendike arbet shtil, behadreygedik, kimat vi mit zeydene finger, fanandershpinendik dinike tsarte gevebn. . . . Shvindzukht hilt zikh ayn in a mistish-filosofisher khupe un trogt in ire hent dem toyt, vi men trogt lekakh af a yontevdike tants. Zeyer veynik krekhtsn hert men in a tuberkuloz-sanatoriye. Oyb yo—zaynen di krekhtsn shemevdike, inerlikhe.*[118]

Charney attributes the quote to Leivick's text *Among the Survivors*, thereby introducing his readership to the tension between life in the sanatorium, life as a refugee, and life in the shadow of the Holocaust that will subtend the entire text.

The epigraph is, in fact, taken from a short account of Leivick's visit to a hospital in the German town of Gauting, where five hundred tubercular Jewish survivors sought treatment after the war. Leivick had arrived there with the intention of hosting a cultural evening. However, he was concerned that the patients would not accept him and that they would tell him, "You are just not from our world, even if you were in the Denver Sanatorium at one time and poeticized [*bazungen*] one of ours—Nathan Newman."[119] Leivick is worried that neither his shared experience of illness nor his "Ballad" will be enough to overcome the experiential barriers between himself and the Gauting patients. But the evening is a success. The patients tell him that they are spiritually hungry.[120] Following the performance, Leivick visits one of the patients and nearly faints. The man, it seems, bears stark similarities to the deceased Newman. Considering that Newman was Leivick's poetic double, this moment of mortal recognition is doubly uncanny.

That this scene in Gauting would subsequently provide the definition of tuberculosis for Charney's exploration of sanatorium life after the war shows that Leivick and his "Ballad" had come to stand between continents. The bioliterary network of the JCRS has now crisscrossed the Atlantic, extended from Denver to Liberty to Gauting and back, from Warsaw to New York, from Cincinnati to Czernowitz, and has become the filter through which Charney wrote himself into the tubercular canon of American Yiddish literature. It is a canon, moreover, that took shape in Denver, that Yehoash nurtured at the JCRS, that Tenenbaum telegraphed to his readers around the world, and that Leivick offered to future generations of Yiddish writers who would continue to compose in the *kenigraykh fun fiber*. Tubercular capital, as it were, mobilized in the name of a Yiddish literary tradition.

While the JCRS was only one of many sanatoria in the United States that welcomed Jewish patients in the first half of the twentieth century, it differentiated itself through its commitments to its literary-medico agenda. It was not simply a place for patients to recuperate physically but to grow aesthetically. The *Sanatorium* went so far as to advise patients to read the great works of literature that took up tuberculosis as theme and subject. "All the great writers of the last century," stated the editorial in 1911, "have made good use of the consumptive." The article then added, "If this is melodrama, then melodrama is part of our life."[121]

This was a lesson long familiar to the subject of the next chapter—David Vogel, the modernist Hebrew writer who sought the cure for his own tubercular diagnosis in Merano, Italy, in the winters of 1925 and 1926. There, in another sanatorium for indigent Jews, Vogel immersed himself in a literary setting and devoted himself to a literary subject that his German-language counterparts had explored for decades: the sanatorium. For Vogel, this would be a sanatorium far different from the JCRS. At the Jüdische Genesungsheim of Merano, he lacked the institutional support that Spivak had shown Mattes, that the *Sanatorium* had offered Yehoash, and that a stream of tubercular literary greats had offered Tenenbaum. Instead, the sanatorium became the setting for an intertextual conversation between Hebrew and German writing—between Vogel's chosen language and his aspirational one. Vogel would go on to look toward his illness, his biography, and his geography as literary resources.

CHAPTER 4

IN THE SANATORIUM

David Vogel between Hebrew and German

> We have allowed ourselves out into the world at large to be fascinated [by it], to dress ourselves as European.
>
> —**David Vogel**[1]

> Vogel was young and very poor. He wrote less and less frequently. He suffered from lung disease. And he had blue eyes, big, white, beautiful teeth, and blushing red cheeks like those with lung disease. I tried to convince Vogel to write prose. First, so that he could make a living, because prose writing earned more. And second, because he told me his life story. I told him, that's material for a novel. Sit and write.
>
> —**Ḥaim Ḥazaz**[2]

In the summer of 1910, Sholem Aleichem took the cure in the famous springs of Badenweiler. Shortly after arriving in the resort town, he visited the Sommer Hotel.[3] It was there, six years earlier, that Anton Chekhov had suffered from tuberculosis, exclaiming "Ich sterbe" before famously drinking a glass of champagne and expiring.[4] No doubt Sholem Aleichem's visit was marked by alternating feelings of excitement and uncanny dread. Two decades later, the poet Raḥel also compared herself to Chekhov in one pitiable moment when she had managed to gather just enough strength to brush her teeth.[5] In a letter to a friend, Raḥel later invoked Sholem Aleichem's ironic medical maxim—"Laughter is healthy. Doctors prescribe laughter"—in both Hebrew and Yiddish as she tried to make light of what would ultimately prove to be a terminal diagnosis.[6] Nearly two decades after Raḥel's death, the Yiddish writer Daniel Charney admired the library at the Workmen's Circle Sanatorium in Liberty, New York, where he found his books sharing space with volumes by none other than Chekhov and Sholem Aleichem.[7] Charney's writing would later occupy one more site in the Leivickian "kingdom of fever," first imagined in Denver and given new poetic currency in Liberty.

Meanwhile, across the ocean in central Europe, a complementary genealogy of tubercular writing had been taking shape since the turn of the century. There, an assemblage of creative accounts of tuberculosis, the recuperative process, and the sanatorium as a space of social illness was flourishing. Tubercular themes found ample representation among German-language writers in works as varied as Arthur Schnitzler's 1896 *Dying* (*Sterben*), Stefan Zweig's 1911 *Burning Secret* (*Brennendes Geheimnis*), Klabund's 1917 *Die Krankheit*, Hermann Hesse's 1925 *Sanatorium Guest* (*Kurgast*) as well as Thomas Mann's *Tristan* (1903) and, most famously, *The Magic Mountain* (*Der Zauberberg*, 1924).[8] Also included were works that were quickly translated into German, such as Knut Hamsun's *Last Chapter* (Norwegian, *Siste Kapital I/II*, 1923; German, *Das letzte Kapital*, 1924). Some of these authors, like Klabund (né Alfred Henschke), experienced a tubercular diagnosis firsthand.[9] Others, like Mann, witnessed the devastating effects of tuberculosis on a loved one.[10] Yet all staged the sanatorium as a space of artistic and philosophical debate conducted among a cohort of international patients.

The language, plot points, and topoi of these German texts make up the intertextual network that girds David Vogel's first Hebrew novella, *In the Sanatorium* (*Bevet ha-marpe*).[11] Born in the Ukrainian town of Satanov in 1891, Vogel studied Hebrew as a young boy.[12] As a teenager, he moved to Vilna, where he immersed himself in the world of modern Hebrew literature that was then gaining traction among intellectuals and burgeoning Jewish nationalists. At the age of twenty-one, he moved to Vienna, where he would live on and off for over a decade, much of it suffering from acute pulmonary tuberculosis.[13] Living in the Austrian capital also brought Vogel into contact with German modernist literature. He read voraciously and, like his fellow

Hebrew writers U. N. Gnessin, Avraham ben Yitzḥak (Sonne), and Gershon Shoffman, drew liberally on the style and themes of the surrounding culture. The result is that scholars and readers have long assessed Vogel's writing in conversation with German literature, whether expressionistic, impressionistic, decadent, or minimalist.[14] His work has been compared to the writing of Else Lasker-Schüler, Peter Altenberg, Georg Trakl, Josef Roth, Arthur Schnitzler, and Thomas Mann.[15] The critic Gershon Shaked went as far as to call Vogel's longest novel, *Married Life* (*Ḥaye nisuim*), "an Austro-Viennese novel written by chance in Hebrew."[16] Robert Alter also noted with no small amount of awe that Vogel took up the "task of creating an authentically European fiction in Hebrew without a national context and without a vernacular base."[17] What Shaked posits as an almost incidental choice (*bemikre*), Alter reads as a volitional attempt by Vogel to distinguish his work from the Hebrew writing produced in the name of Zionism. In fact, Vogel spent less than a year in Palestine from 1929 to 1930 before returning to Europe and to a life of penury and illness. Throughout his career, he also consistently distanced himself stylistically from the maximalist and nationalist aesthetics then dominating Palestinian Hebrew literature.[18]

Vogel's brief trip to Palestine also directs us to reconsider tuberculosis as a constitutive component of Jewish literary history. The writer's decision to travel to and ultimately leave British Mandate Palestine was directly tied to his own (as well as his second wife Ada's) tubercular condition. As early as 1923, Vogel wrote to a friend in America about his desire to travel to Palestine:

> I want to go to the Land of Israel not because I have a specific perspective and not—I must say—because I'm overcome with longing. I'm just so shattered, body and soul, that I have no room for such luxuries. My idea is to go so I may leave behind the troubles of Vienna, I need to rest a bit . . . and because I think that the sun of the Land of Israel will bring relief [*marpe*] to my rotting lung and restore my strength.[19]

Six years later, Vogel arrived in Tel Aviv with Ada, where they were warmly welcomed. Just as the urban literati had procured an ocean-view apartment for Raḥel, so too did they find the Vogel and his wife a residence on the coast.[20] The generous reception, however, did nothing to quell Vogel's near-constant complaining, and the change in air did not ameliorate either his condition or that of his wife.[21] Early in 1930, the couple left Palestine for good with Vogel offering two explanations for their departure: First, the climate had been rough on his wife's health. (As we have seen, the supposedly salubrious effect of the Palestinian climate for the tubercular proved false.) Second, Vogel explained that he preferred to be in Europe. "Zehu avir sheli—*la-neshimah*," he said. "This is my air—*for breathing*."[22] Vogel would locate both his physical and cultural inspiration firmly on European soil.

More than a history of health tourism, Vogel's trips to and from Tel Aviv bring into sharp relief just one way in which tuberculosis would mediate the writer's linguistic and geographic identities, between Europe and Palestine, German and Hebrew. This chapter demonstrates that an awareness of the cultural capital of his disease also played a central role in Vogel's early prose, including his personal diary, which he kept sporadically from 1912 to 1922, and his first novella, *In the Sanatorium*, published in 1927. Vogel completed the text shortly after his second stay in a Jewish sanatorium in Merano, Italy (formerly, Meran, Austria). At the time of its publication, Vogel's novella garnered few laudatory reviews and provoked more curiosity than overt praise. Reassessing the text, however, reveals that Vogel directed his early writing toward a critique of German-Hebrew literary and linguistic symbiosis. It was tuberculosis, moreover, that would provide the cultural context and intertextual touchstones of this critique.

Vogel: Between German and Hebrew

Vogel's engagement in German-Hebrew cultural debates was far from predestined. In his hometown of Satanov, Yiddish was the language of everyday life and Russian the language of the governing authorities. Despite some claims to the contrary, Vogel was able to write in Yiddish.[23] While living in Vienna, he helped organize a collection of Yiddish literary reflections, *Death Cycle* (*Toyt-tsiklus*). Later, he published a Yiddish article about the work of Y. H. Brenner and drafted a fictionalized if heavily autobiographical account of an Austrian citizen interned in France during World War II.[24] Vogel never abandoned Yiddish completely. However, he did ultimately choose Hebrew as the primary vehicle for his creative expression. As Alter explains, "Paradoxical though it may seem, [Vogel] chooses Hebrew because it is the one avenue open to him for being European, for joining European high culture."[25] Modern Hebrew, Alter recognizes, bore with it the allure of a modernizing language, emboldened by a long pedigree of liturgical writing while actively being resignified as the language of contemporary intellectual achievement.[26] Alter further reasons that Yiddish, dismissed as the jargon vernacular of the Jewish masses, could not have served Vogel as the language by which to enter the European literary republic.

Although not incorrect, Alter's statement is incomplete. Shortly after Vogel began to engage modern Hebrew literature, he cast his sights on studying German. In the fall of 1912, he left Vilna, noting in his diary that he desired to study with a *moreh ashkenazit*, a German teacher.[27] Some two weeks later, he began to study the language on his own, using Dr. Shimon Bernfeld's German translation of the Hebrew Bible. Working with a text that he knew well, Vogel progressed rapidly with his German lessons.[28] "My vocabulary resources increase [*mitrabe*] by the hour," he reflected. These German skills, however, came with a compromise. As Vogel records, "I have to contract [*lehitkavets*] in order to continue . . .—and my Hebrew language is forgotten [*mishtakhaḥat etsli*] by the hour for I'm not engaging Hebrew literature or strengthening my memory, but I have no other choice."[29] In his diary, Vogel describes the diminishment of his Hebrew in the passive voice (*mishtakhaḥat etsli*), as if the language were "being lost to him" by an external force. Yet the reason for that loss is clear. Improving his German comes directly at the cost of his Hebrew. He must "shrink/contract himself" (*hitvakets*) to make room for the German language to grow (*mitrabe*). Vogel here contributes his own bodily metaphor of bilingual life to a growing corpus of such distinctions of complementarity and antagonism. Mendele described his practices of Yiddish and Hebrew writing as being as natural as breathing through both nostrils; Sholem Aleichem described the bilingual contest between Hebrew and Yiddish as akin to twins battling in the womb; and Bialik compared the plight of the Hebrew writer burdened by another language to someone forced to limp and unable to move freely.[30] Bialik's words perhaps would have resonated strongly for Vogel, for whom the effort to learn German impinged on his Hebrew fluency.

German, of course, did not push out all of Vogel's Hebrew, nor would he lose his flexibility with his literary language. These diary lines, after all, are written in a poetic Hebrew idiom. But the passage points to a recurrent theme in his diary: Hebrew and German are antagonistic. To increase familiarity with one necessitates the depletion of the other. After Vogel moves to Vienna, he reflects in his diary that he now leads a life buried in literature, reading German books all day and "Hebrew—I barely read it at all."[31] Elsewhere he explains that he has "entered a new period in life, in which the central point is—German culture."[32] He subsequently writes in an excited tone of the works of philosophy he has yet to read and of his rhetorical thirst for knowledge and enlightenment. He also writes that he has seemingly entered "into a foreign life, into a foreign language" while adding that it pains him to see his Hebrew so depleted. In his words, he is "thirsty" (*tsame*) for European writing at the same time as he has nothing with which "to nourish" (*le-hazin*) his Hebrew inclinations.[33] By June 1914, Vogel poses the simple question, "What else is there to study besides German [*germanit*]?" His access to Hebrew literature is constrained, as he explains, "first, because of the lack of books and second because of all the German reading."[34] With his access to Hebrew materials limited and his time at a premium, Vogel chooses to study German.

In Vogel's intellectual life, German and Hebrew seesaw back and forth in a proportionate relationship of power and influence, yet it is Hebrew that maintains its position as the chosen language of Vogel's oeuvre. After all, save a single German poem and a brief effort to translate his later novel *Married Life*, Vogel chose to produce his creative works in Hebrew. Nevertheless, the tug between German and Hebrew should not be underestimated. On the one hand, according to Vogel's diary, German has the power to occlude Vogel's access to Hebrew. On the other hand, by writing in an increasingly flexible Hebrew, Vogel's diary presents the language as a therapeutic response to the susceptibility to German infection. To extend the medical metaphor, the Hebrew language of his diary works to immunize Vogel from the contagious transmission of German. Rather than see his Hebrew capacities shrink, the language of the diary expands to encompass and narrate the entire experience of learning German. Still, the question of the lingering impact of Vogel's German persists. What, for example, does Vogel's attraction to German mean for analyzing his position in a German literary milieu? And what does it mean for articulating Vogel's understanding of the cultural capital attending his disease?

Vogel: Between Literature and Disease

These questions linger when we consider the resonances of tuberculosis that were then extant in Vogel's German milieu. In 1933, the literary critic Hermann Weigand announced a lineage of pathology and creativity that extended from Johann Wolfgang von Goethe to Thomas Mann. Goethe, noted Weigand, "squarely credits disease with effecting spiritual awakening."[35] According to Weigand, Novalis followed suit, associating illness with mental alertness.[36] Alongside Novalis stood Nietzsche, who had offered his own reflection on the linkage between illness and creativity. "It is exceptional states that determine the artists," wrote the philosopher in *The Will to Power*, and "such states are all intimately related and entwined with morbid symptoms, so that it would seem almost impossible to be an artist and not be a sick man."[37] Nietzsche's legacy certainly loomed large among German writers well into the twentieth century. One did not merely read him, as Thomas Mann explained, as much as one "experienced him."[38] In 1922 and again in 1945, Mann relied on precisely this Nietzschean framework to understand Dostoyevsky's epilepsy. According to Mann, Dostoyevsky's condition served as an intensifying agent of his literary genius. The talent of great artists, reasoned Mann, was only "genialized" by disease.[39]

For Vogel, the connection between one's illness and one's literary identity also remained front and center. "The fact is," Vogel wrote in a diary entry from 1913, "I'm not qualified to live a natural and healthy life. A man of the book [*ish ha-sefer*] . . . I'm not like everyone—that's an existential fact [*uvdah kayemet*]." After spending several lines describing how disconnected he feels from the world, he comes to the conclusion, "I'm not healthy [*Eni bari*]."[40] Less than five years after Sholem Aleichem's jubilee celebrations, Vogel accepts the terms of an authorial career that the Yiddish author had refused. Beginning in 1908, Sholem Aleichem and his supporters criticized what they saw as the plight of Jewish writers caught in a cycle of material insecurity and physical incapacitation. They vehemently rejected the tubercular fate as Jewish literary destiny. In contrast, Vogel accepts his sickly condition as an immutable fact.

More than just accept his condition, Vogel seems almost to relish the connections he finds between literature and suffering. Throughout his diary, he writes repeatedly of his fruitless attempts to find work and food. At one point, he even compares himself to the protagonist of Hamsun's novel *Hunger* (1890), for he too has lost hair from malnourishment.[41] Analyzing the diary, Robert Alter has written that what is "compelling about [V]ogel's diary is the palpable feeling it conveys of fashioning a living language, a language that, though not the writer's actual vernacular, is able to trace the twisting contours of his inner life, to body forth a thoroughly modern and European sense of self and other, motive and identity."[42] Here, Vogel is able to "body forth" into the modernist canon by means of his own emaciation. Having immersed himself in a German modernist context, Vogel came to appreciate disease as a literary precondition. The question that we must now pursue is how Vogel would mobilize this form of tubercular capital. More specifically, how would he use the tools of German modernism to evaluate his own position in this cultural and linguistic milieu?

Vogel in Merano and in a Tubercular Literary Tradition

By January 1925, neither Vogel's physical nor financial situation had improved. He had recently published his first book of poems, *Before the Dark Gate* (*Lifne ha-sha'ar ha-afel*), as well as a Hebrew translation of Gerhart Hauptmann's *The Heretic of Soana* (*Der Ketzer von Soana*). Only a few copies of both were sold and only a few reviews appeared in the Hebrew press. Neither granted the destitute and ailing writer any relief. In letters to his friend Shimon Pollack, who was then living in America, Vogel bemoaned his illness as well as his helplessness. He even explored the possibility of moving to New York on the condition that Pollack could find him work before he left Europe.[43] He was too poor, as he wrote, to do anything on his own.[44]

But Vogel was not destined to land in America. Rather, with the support of a Viennese charitable organization, he acquired the funds to take the cure in the town of Merano in the Tyrolean mountains.[45] Merano had long held an allure for a variety of Jewish and non-Jewish health seekers who arrived in the mountain town eager to take the cure in the thermal baths. Many tourists also came to the region to try a variety of grape-based homeopathic remedies.[46] Like Marienbad and Carlsbad, Merano also became a hub for middle-class Jewish tourists despite, as Sabine Mayr has shown, the Catholic, antiliberal, and oftentimes anti-Semitic sentiments of local inhabitants.[47] Freud, Schnitzler, Zweig, and Kafka all found their way to this Tyrolean town, the latter on account of his own laryngeal tuberculosis.[48] And so too did the consumptive Hebrew writer Perets Smolenskin.[49] When he died there in 1885, he was buried in the local Jewish cemetery.

Like Vogel, Smolenskin made the trip to Merano thanks to the generosity of Viennese charities. As indicated by his correspondence record, Vogel was not shy about asking for money. In the winter of 1925, Vogel asked friends in Vienna directly for help, requesting funds to support a two-month stay in Merano.[50] One of those friends was Meir Wiener, the Yiddish and German critic and soon to be Soviet Yiddish literary scholar. Recognizing Vogel's illness, Wiener worked hard on his colleague's behalf.[51] Specifically, he called on the help of Hugo Knöpfmacher, a Viennese lawyer who had recently begun to make a name for himself as a German translator of Hebrew literature.[52] With Knöpfmacher's support, Vogel was admitted in January 1925 to a sanatorium for indigent Jews in Merano, known alternately as the Sanatorio Israelitico, the Jüdische Genesungsheim, or the Asyl für Israelitische Kranke.[53]

Interestingly, on December 11, 1925, Knöpfmacher also published a review of Vogel's Hebrew poetry in the Berlin weekly *Jüdische Rundschau*, accompanying his remarks with German translations of three of Vogel's poems.[54] Though far from his counterparts in Denver, Vogel's tubercular diagnosis also afforded him the opportunity to see his work translated—not into English but into German. The first of the three poems chosen by Knöpfmacher was Vogel's most famous work, "Black Flags Flutter" (Degalim sheḥorim mefarperim).[55] "We," the poem declares, will stand before "the dark gate [*ha-sha'ar he-afel*]" of Vogel's first poetry collection. "We," the poem explains, will stand "like black flags that flutter / in the wind / like the wings of imprisoned birds [*ke-khanfe tsiporim asurot*]"—in Knöpfmacher's rendering, "Wie Flügel gefangener *Vögel*."[56] In this German translation, the restrained *Vögel* points back to the poet, David Vogel. Vogel himself insisted that his name be spelled in Roman letters as "Vogel" rather than "Fogel"; although the latter would also have transliterated his Hebrew/Yiddish last name, the former rendered his identity Germanic.[57] In Vogel's diary, German language was depicted as having the power to occlude his access to Hebrew. Here, in translation, the German text works in the opposite manner, rendering Vogel visible to his non-Hebrew reader. At the same time, the poet does not describe a *Vogel* able to move freely. His wings are constrained, his vista is dark, and it is unclear whether the dark gate stands opened or closed.

Figure 7. Asyl für Israelitische Kranke, Meran, undated. Source: The Jewish Museum of Meran. Reprinted with permission.

Vogel would travel to Merano for a second time in the winter of 1926, once again with the financial backing of Knöpfmacher. After this second stay, Vogel turned his attention to *In the Sanatorium*. The text was completed in 1926 and published in Palestine the following year.[58] The text follows two characters during their stay in a tuberculosis sanatorium in South Tyrol. The first character, Irme Ornik, is a business school student who initially keeps to himself and follows the sanatorium health regime with extreme precision.[59] In the end, however, he commits suicide after his romantic overtures to a female patient are rebuffed. The second character is named Shevaḥ Adler. Unlike quiet Ornik, Adler is an urban dandy who is ultimately expelled from the sanatorium after he seduces one of the institution's employees.

While we know nothing of Vogel's own romantic dalliances during his convalescence in Merano, his stay at the local Asyl certainly influenced the novella.[60] Both institutions were supported by wealthy benefactors from the former Austro-Hungarian Empire. In 1873, a small sanatorium opened in Austrian Meran with the financial support of the Königswarter Stiftung. By the time of Vogel's arrival, the local Genesungsheim had grown into a state-of-the art treatment center.[61] At that point, the Königswarter family had also spread across Europe, in a manner not dissimilar to that of the officers and chief benefactors of Vogel's fictional sanatorium, who send along donations from Prague, Vienna, and Ostrau.[62]

In the Sanatorium also reflects Vogel's intimate knowledge of the paradigm of *Kurort* prose then common in modernist German literature—its setting, character profiles, plot points, and motifs. Consider, for example, the Tyrolean landscape. The setting similarly anchors Arthur Schnitzler's 1896 novella, *Dying*. Vogel's characters look out and comment on the same mountains, brisk air, and bright sun that Schnitzler elaborates in his work. Yet while Schnitzler's text makes brief reference to the town (Meran) and the nearest city (Bolzan), Vogel's text works obsessively to map the topography of the area. His characters amble along the Tappeinerweg, look out on the ruins of the San Zeno Castle, walk down Goethestraße, take the tram to the village of Lana, cross over the Passer River, and stroll along the Gilf Promenade. The text functions as a veritable travel guide to the sights and paths of Merano. These detailed directions assert Vogel's authority over the landscape and, by extension, over the narrative of sanatorium life.

In short, Vogel introduces himself as an author intimately familiar with the subject of the health resort, its town, inns, and institutions. Various plot details also recall three prominent texts of sanatorium genre writing that would have been available to Vogel during his stay in Merano. The first is Klabund's 1917 expressionist novella, *Die Krankheit*.[63] The novella, set in various sanatoria and inns around Davos, follows the protagonist Sylvester Glonner as he falls in love with the beautiful tubercular actress Sybil Lyndquist. After she dies, he continues to admire her tubercular face onscreen at the local cinema. Although ostensibly a love story, Klabund's text focuses on the ugly and degrading physical consequences of tuberculosis and the psychological devolution of its victims.[64]

Closer to the time of his stay in Merano, two additional books were published that were of consequence to Vogel. The first was a German translation of Hamsun's 1923 two-volume novel, *The Last Chapter*. Like many Hebrew and Yiddish writers, Vogel admired Hamsun's modernist sensibility. Recall that as a young man in Vienna he had even described his own physical state of deprivation by comparing himself to the protagonist of Hamsun's *Hunger*. *The Last Chapter* would have been of interest to Vogel not because of its modernist style but because of its subject. The text focuses on an international cast of characters and their various romantic dalliances, financial chicanery, and deviant behavior at the Torahus Sanatorium in Norway.

Most significantly, Thomas Mann's novel *The Magic Mountain* also entered the market in November 1924. The modernist bildungsroman narrates the three-week–turned–seven-year-long stay of Hans Castorp at the International Sanatorium Berghof in Davos, Switzerland. The novel allegorizes the dissolution of the European world order in the lead-up to the Great War, transporting representatives from across class lines to the space of a tuberculosis sanatorium.

Although Vogel's reading habits during his stay in Merano remain unknown, a series of specific details and thematic echoes in his novella suggest that Vogel was familiar with Klabund, Hamsun, and, most noticeably, Mann's text. At twenty-three years old, Irme Ornik is the same age as Hans Castorp when he first entered the sanatorium on *The Magic Mountain.* Ornik's personality and physical presence also recall a similarly large and suicidal character from Hamsun's *The Last Chapter.* Leonhard Magnus, known as "The Suicide," is a perpetual misanthrope who repeatedly threatens to kill himself. His depressed personality presages Ornik's own pessimistic outlook, and his physical girth recalls Ornik's own lumbering body.

Unlike Magnus, however, Ornik carries through with his suicide, which he commits after being rebuffed by Gerte Finger, a fellow patient and resident flirt. Like the characters in *Die Krankheit* and *The Magic Mountain,* Ornik becomes entangled in a relationship that is far from health inducing. In *Die Krankheit,* Sylvester rides in a horse race at Sybil's request, despite his ailing health. In *The Magic Mountain,* Castorp imagines himself to be increasingly infirmed only to prolong his stay at the sanatorium and thereby increase his chances to seduce his fellow patient Claudia Chauchat. In a manner echoing both of these lovesick narratives, Ornik chases after Finger until the point when he is so hurt by her rejection that suicide appears to be the only viable solution.

This tension between the erotic and deadly, between lust and disease, saturates the atmosphere of Vogel's sanatorium even beyond Ornik's suicidal attraction to Finger. The text alerts us to the lascivious intentions of the in-house physician, Dr. Maḥlis, who is suspected of injecting female patients in their bare thighs for no apparent reason. Like Hofrat Behrens of *The Magic*

Mountain, Maḥlis allegedly abuses his position of professional authority to molest female patients. As a rhetorical move, turning the place of healing into a threatening setting only serves to heighten the anxiety at the center of the novella: a space intended for care and recuperation has been rendered physically and sexually unsafe.

Vogel also depicts his Tyrolean sanatorium as a cross section of European patients. The guests who arrive at the sanatorium hail from across central Europe. Herr Minzel arrives from the Czech lands, and Frau Wiesel and Dr. Schamhof travel from Prague. Little Windel has arrived from Vienna, as do his fellow urbanites Herr Kisch, Herr Ritter, and Herr Adler. Lyuba Goldis journeys to the sanatorium from a Russian-speaking household, origins unknown. And the list goes on. Vogel's novella overflows with new names, characters, and geographic places on nearly every page. Aharon Komem, one of Vogel's most sensitive readers, puts the number of characters in this decidedly small narrative at nearly thirty.[65]

The cross section of Europe and the bordering Russian Empire calls to mind the select few who enter and exit Mann's *Magic Mountain*: Hans Castorp arrives from Hamburg, Claudia Chauchat from the Eurasian steps, and Mynheer Peeperkorn from Holland. In Klabund's texts, a geographically diverse array of characters such as "the handsome Russian," "the Japanese," and the "Bulgarian officer" also interact. Vogel's Tyrolean sanatorium similarly gathers patients from across the map, albeit focusing the majority of its attention on those coming from the former Austro-Hungarian Empire. Irme Ornik is even described as "a tangled and complicated jumble of Budapest and Vienna."[66]

For some of Vogel's first readers, this excessive number of characters was more of a hindrance to the novella than a productive literary conceit. Reviewing the book in 1929, Shlomo Tsemaḥ accused Vogel of an inability to penetrate the lives of his characters. The result, he explains, is a boring novella—"a story (that in truth isn't a story)"—but rather a series of moments in various characters' lives. Tsemaḥ also cautions that the style may be a permanent defect of Vogel's "spirit" rather than just "the heavy movement of [Vogel's] first steps" into literature.[67] Decades later, Gershon Shaked offered a similar assessment, critiquing the novella for lacking a strong plot or clear purpose. As Shaked suggested, perhaps the novella was only practice for his subsequent prose efforts.[68]

To be sure, there are moments in the plot that are decidedly slow. What Menachem Perry has called Vogel's "life in parenthesis" style, where the narrative lacks motifs to advance it and time seemingly proceeds without any catalysts, appears in the novella in its least refined iteration.[69] And neither Ornik nor Adler is a particularly compelling character. Their personalities are sketchy, and it is hard to sustain sympathy for them even in the face of their terminal diagnoses. Nevertheless, what is ultimately flawed in these readings is that they do not pay enough attention to the intertextual network into which Vogel actively places himself. Even the "boring" quality that Tsemaḥ identifies in the novella may be a response to the examination of monotony and disinterest fundamental to sanatorium life explored in Mann's *Magic Mountain*. As Katrin Max had shown, Mann's novel incorporates within it Romantic ideals of tubercular suffering, beauty, and literary inspiration while at the same time demonstrating a notion ever more common in German medical discourse of the 1920s—that tuberculosis leads to a general crankiness that constricts the dynamism basic to a healthy life.[70] Indeed, Vogel's text draws directly on established archetypes of the sanatorium/*Kurort* drama—be it a location (Schnitzler), an international population (Klabund, Hamsun, Mann), an erotic plot conceit (Klabund, Schnitzler, Mann), an attention to the sexual power dynamics of doctor/patient privilege (Mann), the presence of suicide as a final outlet (Hamsun), or the age of the protagonist (Mann).

For Vogel, however, the importance of entering this intertextual network was not solely to situate himself in a literary tradition. Rather, the position opened up a productive space of critique. For while *In the Sanatorium* participates in the general paradigm of *Kurort* prose, it does so with an eye toward difference. Unlike Mann, Klabund, Hamsun, or Schnitzler's characters, Vogel's cohort of patients has more in common than a shared diagnosis. They are all recognizably Jewish. With a Jewish accent here, a Hebrew name there, a crass Yiddish joke in between, Vogel's patients reveal their Jewish identity both overtly and discreetly, in their names, in their speech, and even in their faces.[71] Like Mann's Naphta, Vogel's Shevaḥ Adler is identifiable with one embarrassing glance to his nose.[72] The homogeneity of the population is far from incidental. Rather, Vogel carves out in Hebrew an exclusively Jewish space of convalescence that evokes the German modernist tradition precisely to problematize the possibility of a Hebrew-German conversation. More than simply a Judaized retelling of *The Magic Mountain*, Vogel's novella becomes the tubercular occasion in which to allegorize the Hebrew-German struggle he had first announced in his diary.

In the Sanatorium: Between German and Hebrew

In an essay about the Austrian-Jewish writer Arnold Schoenberg's opera *Moses und Aron,* the musicologist Ruth HaCohen locates Schoenberg's work within a German-Jewish milieu of Viennese culture of the late 1920s and early 1930s. One of the touchstones of her analysis is David Vogel's longest prose text, *Married Life*. Trying to understand the sociocultural positioning of Schoenberg's work, HaCohen analyzes Vogel's effort to write a Hebrew novel about German-speaking Viennese characters. The discrepancy between the novel's textual language (Hebrew) and the language of its characters (German), according to HaCohen, bespeaks the theme of "transcendental homelessness" mobilized in the work.[73] Drawing on the terminology of sociolinguist Ghil'ad Zuckerman, HaCohen posits moments of "phono-semantic transposition" as particularly important. In these instances, the German language behind and/or motivating the Hebrew language of the text is perceptible to the sensitive reader.[74] These are moments when the Hebrew narratival fourth wall is peeled back to uncover the German cultural substrate.

Such moments of Hebrew-German crossing are not unique to Vogel's prose, yet it is only recently that the literary phenomenon has captured the widespread attention of scholars of central European Hebrew writing. Na'ama Rokem, Amir Eshel, Rachel Seelig, and Maya Barzilai have all devoted attention to interpreting precisely this "Hebrew-German conversation."[75] Reading a variety of works, these scholars look to the texts of Hebrew writers who were also German speakers and/or German authors to understand the historical interplay between the two linguistic and literary systems. This category of Hebrew writers includes such major figures as writer and anthologist Mikhah Yosef Berdyczewski and the Israeli poet Yehudah Amichai, as well as the lesser-known German and Hebrew poet and prose writer Ludwig Strauss.

Strauss and Vogel were contemporaries. Yet unlike Strauss, Vogel was not a bilingual writer. He also did not put forth a public opinion about the merits of a transnational and multilingual Jewish literature.[76] However, as the following reading of *In the Sanatorium* demonstrates, this did not prevent Vogel from navigating the German-Hebrew cultural border to expose its weakest points. Vogel punctuates the novella with intertextual and linguistic gestures that identify, examine, and problematize just that potentially creative symbiotic space. The result is that *In the Sanatorium* reads as the staging ground for Vogel's investigation into the compatibility of Hebrew and German as languages and literary traditions. His investigation will also not ignore the ever-lurking presence of Yiddish between the two systems. Concerned with language hierarchies, Vogel refused to overlook the Yiddish "other" that haunts his text. In short, Vogel inserts his text into the genre of the German *Kurort* narrative and from there examines his position as both insider and outsider to the literary tradition and language. This becomes clear in four rhetorical decisions that Vogel makes, the first of which concerns the name of Irme Ornik's roommate: Engineer Tseberg.

Tseberg, Zauberberg, Zwerg

Unlike many of the patients of *The Magic Mountain* or *The Last Chapter*, the tubercular characters in Vogel's work are more often than not indigent. They are being treated, after all, in a "Sanatorium for Those of Limited Resources." Ornik, for example, is so concerned with money that he even monetizes his back pain, localizing it in a space he compares to the size of an "Austrian Krone."[77] Unable to afford private accommodations, Ornik also shares his room with an engineer named Tseberg. Their relationship is tense. Unlike Ornik, Tseberg is relaxed. He appears throughout the text as a figure akin to Ornik's devil-on-the-shoulder or, in the Hebrew tradition, his *yester ha-ra* (evil inclination). And it is a role he has ample opportunity to practice. As Ornik's roommate, he is privy to all of the latter's obsessive health machinations. Tseberg frequently encourages Ornik to ease up on his rigid regime, to enjoy himself, and to flirt with the female patients. At one point Tseberg yells at Ornik to "read" and "let your mind wander! You'll see," he adds, "after a week you'll feel better!"[78] Before Tseberg's urging, Ornik had not considered engaging in such indulgent activities. During the first year and a half of his stay, Ornik had refrained from reading entirely and had devoted all of his energy to recuperating.[79] Tseberg, however, encourages Ornik to branch out and to engage the social life of the sanatorium.

In addition to being Ornik's foil, Tseberg is also an engineer. His name aurally gestures back to the "Zauberberg" where Mann's Hans Castorp would dwell for seven years. This is a point emphasized in all printed editions of the novella, where the first instantiation of his name is vocalized as *Tseberg* (צֶבֶּרג). Engineer Tseberg haunts Vogel's *bet-marpe* as a specter of Mann's great novel, pushing Vogel's text and characters into communion with—or, more precisely, into the same room as—German modernist literature. Yet the inclusion of the engineer also suggests that when pushed, Ornik and his creator may likely stumble. After all, following a discussion with Tseberg, Ornik initiates a series of actions that leads to his dalliance with Gerte Finger, which, in turn, results in unreciprocated love and suicide.

A singular reading of Tseberg's name, however, is challenged by the nature of Hebrew itself. When, as in various parts of the novella manuscript, the surname is unvocalized (צברג), the pronunciation is flexible. It may be rendered in English as Tseberg, Tsebarg, or Tsobarg. It might also be rendered as Tsverg, akin to the German word *Zwerg*, meaning "dwarf." In Ruth Achlama's 2013 German translation, for example, Ornik's roommate is none other than "Ingineur Zwerg."[80] The engineer's name now reads as a none-too-subtle onomastic commentary on Vogel's work in comparison with Mann's. How can a thin novella written in a literary language read by few compare to a multivolume, thousand-page novel in German? How can its characters not be dwarfed by the intertextual giant with whom they share a room?

One is reminded of a letter that the Yiddish poet Mani Leib wrote while recuperating from tuberculosis at the Deborah Sanatorium in New Jersey in 1935, over a decade after Vogel's first stay in Merano. While there, he read *The Magic Mountain*. Addressing his friend and fellow poet Meir Shtiker, he put his own life in stark relief with the text. In comparison to the "world of ideas" that opened up to Hans Castorp on the *tsoyberbarg* (magic mountain), Mani Leib explains that his life as a Yiddish poet in the *tsoybertol* (magic valley) was only of the smallest of the smallest (*der mindster fun di mindste*) consequence.[81] "In my magic valley," Mani Leib wrote, "the whole human world comes to life for me in keener miniature. . . . I am not Goethe, nor even Heine. I am a limited Jewish artist will all the shortcomings of a Jew, with his poor cultural inheritance and closeted jargon of a language."[82]

Mani Leib allegorizes cultural hierarchies using the variables of German and Yiddish literature. Unlike his German colleagues, Mani Leib is a Yiddish writer. He is not the great German *Mann* but rather the minimized Yiddish *Mani Leib*. He describes a poetic life lived in the flatlands, down below, where every effort proves futile in his attempt to leave a lasting literary legacy. Writing in Hebrew, Vogel may have been nervous about succumbing to a similar linguistically parochial fate and being dwarfed by the German icon. It would be shortsighted, though, not to acknowledge that the engineer's surname may also be read along exactly the opposite allegorical lines. Perhaps Tseberg/Zwerg appears to suggest not that Mann's German texts dwarf Vogel's but that Vogel's dwarfs Mann's. Earlier in this chapter, we read Vogel's admission that he learned German to the detriment of his Hebrew, which shrank proportionately. "My vocabulary resources increase [*mitrabe*] by the hour," he wrote in his diary upon first studying German. "I have to practice in order to travel to Vienna—in all aspects; I have to contract [*le-hitkavets*] in order to continue."[83] Here, however, he has literally contracted a giant of German literature and placed him within a Hebrew frame. He has similarly reduced the title of Mann's masterpiece to its bare consonants, rendering *Der Zauberberg* into *Der Zwerg* into *TsBRG*. The engineer's presence introduces a moment of indecipherability into the text where Vogel reads not only as Mann's interlocutor but simultaneously as both his superior and his subordinate.

Hansel, Hermann, Herr Mann

The tense relationship between *In the Sanatorium* and *The Magic Mountain* further animates a politics of names during a series of events that leads to the dismissal of Shevaḥ Adler from the sanatorium. Again, alongside Ornik, Adler is the second most developed character in the novella. Aharon Komem has gone as far as to declare that the novella presents Ornik and Adler together as one divided hero.[84] The characters themselves each comprise two conflicting yet complementary empires. While Ornik embodies Vienna and Budapest, Adler incorporates Vienna and Jerusalem. His last name—the Germanic "Adler"—points to the double-headed eagle adorning the crest of the imperial coat of arms of the Austrian Empire. His first name—Shevaḥ—is the Hebrew word meaning "praise." His name, accordingly, seems to be a pronouncement of his patriotic loyalty. Less a zealous nationalist, however, Adler is most comfortable in the sanatorium as one of many unyielding Lotharios.[85]

Like his fellow patients, Adler has a particular affection for the non-Jewish women in his midst. Little Windel, for example, takes particular pleasure in touting the merits of the "*shiksah*" whom he meets on the *Kurpromenade*. Unlike "the kosher daughters of the sanatorium," he explains, the non-Jewish object of his affection is fleshier, the embodiment of health compared to the gaunt Jewish female patients.[86] The sanatorium chambermaid, Anni, is described in similar terms. In order to capture her attention, Adler grabs Anni by her fleshy arm and pushes his hand against her overflowing breast.[87] She is neither diminutive nor submissive. She also does not contract in the face of Adler's overtures but rather responds with an encouraging laugh.

After some scheming, a plan is hatched. One night, while the patients are supposed to be sleeping, Adler and a fellow patient named Fleischmann (literally, "Flesh-man") sneak out of the sanatorium to meet up with two chambermaids, Anni and Betti. After the two couples rendezvous, they share several bottles of red wine at a local inn. Alerting readers to the disruption that is to come, Vogel interrupts this drinking scene with the inclusion of a folk poem that is engraved on the wall of the inn. The quatrain reads: "Rebensaft / Gibt uns Kraft, / Regt das Blut, / Macht uns Mut [The juice of the vine / Gives us strength, / Stirs the blood, / Gives us courage]."[88] The lines appear in Roman letters within the Hebrew text orthographically intruding into the literary space. These letters visibly alert readers to the potential incompatibility of German and Hebrew. Vogel must include a Hebrew translation of the folk song in a footnote, signposting the fact that his readers might not understand the German phrases or be able to read the German lettering.

Rebensaft, as previously mentioned, was also part of a variety of therapeutic treatments for tubercular patients in South Tyrol. Yet here, rather than curative or palliative, the juice of the vine linguistically attests to just how far the Jewish patients are from being cured. Like the ailing English "Lung-Fellow," Vogel's quatrain appears on the page in Roman letters—far from the implied safety of the Hebrew sanatorium. The "juice of the vine" will not ameliorate their condition but, rather, bespeaks the drunken folly that Adler and Fleischmann are pursuing.[89] The German folk song further warns readers of the potential danger that will result from the coupling of the two Jewish patients with the non-Jewish women. Throughout the novella, the relationship between German and Hebrew is allegorized as the relationship between non-Jews and Jews. Having crossed the threshold of the sanatorium, the warning appears all the more overtly, emblazoned in German on the wall of the inn.

The ominous warning sign, however, goes unheeded. Rather, following this eruption of German language, the two couples pair off, eventually retiring to Betti's apartment, which, unlike the sanatorium, is dark, stuffy, and dirty. The air, notes the narrator, "was heavy and dense [*atum*], a few days old."[90] Once again, environmental clues should set off warning signs for the tubercular Adler. Neither the *Rebensaft* of the inn nor the suffocating atmosphere of Betti's apartment will bode well for the Jewish patient, short of breath yet insistent on the sexual conquest. Early the next morning, they return to the sanatorium, but the night of passion does not go unnoticed. Romantic dalliances are not to be tolerated, and by breakfast, Adler is expelled. Hermann, the non-Jewish sanatorium orderly, is sent to help Adler pack.

Adler then begins to wonder who was responsible for his dismissal. While he knows that such relationships among patients are not sanctioned, he does not know how the affair has come to the attention of the institution's superintendent. Before Hermann arrives to help with the packing, Adler realizes that it was none other than the janitor himself who had played the role of informant. As readers learn earlier, Anni is also seeing Hermann; it is he whom she had asked to leave the gate open the night before. Anni's relationship with the janitor might have flown under the readers' radar were it not for a conversation that Adler held with Anni at the pub. In a flirtatious move, he asks Anni whether she loves him more than "that Hansel [*he-Hansel*]."[91] After some confusion, Anni realizes that he is speaking about Hermann. Between little Hans and Hermann, Vogel's reader again begins to see an ever-larger figure hovering in the text. It is none other than *Herr Mann* himself, whose own little Hans had spent seven long years living and lusting in a mountaintop sanatorium for tuberculars. And it is that Hansel/Hermann who is, in the end, responsible for Adler's dismissal from the sanatorium.

With the introduction of Engineer Tseberg on the third page of the story and this final act by Hermann/Hansel toward the novella's conclusion, Vogel's text now appears to have been bookended by the players and language of *The Magic Mountain*. Tseberg may have encouraged Ornik to go out into the world republic of letters—to read, flirt, and relax—but when Adler does just that, he is kicked out by none other than *Herr Mann* himself. Should we understand Hermann's intrusion into the text, therefore, as a symbolic gatekeeper of modernist German writing? Will Adler along with Vogel—whose name, coincidentally, shares an avian agenda—be excluded from the literary tradition? Again, the complexities of the text preclude a clear answer. On the one hand, Adler has successfully wooed his non-Jewish lover. Read symbolically, he has been allowed access to German culture through an erotic encounter first initiated in a space of disease and illness. On the other hand, Adler has been expelled from the sanatorium on account of Hermann's jealousy and betrayal. *Herr Mann* has kicked Adler out of the literary sanatorium. At the same time, *Herr Mann* has also kicked Adler out of an exclusively Jewish/Hebrew recuperative space. The affair has rendered Adler's place within both the German tradition and Hebrew tradition equally tenuous. Adler's expulsion reminds us that he is not playing a game in which he is able to set his own rules. When Hebrew (i.e., Jewish) and German (i.e., non-Jewish) mix, asserts the text, Vogel's character will find neither physical nor literary stability. Reading Adler as a Vogelian avatar, we must ask whether the text is concerned that Vogel will meet with a similar fate. Will *In the Sanatorium* ever find a settled relationship vis-à-vis the German literary tradition? Vis-à-vis Hebrew?

Sun, Sonne, Zoneh

These questions take on added significance as we continue to consider precisely how German language functions in Vogel's Hebrew. Specifically, throughout the text, Vogel engages in German-Hebrew wordplay. For example, toward the beginning of the novella, readers encounter a brief exchange between patients. It is the beginning of the rest hour and they are preparing for their afternoon sunbathing. Trudi Wiesel—"the little imp from Prague"—has been tasked with letting her fellow patient Frau Schnabel know whether or not the sun is to be found in the proper position.

"Frau Schn—a—bel," yells Wiesel, "she is still sleeping!" Frau Schnabel asks in reply, "Who is sleeping?" and Wiesel answers, "The sun!"[92]

The brief exchange would likely have gone unnoticed had Adolph Ritter, a male patient resting one floor below, not overheard the women's conversation. As we read:

> And a good idea occurred to Adolph Ritter, who was lying in the middle of the balcony. Turning to his left and right, slightly raising the upper part of the body, he commanded [those around him] in a restrained voice and with helpful gestures, like a general in battle who had already been thrown from his horse:
>
> —One—two—th—r—ee!!!!
>
> And all those lying on the first floor in unison [lit., "in one mouth"]:
>
> —Frau Schna—bel—*Die—So—nne*!
>
> From above came boisterous laughs from the women's mouths.[93]

Ostensibly, this is a scene documenting an afternoon rest cure. But it soon devolves into a comically crass exchange between a variety of orifices. Frau Schnabel (Mrs. Beak) is made fun of by a chorus of mouths that laugh in unison at the command of an aggressive male patient. Were a German reader to have heard the text read aloud, however, the humor of the scene would likely have been lost. In the recent German translation of the novella, the ensuing laughter seems completely unwarranted. What, after all, is so funny, about *die Sonne*? Does it not simply point back to the heliotherapeutic cures prescribed for tubercular patients?

For Vogel's Hebrew readers, the answer would be obvious. The seemingly innocuous German term *Sonne* is rendered in the Hebrew as the vocalized *zoneh,* a "prostitute" or "slut." The vowels added by Vogel in the manuscript also specifically suggest that the reference is to a male prostitute, further augmenting the brunt of the taunt. That which is supposed to heal—the sun—radiates here textually as a locus of derogatory affect. Like the resignified *Rebensaft*, the *Sonne* functions less as a therapeutic presence than that which contributes to the patient's measured pain. And the wordplay further draws us into a world where sexual intrigue and illness are collapsed, where the sun, the whore, and the tubercular Jewish body meet at the intersection of a German and Hebrew pun.

As Maureen Quilligan has shown, the pun offers a productive model for understanding "that instant of ambiguity whereby two meanings are suspended in a single signifier, and two speech communities can coincide in their language, although not in their frames of references."[94] In Vogel's text, the pun both links and distinguishes the German speakers from Hebrew speakers—those who hear *Sonne* and think of celestial light and those who hear *zoneh* and think of disparaging names and sexual impropriety. Most interesting, however, is how the pun of *Sonne/zoneh* alerts us to a third linguistic community of which Vogel was quite aware—Yiddish speakers, for whom both *Sonne* and *zoneh* would have been immediately comprehensible. The slash between *Sonne* and *zoneh* gestures toward the Yiddish *zoyne*. The potential source of healing, the sun, not only becomes a naughty Hebrew sobriquet but also identifies the Yiddish lurking between the Hebrew and German divide. Can German and Hebrew overlap, asks the text, without the situation devolving into one extended sexual joke or, for that matter, into a naughty Yiddish aside? Is meaningful German-Hebrew coupling possible without recourse to Yiddish as a mediator?

Vogel notably did not publicly share in the hostility toward Yiddish, as did many Hebrew and German writers. Mani Leib, himself a Yiddish poet, lamented "the closeted jargon of a language" in which he wrote.[95] Yet Vogel was not overly antagonistic toward Yiddish. While in the sanatorium, he wrote to Melech Ravitch on behalf of a fellow patient named Vishlitski. He beseeched the editor to publish the amateur writer's Yiddish work. Just as Vogel's German-Hebrew literary support network would help fund Vogel's recuperation, so too would Vogel advocate on behalf of his fellow patient-writers.[96] Regardless of his sympathies for the Yiddish literary project and its practitioners, Vogel's novella problematizes the relationship of Hebrew and German as one insistently disrupted by Yiddish. Put differently, Hebrew and German are collapsed into one big Yiddish pun.

This disruptive position of Yiddish between Hebrew and German also registers in the second phrase that Vogel presents to readers in Roman orthography. During a dining room scene, one patient calls another "ein betamter Bursch," "a charming boy."[97] Like the German drinking song adorning the local inn, this sarcastic comment linguistically interrupts the Hebrew page, presenting readers with the *Bursch* (a version of the German word *Bursche*) who is *betamter* (a Yiddish adjective of Hebraic origin meaning "charming"). On the one hand, we might interpret this intrusion as one more reminder to the reader that Vogel's characters are speaking German. On the other hand, we might also understand this phrase as Vogel's way of indicating that the German of these patients would be comprehensible only to the Yiddish reader. Even when the "German" language of the patients appears in "German," it does so with a Yiddish inflection. By extension, even the Hebraized German of these speakers who use a term such as *betamter* must filter their Hebrew through Yiddish. Elaborating on puns, Haun Saussy states that "a connected series of such puns is an *allegory*."[98] With these two scenes of *Sonne/zoneh/zoyne* and *ein betamter Bursch*, Vogel allegorizes the inability of the Hebrew text to fully inhabit the German space of the sanatorium. According to the text, there is always a Yiddish pun lying between Hebrew and German. Yiddish subtends both Hebrew and German orthography, it interrupts both Hebrew and German discourse, and it reinforces the message that *In the Sanatorium* narrates the tension between Hebrew and German rather than their commensurability.

On Jewish Time

The sanatorium in Vogel's text is a liminal space where the potential for German-Hebrew creative symbiosis is posed if only to be critiqued. The text repeatedly disrupts any chance for the two languages and literary traditions to map onto each other harmoniously. In addition to the embedded allusions to Mann's text and the German/Hebrew/Yiddish eruptions, Vogel drives this point home in one of the only scenes of writing in the text. While there are multiple allusions to the novella's literary context, the fictionalized sanatorium is a distinctly uncreative space—the patients spend their days eating, sunbathing, taking walks, and flirting. Save one patient who is handy with a camera, there are no artists, writers, or creative personalities walking through its halls. The most embellished verbal exchanges are relegated to the flirtatious banter of would-be lovers.

The sole account of literary output occurs when Irme Ornik decides to write a letter to Dr. Kalbel in Vienna. Unwilling to trust the in-house physicians, Ornik writes to the Viennese doctor every two weeks, providing him with a report of his treatments as well as appending a detailed chart, titled

"Temperature Chart of Irme Ornik, Student of the Academy of General Commerce." The chart contains information concerning his temperature, pulse, sputum, bowels, weight, medications, and general notes. Vogel includes the table in its entirety in the Hebrew text. Most of the information is relatively quotidian in the life of the tuberculosis patient. Over the course of three days, his temperature fluctuates from 36.6 to 37.8 degrees Celsius. His pulse varies between a low of 80 to a high of 106 beats per minute. And he adds marginalia, such as "restless all night," "bloody nose," and "exhaustion after a ten minute walk."[99] There is also a column for Ornik to mark down the date. There, Ornik records three successive dates that he has been charting his health: the 11th, 12th, and 13th of Shevat. The fifth month of the Hebrew calendar, Shevat roughly corresponds annually to January or February. In 1925, the dates would have corresponded to February 5 through 7 and in 1926, January 26 to 28—both overlapping with Vogel's own stays in the sanatorium.

Ornik's decision to record the date using this notational system is curious. An educated German speaker, Ornik would likely have chosen to mark the date using the terms of the Gregorian calendar. Yet in the novella, he inscribes the chart he will send to his Viennese doctor according to the Hebrew dating system, immediately positioning himself outside the temporal progression of medico-scientific and secularizing time. Were we to assume that the physician Dr. Kalbel was also Jewish, as well as aware of the Hebrew calendar, we might infer that evident here is not only a secret letter being written by Ornik but also an example of Jewish medical in-speak; the patient uses a culturally specific language to communicate his experience of illness. Working in Vienna, it would have been highly unlikely that Dr. Kalbel would organize his daily routine according to the Hebrew calendar. Rather than connect Ornik to the Viennese physician, the Hebrew dates reinforce just how far he is—physically, culturally, and most important, linguistically—from the Austrian cultural center.

Writing about early-modern culture in Europe, Elisheva Carlebach has carefully attended to the significance of the Jewish calendar as an example of "how a minority culture creatively and simultaneously embraced and distanced itself from the majority culture."[100] The constant negotiation of the rhythms of Jewish time over and against the Christian calendar, argues Carlebach, offers strong evidence of the double consciousness of Jewish culture as both an inward- and outward-looking body. Although writing in a far different European climate than Carlebach's subjects, such double consciousness of competing temporal frameworks is legible in Vogel's characters' lives as well as his own. When Vogel first arrived in Vienna, he switched from the Hebrew calendrical system he had used in his diary while in Vilna to the Gregorian system; the new chronological system, as one might expect, appeared more in line with his burgeoning German studies.[101]

The move to Vienna in Vogel's case was marked by this shift from Jewish to Christian time. Ornik's letter from the sanatorium to Vienna, in contrast, is dated according to the Hebrew month of Shevat. At the same time that disease brings Vogel's text close to a tradition of sanatorium writing, his character appears to write himself out of that temporal alignment. Ornik's dating also touches on one of the most prominent concerns of those same sanatorium narratives—specifically, the measurement of time while in the institution. Hans Castorp famously arrives in Davos intending to stay for three weeks but leaves the International Sanatorium Berghof seven years later. Shortly after his arrival, Castorp is shocked to learn that the doctors have recommended that his cousin Joachim remain on the mountain for at least another six months. "Six months? Are you crazy?" replies Castorp. Joachim replies in turn, "Ah, yes, time. . . . You wouldn't believe how fast and loose they play with people's time around here. Three weeks are the same as a day to them. You'll see. You have all that to learn."[102] Several hundred pages later, Castorp, along with the reader, has adapted to the temporal pace of sanatorium life. "Notions of time here," he reflects, "were different from those applicable to trips to the shore or stays at a spa. The month was, so to speak, the shortest unit of time, and a single month played no role at all."[103] As Russell Berman has summarized, above and beyond its status as a bildungsroman, *The Magic Mountain* sits comfortably within the category of the *Zeitroman*; it "poses fundamental questions about its own time, and it is a novel thematically and structurally concerned with time and its duplicities."[104]

Vogel's novella similarly touches on the tension between the progression of time in the sanatorium as well as in the Mannian flatlands below. Ornik, for example, is shocked at one point to realize that he has been hospitalized for over a year and a half. It is Ornik's dating system, though, that most directly distinguishes this Tyrolean sanatorium for indigent Jews from the temporal zone of its geographic setting and its literary context. On the one hand, Ornik inscribes his personal medical history within the Jewish calendar and, in doing so, absorbs the German sanatorium into the Hebrew cycle. He writes his own story using Jewish time in a German space. On the other hand, with this move, the novella chronologically divorces itself from the German temporal-cultural sphere of the text. Read this way, Vogel's work argues against the compatibility of Hebrew and German literature. The bodies share neither a language nor a temporal-experiential context. Rather, Hebrew and German are pitted against each other. When Ornik finishes drafting the letter to Dr. Kalbel, he gives the envelope to the janitor, Hermann, to send out into the world. Once again, *Herr Mann* appears as the gatekeeper of the literary sanatorium.

Conclusion: Tubercular Contraction

Following the scene of Ornik's letter writing, readers find themselves taking stock of the sanatorium bookshelves. The books are old and yellowing, some are classic novels, and some are old, illustrated periodicals. Next to the shelves, a number of patients flip through volumes "that have soaked up the sweat of thousands of sick hands and the tens of thousands of tuberculosis germs."[105] Vogel does not offer any more information about the books or bookshelves, but the rhetorical thrust of the observation is strong. He has pointed readers to consider the work of literature as an infectious agent. The book is a potential site of contagion where tuberculosis may be touched, absorbed, and contracted.

On a rhetorical level, it is precisely a concern for the polyvalent English category of contraction that has motivated my preceding inquiry into Vogel's early writing. Already in his diary, Vogel alerts his readers to his fear that his Hebrew must contract, must shrink, must *hitkavets* to make room for German language and culture. He responds to that threat by growing his own Hebrew prose style, by developing a literary language to describe his daily life, and by rendering his Hebrew flexible enough to endure the encroaching German vernacular. He begins to adopt the Gregorian calendar, to engage German literature, and to assimilate a set of German cultural ideas of disease and creativity, even while remaining committed to Hebrew.

Over a decade after Vogel first began to study German, he would still be engaging the same questions of linguistic and cultural compatibility in his novella, *In the Sanatorium*, which, heavily influenced by Vogel's own experiences, allegorizes the fictional Genesungsheim as a European tradition of writing. This symbolic sanatorium contracts around its Jewish patients. Fictional and linguistic borders are established and, when crossed, alert readers to the tensions directing the Hebrew-German conversation. When Engineer Tseberg/Zwerg enters the Hebrew sanatorium, he brings with him *The Magic Mountain*, dwarfing Vogel's thin novella. The text reacts to this threat by reducing *Der Zauberberg* to its consonantal base, shrinking the novel into its most minimal form, and relegating the Engineer Tseberg to a peripheral role. The German *Herr Mann* kicks the Vogelian counterpart Adler out of the Hebrew sanatorium while Ornik writes himself out of Gregorian time. Vogel's Hebrew narrator ignores the omen of Roman script while a German-Hebrew pun reveals the specter of Yiddish attending the hyphenated exchange. And while the sanatorium itself provides an entrée into a German literary conversation, Vogel's Hebrew repeatedly gestures to the closed borders of that tradition, to orthographic dissimilarities, to proprietary administrators, and to a conversation that is written under the sign of incurable disease, of intercultural unease, and of the emaciating illness of tuberculosis.

Vogel's world is far from a positively troped space of German-Hebrew cultural exchange. Rather, his German-Hebrew conversation is sick, angry, and combative. Even while the novella identifies Vogel's familiarity with the German sanatorium, the rhetorical moves of the text push Vogel precisely out of the tradition. Ornik commits suicide, Adler is expelled from the sanatorium, and the remaining patients are no closer to a cure. In broad strokes, one character leaves of his own volition, one character is kicked out, and the remaining characters are left in an ambiguous zone of conflict and illness.

For more than a vehicle of symbolic capital, tuberculosis would be the literary occasion through which Vogel would enter the German cultural sphere as well as recognize his necessary distance from it. The disease offered Vogel new literary opportunities to see his work translated into German and even to advocate on behalf of a fellow writer, albeit a Yiddish author. It also garnered him the support of the Hebrew-Viennese literary elite. Yet Vogel did not become famous by virtue of contracting a terminal disease. He certainly did not boast the same renown as Sholem Aleichem, and a global appeal was not initiated in his name. His disease also did not render him the central figure of a private salon, as it did for Raḥel. Finally, tuberculosis did not place him in a sanatorium in which both administrators and patients would work together to form a multigenerational writer's colony and fund-raising machine. Rather, tuberculosis proved itself a dynamic cultural actor, mediating Vogel's first steps into a fraught Hebrew-German conversation, situating his text within a network of textual relations, and providing him the literary language to challenge precisely the possibility of that exchange. The sanatorium, as Vogel's work argues, was not simply a place for patients to recuperate but also the allegorized stage of German-Hebrew difference. Tubercular capital, as it were, mobilized and critiqued at the borders of Hebrew modernism.

EPILOGUE

After the Cure

> Let's go back to the sanatorium. People have to go back to where they came from. So they say, if I'm not mistaken.
>
> —**Aharon Appelfeld**[1]

David Vogel left Merano in 1926 and made his way to Paris. Excluding extended stays in Berlin, Vienna, and Tel Aviv, he settled in the French capital and remained there on and off for more than a decade. Throughout his time in Paris, he lived in the manner to which he had grown accustomed: poor, sickly, and underemployed.[2] There was no sign that either financial or physical relief would arrive. Still, he continued to write, and, despite his French surroundings, his prose remained embedded in the German cultural landscape of his early work. When the war broke out in 1939, Vogel left Paris with his daughter and joined his wife in the town of Hauteville in the east of France. Ada Vogel had already moved to the town to enter the Sanatorium de l'Espérance.[3] The institution had been founded in 1926 by Adelaide Rothschild, specifically for women, like Ada, who suffered from pulmonary tuberculosis.[4]

At the outbreak of World War I, Vogel had been living in Vienna. As a Russian subject, he was imprisoned by the Austrian government. Now living in France as an Austrian citizen, he was imprisoned once again. From the fall of 1939 to the summer of 1940, he was moved from internment camp to internment camp, unsure whether or not he would be able to rejoin his wife and daughter in Hauteville. During his incarceration, he wrote dozens of postcards to Ada and, after being released, worked to distill his experiences through a literary lens. To do so, he drafted a Yiddish narrative that might alternately be described as an autobiography, a novel, or a chronicle. The text, *They All Went Out to War* (*Kulam yats'u la-krav*), concerns the imprisonment by the French authorities of an Austrian-Jewish painter named Weichert. Over the course of the narrative, Weichert moves from camp to camp. His living conditions grow successively worse and his Jewish identity increasingly stigmatizing.

Early on in the text, Vogel establishes the link between author and protagonist. In one of the opening scenes, Weichert is arrested. He is told that he will soon be placed in an internment camp despite his protestations that, as a Jew, he could not support Hitler. Recognizing the logic of his claim, the gendarmes suggest that he procure a document from a reputable French citizen to attest to his loyalties. Weichert turns to the local Dr. Bonafé, who is in charge of the sanatorium where Weichart's wife is suffering from tuberculosis. The physician, in fact, shares his name with Dr. Léon Bonafé, then the chief medical officer at the Sanatorium de l'Espérance where Ada Vogel was recuperating. The character Bonafé provides Weichart with the document, and then, from the perspective of Weichart, we read:

> He tried to calm me, saying that I shouldn't lose hope, that I'd return soon, in France we're . . . "the French aren't like that." . . . And it occurred to me that he must use the same strong tone when he pacifies his patients who are hopeless, for whom there is no treatment.[5]

This final line is devastating. Vogel paints the future of the Austrian Jews living in France with the brushstroke of chronic illness. The condition is permanent, incurable, fatal. Shortly after the conversation, Weichert is imprisoned at a camp in Bourg-en-Bresse and then moved to an internment camp in Arandon. There, one of his fellow inmates suffers a tubercular hemorrhage and is released to a hospital in Grenoble. Weichert is gripped by jealousy. "To be liberated by tuberculosis!," he writes; "in my mind, there was only: 'To be liberated.'"[6] For the moment, it is as if Weichert could serve as one of Didier Fassin's interviewees, whom we encountered at the outset of this book; the character's disease seems to offer a glimmer of freedom. Yet as Bonafé's words suggest, a terminal illness could not offer any permanent escape. Considering Vogel's personal experience with tuberculosis as well as his earlier novella, these episodes are all the more unsettling. Once again, the metaphor of disease names the path that the Jewish artist will take through a European landscape, but here that path is not marked by allusions to Mann, Chekhov, or Sholem Aleichem. The dynamism of that potential conversation is lost. There is only a tubercular future with no possible relief.

Vogel's text would not appear in published form until 1990, and then only in Hebrew translation. Since the time of the text's composition and until today, the presence of the tubercular trope has dramatically waned in Hebrew and Yiddish literature. With the introduction of antibiotic treatments for tuberculosis beginning in the 1950s, the sheer number of patients shrank at a rapid rate. By 1955, the so-called Triple Therapy had been implemented. Patients were treated successfully using a combination of three chemotherapeutic agents: streptomycin, PAS (para-aminosalicylic acid), and isoniazid.[7] As fewer individuals in the United States and central Europe suffered from tuberculosis, health institutions around the world were closed or repurposed. Today the Jüdische Genesungsheim in Merano houses municipal offices and apartments.[8] The Jewish Consumptives' Relief Society in Denver was turned first into a cancer research center and then into an art college.[9] Raḥel's apartment on 5 Bogroshov is now a private residence above a real estate brokerage and travel agency. And while there is a small plaque in the town of Nervi, Italy, where Sholem Aleichem once took the cure, tubercular patients no longer flock there en masse.

Over the decades, the disease also lost its cultural currency for Hebrew and Yiddish writers. The former looked elsewhere—to the cancer ward and the AIDS crisis—for the material to generate the narratives of Israeli literature.[10] It was a move echoed in Sontag's companion volume to *Illness as Metaphor* (1978), where she plotted the cultural history of positively troped tuberculosis and negatively troped cancer. Ten years later, in *AIDS and Its Metaphors*, Sontag traced how the stigmatizing metaphoric complex surrounding cancer had been adopted in the linguistic conventions attending AIDS. The discursive spaces of AIDS and HIV, however, would not be explored at length in the postwar Yiddish canon. And, perhaps surprisingly, tuberculosis also was not actively deployed as a metaphor for the decline of Yiddish literature, a tradition that continued to face an ever-dwindling population of writers, readers, and publishers. The Yiddish poet Yankev Glatshteyn, for example, called on the sclerotic motif instead to pathologize the Yiddish literary future.[11] In addition to the literary subjects of cancer and AIDS, contemporary scholars of literature, art, and medicine have turned their attention elsewhere, most recently to the cultural experience of disability as a creative resource, as a theoretical tool, and as that which "[enables] the humanities."[12]

An exception to this rule of tubercular erasure may, however, be found in the canon of Holocaust literature. The prevalence of tuberculosis in internment camps, ghettos, and death camps led writers, including Vogel, to reference the illness in a variety of creative accounts. In 1946, the Yiddish writer Chava Rosenfarb published "The Ballad of T.B.," a poem that follows a teenage girl in the Łódź ghetto on her way to the cemetery.[13] She carries a small note with her that testifies to her terminal diagnosis. The note stands as the final text that this young woman will read. As late as 1992 Rosenfarb returned to the theme of tuberculosis in her autobiographical novel, *Letters to Abrashe*.[14] The text narrates an epistolary exchange between two patients who begin to write to each other after the war. Both patients are located in hospitals in displaced persons camps. The protagonist suffers from typhus and writes to the eponymous Abrashe, whom she believes is suffering from tuberculosis.[15] The hospital functions as a liminal space for the patient-survivors of the Holocaust who hover between life and death. In Rosenfarb's novel, tuberculosis is not a sign of European cultural potential as much as the narrative device that lends some stability to an otherwise homeless person. Both tuberculosis and typhus, moreover, linger as physiological remnants of the Holocaust. The war may have ended, but the disease persists.[16] We might also recall here the tubercular patients whom H. Leivick visited in the Gauting Sanatorium. Many of those survivors spent years in the hospital, too sick to emigrate.[17]

In the world of postwar Hebrew fiction, there is one author in particular who stands out for his allegorical invocation of tuberculosis and the space of the sanatorium: the Israeli novelist Aharon Appelfeld. Born in Romania in 1932, Appelfeld grew up in a German-speaking household.[18] During World War II, he and his family were sent to a concentration camp. Appelfeld escaped and wandered from village to village. In 1944, he joined the Russian army as a kitchen aide.[19] He immigrated to Palestine in 1946, and his first collection of Hebrew short stories appeared in 1962.

Since the publication of his first Hebrew collection, he has continuously set the majority of his texts in the central European landscape of his youth. Health spas, sanatoria, and tuberculosis appear throughout his literary oeuvre, although he himself never suffered from the disease. In his 1995 novel, *Until the Dawn's Light* (*Ad she-ya'aleh amud ha-shaḥar*), the protagonist is a young Jewish woman named Blanca. She grows up in Austria in a petit bourgeois family. They spend every summer in resort town chosen precisely to avoid other Jews. Blanca's father believes that "Jewishness [is] an illness that had to be uprooted," and as a young woman, Blanca had similarly conceived of her identity as "a kind of severe disease, accompanied by fever and vomiting."[20] At first, her mother tries to mitigate her daughter's self-hatred, but later, after being diagnosed with tuberculosis, she tells her daughter that Jews are weak. Blanca goes on to marry a violent non-Jewish man. Adolf, whose name overstates his anti-Semitic predisposition, repeatedly criticizes Jews and refuses to let Blanca visit her mother in the sanatorium. Eventually Blanca kills her husband and begins a life on the road as a serial arsonist, a career that ultimately leads to her demise.

Like other Appelfeld narratives, *Until the Dawn's Light* is a story of failed assimilation, of abusive intermarriages, and of a German-Jewish society that understands Jewish life as a pathological disease. Nowhere are these themes more pronounced than in Appelfeld's 1975 novella, *Badenheim, Resort Town* (*Badenhaim, ir nofesh*), one of the author's most famous texts. The novella introduces Badenheim as a typical spa town of central Europe, not dissimilar to the seaside resort of Nervi where Sholem Aleichem recuperated or from the mountain town of Merano, where Vogel sought medical help. Jews arrive in Badenheim each summer for entertainment and recuperation and as an exercise in proper social behavior. Set in 1939, the typical spa season is interrupted by the increasingly onerous demands of the aptly named Sanitation Department. First the municipal body requires all the Jewish residents and guests to register. Although some are initially hesitant, all eventually acquiesce. Later, the officials institute the forced immigration of Badenheim's Jews to Poland. In the final scene, the characters enter the trains without protest.

After boarding, the local impresario remarks, "If the coaches are so dirty it must mean that we have not far to go."[21] The dramatic irony of the novella is heavy-handed, and readers are left without a doubt that this will be the final train ride for the residents and guests of Badenheim.

Despite, or perhaps because of, its canonical status, it is difficult for the present reader to engage *Badenheim* without wishing to excoriate Appelfeld for his relentlessly overdetermined interpretation of German-Jewish history and culture. The work appears even more troubling when we take into account how frequently Appelfeld is placed in a Hebrew literary tradition alongside Vogel.[22] Appelfeld, in contrast to Vogel, does not engage the German literary tradition to test the boundaries between Hebrew and German cultural production. This is evident, for example, when we examine the rhetorical difference of two characters' names: Engineer Tseberg from *In the Sanatorium* and Frau Zauberblit from *Badenheim*. With his name, Vogel's character initiates a conversation with Thomas Mann's *Zauberberg* that involves a back and forth of power and prestige. Reducing Mann's text to its consonantal base, he dwarfs Mann's epic novel while himself appearing dwarfed by it. Appelfeld's Frau Zauberblit resists such a back and forth. On first reading, the name clearly references Mann's text, both sharing the prefix *Zauber*. But there will be nothing enchanted about Frau Zauberblit's experience of tuberculosis and no extended or dynamic exchange with Mann's work. Rather, Frau Zauberblit's name points to the fact that her fate is sealed in her tubercular *blit*—one Yiddish dialectical variant of the Germanic *Blut*. After arriving in Badenheim from a Jewish sanatorium, she continues to cough up blood and remains feverish throughout the novella; she cannot escape the blood that defines her or the racialized identity that attends it. In short, as her name suggests, Frau Zauberblit's fate is doubly sealed as both ailing and Jewish, and any relation she may have to Mann's magisterial novel is there to be ironized rather than taken seriously. Tuberculosis is simply the physiological manifestation of Appelfeld's understanding of a terminal European-Jewish identity rather than an intertextual mechanism with which to critically engage the German literary canon.

Even after tuberculosis had become a treatable affliction, Appelfeld painted prewar life with an incurable tubercular profile. The disease pointed to an inherent Jewish weakness exacerbated by assimilation, and tuberculosis and the health spa became metaphors for the inevitable destruction of the diaspora.[23] Central Europe, in Appelfeld's literary world, was a topography of graveyards and the health resort, a waiting area before the gas chamber. Appelfeld's writing manifests an understanding of tuberculosis that echoes Sander Gilman's investigations as a cultural historian. Both narrate a history in which tuberculosis metaphorizes Jewish difference as an identity that is always, only, and nothing other than terminal. While not every writer is Kafka, all the tubercular Jewish characters of Appelfeld's oeuvre are already fated to succumb to their pathologized identities.

Appelfeld's novella is perhaps the most famous text explored in this study. Unlike Vogel's *In the Sanatorium*, Sholem Aleichem's "Shmuel Shmelkes and His Jubilee," Raḥel's "I Don't Complain," or Shea Tenenbaum's Denver sketches, *Badenheim, Resort Town* is firmly ensconced in the modern Jewish canon.[24] Yet by limiting the metaphoric range of tuberculosis to the prefiguration of Jewish destruction, Appelfeld flattens out the opposing valences that have attended the disease throughout this study. Tuberculosis impinged on the health of the Jewish writer while conditioning his or her literary horizons. It was both physically debilitating and literarily generative. It isolated writers even as it expanded their readerships and translated their texts for new audiences. It confined them to hospital beds as well as introduced their work to new geographic settings and subjects. The disease mobilized authors, poets, readers, editors, publishers, and critics as it managed a variety of anxieties about the future of Yiddish and Hebrew literature. It assumed a Romantic patina as well as a socialist edge; it looked out at the world through a Zionist lens and from a modernist sanatorium; and it was expressed by authors who peppered their words with humor and by those who could not avoid crying in a melancholic tone.

What Appelfeld ignores in his literary map of central Europe is precisely the paradox of tubercular capital. For him, the disease means only one thing—only one vision of Jewish cultural and corporeal failure. But for the writers of this study, a diagnosis of tuberculosis was a physical reality, an aesthetic possibility, a literary subject, and a sociocultural resource. It led them down unpredictable pathways of creativity and experimentation. "Let it be a consumption," declared Peretz's protagonist. "At least something should happen." What the histories and texts of Sholem Aleichem, Raḥel, the writers of the JCRS, David Vogel, and others have demonstrated is precisely that *something did happen*. And that *something* was neither homogeneous nor predetermined but dynamic, historically contingent, and adaptive. The question of tuberculosis has become a matter of the past for contemporary Jewish writers, but for the authors and poets of the early twentieth century, it was always a matter of the future, its risks, its obstacles, and its rewards.

NOTES

Introduction

1. I. L. Peretz, "Mayses," in *Di tsayt*, vol. 2, *Ale verk fun Y. L. Perets* (New York: Morgn-Frayhayt with the Permission of B. Kletzkin Farlag, Poland, 1920), 178.

2. For a medical overview of tuberculosis, including basic facts about the disease, its pathology, and treatment practices, see Centers for Disease Control and Prevention, "Tuberculosis (TB)," accessed December 26, 2014, http://www.cdc.gov/tb/.

3. My use of the term "mediator" here draws on the work of Bruno Latour, who defines the "mediator" as that which "render[s] the movement of the social visible to the reader." Bruno Latour, *Reassembling the Social: An Introduction to Actor-Network Theory* (Oxford: Oxford University Press, 2007), 128.

4. World Health Organization, "TB: Reach the 3 Million," WHO Document Production Services, 2014, 5, http://www.stoptb.org/assets/documents/resources/publications/acsm/WORLD_TB_DAY_BROCHURE_14March.pdf.

5. Ibid., 3; World Health Organization, "Tuberculosis: WHO Global Tuberculosis Report," 2014, 1, http://www.who.int/tb/publications/factsheet_global.pdf?ua=1.

6. Richard Luscombe, "Florida Closes Only Tuberculosis Hospital amid Worst US Outbreak in 20 Years," *The Guardian*, July 9, 2012, US edition, http://www.theguardian.com/world/2012/jul/09/florida-closes-tuberculosis-hospital-outbreak?newsfeed=true.

7. Recognizing that a modern medical vocabulary to describe various aspects of tuberculosis would not be available to his readers, Zagorodski at times translates his terminology into Yiddish. For example, he follows the Hebrew term *ha-shi'ul* with the parenthetical Yiddish *hustn*, both referring to coughing. See Y. Ḥ. Zagorodski, "Ḥayenu ve-'orekh yamenu: 'Etsot ve-ḥukim li-shemor beri'ut ha-guf" (Warsaw: Schuldberg, 1898), 106.

8. René J. Dubos and Jean Dubos, *The White Plague: Tuberculosis, Man, and Society* (New Brunswick, NJ: Rutgers University Press, 1996), 142–44.

9. M. Gotlieb, *Zayt gezund* (Warsaw: Tsukermans Folksbibliotek, 1899–1900).

10. David S. Barnes, *The Making of a Social Disease: Tuberculosis in Nineteenth-Century France* (Berkeley: University of California Press, 1995), 4, 13; Michael Zdenek David, "The White Plague in the Red Capital: The Control of Tuberculosis in Russia, 1900–1941" (PhD diss., University of Chicago, 2007) ProQuest/UMI (Publication No. 3287026), 1; Dubos and Dubos, *The White Plague*, 10; "Ten Leading Causes of Death in the United States, 1900, 1940, 1976," in *From Consumption to Tuberculosis: A Documentary History*, ed. Barbara Gutmann Rosenkrantz (New York: Garland Publishing, 1993), 3–4.

11. As reported by Joseph Marcus, *Social and Political History of the Jews in Poland, 1919–1939* (Berlin: Walter de Gruyter, 1983), 191. As Marcus notes, however, these statistics are based on official death certificates and likely do not account for all death from tuberculosis (ibid., 493n17).

12. Barnes, *The Making of a Social Disease*, 4, 258n9.

13. For narration of his discovery of *Mycobacterium tuberculosis* as well as the near-simultaneous discovery by other scientists, see Dubos and Dubos, *The White Plague*, 101–4.

14. The article first appeared in English in the *American Veterinary Review* 13 (1884): 54–59, 106–12, 202–4. For a reprint, see Robert Koch, "Aetiology of Tuberculosis," trans. Rev. F. Sause, in *From Consumption to Tuberculosis: A Documentary History*, ed. Barbara Gutmann Rosenkrantz (New York: Garland Publishing, 1994), 197–224.

15. Gershn Levin, "Der kamf mit der shvindzukht," *Haynt*, February 20 [March 5], 1909, 6.

16. The Duboses date the first printed record of the term "tuberculosis" to 1840. Dubos and Dubos, *The White Plague*, 6–7.

17. As quoted in Muki Tsur, "Ke-ḥakot Raḥel: Kavim biyografiyim," in *Ha-shirim*, by Raḥel (Bene Barak: Ha-Kibuts Ha-Me'uḥad, 2011), 66.

18. David Barnes has also recently shown that, in the case of France, "the redemptive-spiritual view persisted long after the sociomedical understanding arose that (far from being mutually exclusive) the two sets of meanings coexisted, at once complementing and contesting each other throughout the Belle Epoque." As Barnes proves, the shift from an understanding of "consumption" to an understanding of "tuberculosis" in France was not a decisive break. Barnes, *The Making of a Social Disease*, 51.

19. For example, I do not include an analysis of Uri Nissan Gnessin, who suffered from a variety of heart and chest ailments but never specifically named his disease as tuberculosis or consumption. On Gnessin's heart disease (*maḥalat ha-lev*), see Bentsiyon Benshalom, *Uri Nisan Genesin: Monografiyah* (Krakow: Miflat, 1934), 104; Sh. Bikhovsky, "Uri Nisan Genesin," in *Ha-tsidah: Kovets zikaron le-A. N. Genesin*, by Uri Nis-

san Gnessin (Jerusalem: Defus Aḥdut, 1913), 89–91; Zalman Shneur, "Al Uri Nisan Genesin," in *Ḥ. N. Bialik u-vene doro* (Tel Aviv: Devir, 1958), 405.

20. Clark Lawlor, *Consumption and Literature: The Making of the Romantic Disease* (New York: Palgrave Macmillan, 2006), 15–27.

21. Ibid., 8. See also, Katherine Byrne, *Tuberculosis and the Victorian Literary Imagination* (New York: Cambridge University Press, 2011), 4.

22. Susan Sontag, *Illness as Metaphor and AIDS and Its Metaphors* (New York: Picador USA, 2001), 33.

23. Byrne, *Tuberculosis and the Victorian Literary Imagination*, 96–99.

24. Thomas Mann, *Tristan*, in *Death in Venice and Other Stories*, trans. H. T. Lowe-Porter (New York: Alfred A. Knopf, 1947), 320.

25. Sander L. Gilman, *Franz Kafka: The Jewish Patient* (New York: Routledge, 1995), 187–89.

26. Dubos and Dubos, *The White Plague*, 59.

27. Robert Diedrich Wessling, "Semyon Nadson and the Cult of the Tubercular Poet" (PhD diss., University of California, Berkeley, 1988), 2, ProQuest (Order No. 9923103).

28. Erich Ebstein, *Tuberkulose als Schicksal: Eine Sammlung pathographischer Skizzen von Calvin bis Klabund, 1509–1928* (Stuttgart: Ferdinand Enke Verlag, 1932).

29. Lewis Jefferson Moorman, *Tuberculosis and Genius* (Chicago: University of Chicago Press, 1940), xi.

30. Thomas Moore, *The Life of Lord Byron* (London: John Murray, 1844), 113. See also Sontag, *Illness as Metaphor*, 31.

31. Dubos and Dubos, *The White Plague*, 65.

32. Barnes, *The Making of a Social Disease*, 31, 36.

33. David, "The White Plague in the Red Capital," 59.

34. Irving Howe, *World of Our Fathers: The Journey of the East European Jews to America and the Life They Found and Made* (New York: Simon & Schuster, 1976), 149.

35. G[ershn] Levin, *Lungen-shvindukht iz heylbar!* (Warsaw: TOZ, 1925), 32–33.

36. Sholem Asch, *Ist river: Roman* (New York: Elias Laub, 1946), 39.

37. Morris Rosenfeld, "A trer afn ayzn," in *Gezamelte lider* (New York: International Library, 1906), 14–15. I have drawn on Marc Miller's translation and modified it slightly. Marc Miller, *Representing the Immigrant Experience: Morris Rosenfeld and the Emergence of Yiddish Literature in America* (Syracuse, NY: Syracuse University Press, 2007), 123.

38. Morris Rosenfeld, *Lieder des Ghetto*, trans. Berthold Feiwel (Berlin: S. Calvary, 1903), 36.

39. . Gilman, *Franz Kafka*, 173.

40. Ibid., 7–8.

41. Ibid., 12.

42. Ibid., 51, 212–13.

43. See also John M. Efron, *Medicine and the German Jews: A History* (New Haven, CT: Yale University Press, 2001), 126–32.

44. Of particular importance here is the contribution of historian Mitchell Hart, whose research shows that, at the same time that Jews were considered categorically tubercular, they were also being studied for their statistically lower rate of tubercular infection. These low rates were explained at different times using different reasons, such as the prevalence of kosher food practices. Some scientists, drawing on social Darwinist theories, concluded that centuries of urban living rendered the Jews less susceptible to the disease. Mitchell Bryan Hart, *The Healthy Jew: The Symbiosis of Judaism and Modern Medicine* (New York: Cambridge University Press, 2007), 143–72.

45. Efron, *Medicine and the German Jews*; Michael Gluzman, *Ha-guf ha-tsiyoni: Le'umiyut, migdar u-miniyut ba-sifrut ha-ivrit ha-ḥadashah* (Tel Aviv: Ha-Kibuts Ha-Me'uḥad, 2007); Todd Samuel Presner, *Muscular Judaism: The Jewish Body and the Politics of Regeneration*, Routledge Jewish Studies Series (New York: Routledge, 2007).

46. Presner, *Muscular Judaism*, 16.

47. Asch, *Ist river*, 39.

48. Naomi Seidman, *A Marriage Made in Heaven* (Berkeley: University of California Press, 1997), 124–31.

49. A[vraham] Shlonsky, "Al 'ha-shalom,'" *Ketuvim*, May 11, 1927, 1. Also quoted by Naomi Rebecca Brenner, "Authorial Fictions: Literary and Public Personas in Modern Hebrew and Yiddish Literature" (PhD diss., University of California, Berkeley, 2008), ProQuest (Order No. AAT3331524).

50. Bashevis Singer's text *Der hoyf* appeared in the Yiddish daily *Forverts* from January 10, 1953, to February 12, 1955. The serialized novel was translated into English as two novels, *The Manor* (1967) and *The Estate* (1969). For a translation of the text in one volume, see Isaac Bashevis Singer, *The Manor and The Estate*, trans. Joseph Singer, Elizabeth Gottlieb, and Herman Eichenthal (Madison: University of Wisconsin Press, 2004). For Baron's text, see Dvora Baron, "Be-sof kayits," in *Parashiyot: Sipurim mekubatsim*, ed. Nurit Govrin and Avner Holtzman (Jerusalem: Mosad Byaliḳ, 2000), 631–35. For Gnessin's, see Uri Nissan Gnessin, *Etsel* (Tel Aviv: Yaḥdav̱, 1965).

51. Shlomo Damesek, *Be-gorali* (New York: Hotsa'at Bitsaron, 1945); Yisroel Rabon, *Di gas: Roman* (Warsaw: L. Goldfarb, 1928).

52. Sholem Aleichem, "In di varembeder," in *Zumer-lebn*, vol. 11, *Ale verk fun Sholem-Aleykhem* (New York: Morgn-Frayhayt, 1937), 73–118; Ben K. Blake, dir., *Two Sisters: Tsvey shvester* (1938) (Waltham, MA: National Center for Jewish Film, Brandeis University, ca. 2006), DVD, 82 min.

53. Sontag, *Illness as Metaphor*, 3.

54. Cancer, demonstrates Sontag, has been defined by the metaphoric language of war (i.e., cancer "invades"), and AIDS has been stigmatized through the lan-

guage of delinquency (i.e., the victim is blamed for sexual impropriety). Ibid., 14, 113, passim.

55. Pierre Bourdieu, *The Field of Cultural Production: Essays on Art and Literature*, ed. Randal Johnson (New York: Columbia University Press, 1993); Pierre Bourdieu, "The Forms of Capital," in *Handbook of Theory and Research for the Sociology of Education*, ed. John G. Richardson (New York: Greenwood Press, 1996), 241–58.

56. Amos Ron, "A Rachel for Everyone: The Kinneret Cemetery as a Site of Civil Pilgrimage," in *Sanctity of Time and Space in Traditions and Modernity*, ed. Alberdina Houtman, Marcel Poorthuis, and Joshua Schwartz (Boston: Brill, 1998), 349–59.

57. Sholem Aleichem, "Shmuel Shmelkes un zayn yubileum," in *Fun Kasrilevke*, vol. 19, *Ale verk fun Sholem-Aleykhem* (New York: Morgn-Frayhayt, 1937), 205.

58. My use of the term "network" here has been greatly influenced by the work of actor-network theorist Bruno Latour. A network is a "string of actions where each participant is treated as a full-blown mediator," and a mediator is that which "render[s] the movement of the social visible to the reader." Put simply, a network is a chain of associations that can be traced. Something works on something else, *mediates* it, transforms it, causes it to change. That object, in turn, performs an action on another object, and a link in the associative chain is generated. This network may only be identified as the various actants associate with each other, impinge on each other, and effect change in the other's presence. Most important, the network considers both humans and nonhumans as mutually affective actants constituted in relation to each other. This is key for understanding the role of tuberculosis and its institutions in directing the history of modern Jewish literature. My research takes as its agenda the process of making visible the association of tuberculosis (nonhuman), literary institutions (nonhuman), and the Yiddish or Hebrew writer (human). By tracing these associations, the bioliterary network becomes observable and links together authors, poets, editors, readers, philanthropists, sanatoria, and, of course, illness. Latour, *Reassembling the Social*, 93–99, 128. See also Bruno Latour and Steve Woolgar, *Laboratory Life: The Construction of Scientific Facts* (Princeton, NJ: Princeton University Press, 1986).

59. I draw here on the definition of "self-fashioning" offered by Stephen Greenblatt that is central to New Historicist thinking. In this model, authorial self-fashioning is "a manifestation of the concrete behavior of its particular author, as itself the expression of the codes by which behavior is shaped, and as a reflection upon those codes." Stephen Greenblatt, *Renaissance Self-Fashioning: From More to Shakespeare* (Chicago: University of Chicago Press, 2005), 3–4.

60. Daniel Charney, "Fun Eyrope keyn Elis Aylend un tsurik (Part 1)," *Der tog*, November 15, 1925; Daniel Charney, "Fun Eyrope keyn Elis Aylend un tsurik (Part 2)," *Der tog*, November 22, 1925; Daniel Charney, "Fun Eyrope keyn Elis Aylend un tsurik (Part 3)," *Der tog*, November 29, 1925; Daniel Charney, "Fun Eyrope keyn Elis Aylend un tsurik (Part 4)," *Der tog*, December 6, 1925; Daniel Charney, "Fun Eyrope keyn Elis

Aylend un tsurik (Part 5)," *Der tog*, December 14, 1925; Daniel Charney, "Fun Eyrope keyn Elis Aylend un tsurik (Part 6)," *Der tog*, December 21, 1925. For an overview of the politics and rhetoric of border control at Ellis Island, see Alan M. Kraut, *Silent Travelers: Germs, Genes, and the "Immigrant Menace"* (New York: Basic Books, 1994), chaps. 2, 3.

61. Didier Fassin, "Another Politics of Life Is Possible," *Theory, Culture & Society* 26 (2009): 51.

62. Didier Fassin, "Ethics of Survival: A Democratic Approach to the Politics of Life," *Humanity: An International Journal of Human Rights, Humanitarianism, and Development* 1, no. 1 (2010): 91.

63. Fassin, "Another Politics of Life Is Possible," 51.

Chapter 1

1. O. Henry, "A Fog in Santone," in *The Complete Works of O. Henry* (Garden City, NY: Doubleday, 1953), 992–97.

2. Gershn Levin also recounts his surprise that Peretz attended the Warsaw celebration of Sholem Aleichem's jubilee in 1908, as Peretz had previously refused to include Sholem Aleichem's work in a Hanukkah performance under Peretz's supervision. In response to Levin's surprise, Peretz explained: "Sholem Aleichem is still Sholem Aleichem." His reputation still demanded Peretz's attention. See Gershn Levin, "Mayne zikhroynes vegn Sholem-Aleykhem," in *Dos Sholem-Aleykhem-bukh*, ed. Yitsḥak Dov Berkowitz (New York: Ikuf, 1958), 259–82; Gershn Levin, "Sholem-Aleykhems krankhayt un zayn 25-yeriker yoyvl: Fun der seriye, 'Varshe far der milkhome,'" *Haynt*, September 11, 1938, 6. For an account of Peretz's attempt to usurp Sholem Aleichem's position in Yiddish literature, see Ruth R. Wisse, *I. L. Peretz and the Making of Modern Jewish Culture* (Seattle: University of Washington Press, 1991), 28–29.

3. Joseph Marcus, *Social and Political History of the Jews in Poland, 1919–1939* (Berlin: Walter de Gruyter, 1983), 191.

4. The TOZ (Towarzystwo Ochrony Zdrowia Ludności Żydowskiej, the Society for Safeguarding the Health of the Jewish Population) was a branch of the Saint Petersburg–based OZE (Russian: Obshchestvo Zdravookhraneniia Evreev, Society for the Protection of Jewish Health). The organization worked to educate and provide health care to the Jewish population of Poland, particularly in response to the growing need for health care in the wake of World War I. Gershn Levin, "Der kamf mit der shvindzukht," *Haynt*, February 20, 1909; Gershn Levin, *Higeniye bay iden amol un atsind* (Warsaw: TOZ, 1925); G[ershn] Levin, *Lungen-shvindukht iz heylbar!* (Warsaw: TOZ, 1925).

5. Now known as Baranavichy, Belarus.

6. Sholem Aleichem, "Di vibores," *Yudishes folks-blat*, October 19 [31], 1883, 623–

26. Throughout this chapter, I include both the Julian and Gregorian dates when both are listed in the publication.

7. For a description of the author's skill at public readings, see Ken Frieden, *Classic Yiddish Fiction: Abramovitsh, Sholem Aleichem, and Peretz* (Albany: State University of New York Press, 1995), 130. In 1906, he had traveled throughout western Europe giving readings with general success. Jeremy Dauber, *The Worlds of Sholem Aleichem* (New York: Nextbook & Schocken Books, 2013), 179.

8. Otwock was home to Jewish sanatoria for both tubercular patients and those who were mentally ill. In 1890, the first sanatorium was established in the town. For information on the establishment of the sanatorium, see Shimen Kants, "Di geshikhte fun alt-un nay Otvotsk," in *Yizker-bukh tsu fareybiken dem ondenk fun di khorev-gevorene yidishe kehiles Otvotsk, Kartshev* (Tel Aviv: Irgun Yotse Otvotsk Be-Yisra'el, 1968), 86–87. For general information on the city, see Binyomen Orenshteyn, *Khurbn: Otvotsk, Falenits, Kartshev* (Bamberg: Farvaltung fun Otvotsker, Falenitser un Kartshever Landslayt in der Amerikaner Zone in Daytshland, Published under EUCOM Civil Affairs Division Authorization Number UNDP 219, 1948).

9. The author describes himself and fellow patients as "half-men, (simply tuberculars) [*halbe mentshn (poshet sukhotnikes)*]." Otwock Sanatorium Patients, "Letter to Sholem Aleichem," May 30, 1908, Box 10, Folder lamed-alef 18/1, Beth Shalom Aleichem Archive.

10. "Fun varshever lebn: Sholem-Aleykhem in Varshe," *Unzer lebn* (Warsaw), May 18 [31], 1908, 3. In Łódź, he was met with fifteen minutes of applause. For additional records of the Łódź reading, see "Lodzher kronik: Sholem-Aleykhem in Lodzh," *Lodzher tageblat*, May 18 [31], 1908, 3; "Lodzher kronik: Tsum Sholem-Aleykhem," *Lodzher tageblat*, May 26 [June 8], 1908, 3; "Der ershter Sholem-Aleykhem ovnt in Lodzh," *Lodzher tageblat*, May 29 [June 11], 1908, 3. For an exuberant first-person account of the reading, see Yud-Alef, "Sholem-Aleykhem in Lodzh," *Lodzher tageblat*, June 29, 1938, 2.

11. In Minsk, an additional reading was planned after the first sold out. Tsvey-un-nayntsik, "Provints (fun unzere korispondenten): Minsk: Davke af yudish," *Der fraynd*, July 7 [20], 1908, 4. The three evenings in Warsaw were also sold out. "Fun varshever lebn: Yudishes," *Unzer lebn*, May 30 [June 12] 1908, 4.

12. Marie Waife Goldberg, *My Father, Sholom Aleichem* (New York: Simon & Schuster, 1968), 237.

13. Yankev Tsernikhov, "Vos makht Sholem-Aleykhem? A briv in redaktsiye," *Unzer lebn*, September 3 [16], 1908, 2.

14. "Be-Rusiyah," *Hashkafah*, September 4, 1908, 3; "Baranovitshi," *Hed ha-zeman*, August 17, 1908, 3.

15. "Telegramen: Spetsiel tsu 'Unzer Lebn,'" *Unzer lebn*, July 30 [12 August], 1908, 1.

16. Tsernikhov, "Vos makht Sholem-Aleykhem?," 2.

17. The exact timing is hard to determine as conflicting reports exist. Tsernikhov maintains that he fell ill three days after the performance. Waife-Goldberg recalls that he fell ill immediately after the performance. Ibid., 2; Goldberg, *My Father, Sholom Aleichem*, 237.

18. For an account of the doctor's first arrival, see Tsernikhov, "Vos makht Sholem-Aleykhem?," 2. For an account of Sholem Aleichem's protective young guards and nurses, see Vilnai, "Al-yad mitato shel Shalom Alekhem," *Hed ha-zeman*, September 2, 1908, 1. For a description of their diligent watch over Sholem Aleichem, see "Telegramen: Baranovitsh (spetsiel tsu 'Unzer Lebn')," *Unzer lebn*, August 7 [20], 1908, 1.

19. Binyomen Rabinovitsh, "Vegn Sholem-Aleykhems krankhayt," *Unzer lebn*, August 11 [24], 1908, 3; Tshernikhov, "Fun der letster minut," 1. An alternative account was later recorded in 1930 in the Soviet journal *Di royte velt*. The author claims that the Russian police provided "protektsiye" for Sholem Aleichem and that it was a Dr. Lunts from Minsk who attended to the sick writer. Shloyme-Yankev Nepomniashtshi, "Naye materialn vegn Sholem Aleykhem (1908–1909)," *Di royte velt* 6, no. 1–2 (1930): 181.

20. Yitsḥak Dov Berkowitz, *Ha-rishonim ki-vene adam: Sipure zikhronot al Shalom Alekhem u-vene doro* (Tel Aviv: Devir, 1975), 605; Goldberg, *My Father, Sholom Aleichem*, 238.

21. Italy was a common destination for consumptive patients in the nineteenth century. In 1852, Thomas Henry Burgess wrote extensively on the subject of climatology and attempted to debunk the myth that all locations in Italy were necessarily salubrious for consumptives. See Thomas Henry Burgess, *Climate of Italy in Relation to Pulmonary Consumption with Remarks on the Influence of Foreign Climates upon Invalids* (London: Longman, Brown, Green & Longmans, 1852). Clark Lawlor has also written about the equation of La Grande Tour with health tourism in and around Italy, paying specific attention to Tobias Smollett's *Travels through France and Italy* of 1766. See Clark Lawlor, *Consumption and Literature: The Making of the Romantic Disease* (New York: Palgrave Macmillan, 2006), 4, 143.

22. The public letter was reprinted in multiple newspapers. Sholem Aleichem, "A briv in redaktsiye," *Der fraynd*, September 9 [22], 1908, 3; Sholem Aleichem, "A briv in redaktsiye," *Unzer lebn*, September 12 [25], 1908, 3; Sholem Aleichem, "A briv fun Sholem-Aleykhem," *D"r Birnboyms vokhenblat*, September 25, 1908, 16–17.

23. Johann Wolfgang von Goethe, *Wilhelm Meister's Apprenticeship*, ed. and trans. Eric A. Blackall (New York: Suhrkamp Publishers, 1983), 9:83.

24. Yankev Dinezon, "Letter to Sholem Aleichem," August 12, 1908, Box 10, Folder lamed-dalet 10/52, Beth Shalom Aleichem Archive. Jeremy Dauber has done the most work in English to summarize the various financial crises that occurred throughout Sholem Aleichem's life and career. Dauber, *The Worlds of Sholem Aleichem*, passim.

25. Berkowitz, *Ha-rishonim ki-vene adam*, 605; Goldberg, *My Father, Sholom Aleichem*, 239.

26. On the history of Mendele's adoption of a pseudonym, see Dan Miron, *A Traveler Disguised: The Rise of Modern Yiddish Fiction in the Nineteenth Century* (Syracuse, NY: Syracuse University Press, 1996).

27. For a sample of reports regarding jubilee celebrations in Mendele's honor held in 1906 and 1907, see Kh. Aleksadrov, "Amerike un Mendeles yubileum (a briv fun Nu-York)," *Der fraynd* (Warsaw), February 12 [25], 1906, 1; Moyshe Kleynman, "Di vokh fun Mendele Moykher Sforim: Der Zeyde zol lebn, I," *Gut morgn*, December 22, 1910; Moyshe Kleynman, "Di vokh fun Mendele Moykher Sforim: Der zeyde zol lebn, II," *Gut morgn*, December 23, 1910; Moyshe Kleynman, "Di vokh fun Mendele Moykher Sforim: Der zeyde zol lebn, III," *Gut morgn*, December 24, 1908; Moyshe Kleynman, "Di vokh fun Mendele Moykher Sforim: Der zeyde zol lebn, IV," *Gut morgn*, December 26, 1908; Yoysef Luria, "Sholem Yankev Abramovitsh," *Dos yudishe folk* (Warsaw), December 25, 1906, 1–2; "Oysland: Berlin," *Di tsayt* (Vilna), February 2, 1906, 2; "Rebi Mendele Moḥer Sfarim (hirhurim u-maḥshavot le-yovel shenat ha-shiv'im shelo be-yom dalet tet"vav tevet), I," *Hashkafah* (Jerusalem), January 23, 1907, 6; "Rebi Mendele Moḥer Sfarim (hirhurim u-maḥshavot le-yovel shenat ha-shiv'im shelo be-yom dalet tet"vav tevet), II," *Hashkafah* (Jerusalem), January 25, 1907, 3; Sholem Aleichem, "Tsu Mendele Moykher-Sforims yubileum," *Der veg*, January 19, 1906, 1.

28. Berkowitz, *Ha-rishonim ki-vene adam*, 606; Goldberg, *My Father, Sholom Aleichem*, 240.

29. The date was October 11 [24], 1908. Berkowitz, *Ha-rishonim ki-vene adam*, 608.

30. For the first letter, see Moshe Weizmann, "A briv in redaktsiye," *Der fraynd*, September 3 [16], 1908, 2; Moshe Weizmann, "Sholem-Aleykhems yubileum," *Haynt*, September 5 [18], 1908, 4. For the second letter, see Moshe Weizmann, "A briv vegn 'Sholem Aleykhem,'" *D"r Birnboyms vokhenblat* 1, no. 6 (October 9, 1908): 15–16; Moshe Weizmann, "Sholem Aleykhems yubileum," *Der morgn-zhurnal*, October 15, 1908, 5. For mention of the letter, see "Yubileum far Sholem Aleykhem," *Der morgn-zhurnal*, September 30, 1908, 1.

31. My emphasis. Weizmann, "A briv in redaktsiye," 21.

32. Weizmann, "Sholem Aleykhems yubileum," *Der morgn-zhurnal*, 5.

33. Sholem Aleichem was particularly fond of the Gogolian phrase regarding "laughter through tears" and kept the passage on his desk. The idea has now become shorthand for the force and method of the Yiddish writer. The passage from *Dead Souls* reads, in George Reavey's translation: "For a long time to come I am destined by the magic powers to wander together with my strange heroes and to observe the whole vast movement of life—to observe it through laughter which can be shared by all and through tears which are unknown and unseen!" See Nikolai Vasilevich Gogol, "Dead Souls," in *Dead Souls: The Reavey Translation, Backgrounds and Sources, Essays in Criticism*, trans. George Reavey (New York: W. W. Norton, 1985), 141. Berkowitz writes that Sholem Aleichem kept a translation of this passage, which he wrote himself, on

an envelope on his desk as a type of talisman. See Yitsḥak Dov Berkowitz, "Mit der mishpokhe fun shriftshteler," in Sholem Aleichem, *Dos Sholem-Aleykhem-bukh*, ed. Yitsḥak Dov Berkowitz (New York: Ikuf, 1958), 188–89. On Sholem Aleichem's literary relationship to Gogol, see Amelia Glaser, *Jews and Ukrainians in Russia's Literary Borderlands: From the Shtetl Fair to the Petersburg Bookshop* (Evanston, IL: Northwestern University Press, 2012), 107–8; David G. Roskies, *A Bridge of Longing: The Lost Art of Yiddish Storytelling* (Cambridge, MA: Harvard University Press, 1995), 154. For an example of the use of the phrase in Sholem Aleichem criticism, see Frieden, *Classic Yiddish Fiction*, 109.

34. Similar brief mention is made to Rabinovitsh in the second letter, where Weizmann first introduces Sholem Aleichem and then puts Rabinovitsh's name in parentheses. Later, he makes clear that the jubilee will celebrate twenty-five years since "Rabinovitsh has become for us 'Sholem-Aleykhem' [*Rabinovitsh iz gevorn far unz 'Sholem-Aleykhem'*]." The emphasis, as in the first letter, shows a progression from Rabinovitsh to Sholem Aleichem.

35. Pierre Bourdieu, *The Field of Cultural Production: Essays on Art and Literature*, ed. Randal Johnson (New York: Columbia University Press, 1993), 75. My emphasis.

36. Dan Miron, "Sholem Aleichem: Person, Persona, Presence," in *The Image of the Shtetl and Other Studies of Modern Jewish Literary Imagination* (Syracuse, NY: Syracuse University Press, 2000), 136–39, 134–35.

37. Ibid., 154.

38. Of particular importance here is Naomi Brenner's recent intervention into the Mironian debate. Brenner has argued for the need to assign Sholem Aleichem more authorial agency. While Brenner agrees that there exists an "ontological difference between author and persona," she contends that "Rabinovitsh/Sholem Aleykhem makes this distinction difficult to recognize and sustain." Sholem Aleichem's "near-constant literary *presence* unifies Rabinovitsh's vast fictional world," writes Brenner, yet the Yiddish writer's literary style changes throughout his career. In Brenner's understanding, Miron is not wrong as much as he does not allow Sholem Aleichem as persona the necessary agency to displace Rabinovitsh from the authorial position. She reads Rabinovitsh as an author who has created a new author, a "canonical fictional [being]" who was a "stylized spokesm[a]n for the Jewish folk and Jewish tradition." In other words, the distance between author and persona may be true in the sense that the author is not the persona, but Sholem Aleichem as persona has his own authorial authority. Naomi Rebecca Brenner, "Authorial Fictions: Literary and Public Personas in Modern Hebrew and Yiddish Literature" (PhD diss., University of California, Berkeley, 2008), 47, 26, ProQuest (Order No. AAT3331524).

39. "Groyser oylem bay'm Sholem Aleykhem ovent," *Der morgn-zhurnal*, December 29, 1908, 7; "Literatur un kunst: Dem 11tn Oktober," *D"r Birnboyms vokhenblat*, September 18, 1908, 16; "'Sholem-Aleykhem' darf hilf fun Amerike," *Der morgn-zhurnal*,

December 9, 1908, 4; "Sholem Aleykhem: Oyser gefer," *Der morgn-zhurnal*, September 2, 1908, 8; "Sholem-Aleykhems yubileum," *Haynt*, September 5 [18], 1908, 4; "A Yiddish Literary Anniversary: A Character Sketch of 'Shalom Alechem,'" *Jewish Chronicle*, October 23, 1908, 14; Israel Cohen, "Shalom Aleichem: Letter from Israel Cohen," *Jewish Chronicle*, November 20, 1908, 26; Gershn Levin and Avrom Podlishevski, "Tsu Sholem-Aleykhems fererer," *Haynt*, September 25 [October 8], 1908, 1.

40. Justin Cammy, "Judging *The Judgment of Shomer*: Jewish Literature versus Jewish Reading," in *Arguing the Modern Jewish Canon: Essays on Literature and Culture in Honor of Ruth R. Wisse*, ed. Justin Cammy et al. (Cambridge, MA: Harvard University Press, 2008), 85–127.

41. On the development of a mass reading audience in Yiddish, see Alyssa Quint, "Yiddish Literature for the Masses? A Reconsideration of Who Read What in Jewish Eastern Europe," *AJS Review* 29, no. 1 (2005): 61–89.

42. Folk writer: H. Epelberg, "A yontef vokh: Tsu Sholem Aleykhems 25 yorikn yubileum," *Teatr velt* 3 (October 16, 1908): 4; Ployni ve-koyen, "Tsu Sholem-Aleykhems yubileum: Eynige algemeyne shtrikhen vegn dem literarishn verte fun dem grestn yidishn humorist," *Der amerikaner*, November 20, 1908," 1; Sh., "Le-yovelo shel Shalom Alekhem," *Hed ha-zeman*, October 7, 1908, 1. *Folksshrayber*: Y. Ug, "Tsu Sholem-Alekhems Yubileum," *Lodzher tageblat*, October 8 [21], 1908, 2. From the people: Emphasis in original. "Yubileums: Sholem-Aleykhem," *Lidskis familiyen kalender: Almanakh* (1909–10): 52.

43. Y. Ug, "Sholem-Aleykhem (tsu zayn 25-yeriken yubileum): I," *Lodzher tageblat*, October 13, 1908, 2.

44. Emphasis in original. Niser-azl, "Sholem-Aleykhem (tsu zayn yubileum)," *Di tsukunft* 8, no. 12 (1908): 6. Noah Pryłucki also wrote that "there are names that symbolize the folk to which they belong. Such a symbol is the dear name—Sholem Aleichem. The whole epoch of modern Jewish life is associated with him." Noah Pryłucki, "Sholem-Aleykhem (Part 1)," *Teatr velt*, no. 3 (October 16, 1908): 5.

45. Emphasis of "ours" in original. Emphasis of "with his sickness" is mine. R., "Ekspropri'irt Sholem-Aleykhemen!," *Der fraynd*, September 18 [October 1], 1908, 1.

46. Gershn Levin, "Tsu Sholem-Aleykhems yubileum," *Haynt*, September 10 [23], 1908, 1. This was echoed in an article in the New York–based *Der amerikaner*, in which the author declared it the "holy duty" (*heylike flikht*) of each reader to do his part for the fate of the writer and humorist. Ployni ve-koyen, "Tsu Sholem-Aleykhems yubileum," 5. Writing from the Polish industrial town of Łódź, Y. Lazar clarified that "repaying our debt [*khov*] to Sholem Aleichem—that is our holiest duty [*heylikste flikht*] at the moment." Izidor Lazar, "Sholem-Aleykhems 25 yoriker yubileum," *Lodzher tageblat*, October 10 [23], 1908, 2.

47. On the social role of philanthropy, in Germany and the Russian Empire, respectively, see Marion Kaplan, *The Making of the Jewish Middle Class: Women, Family, and*

Identity in Imperial Germany (New York: Oxford University Press, 1991); Brian Horowitz, *Jewish Philanthropy and Enlightenment in Late-Tsarist Russia* (Seattle: University of Washington Press, 2009).

48. Lisa Rae Epstein, "Caring for the Soul's House: The Jews of Russia and Health Care, 1860–1914" (PhD diss., Yale University, 1995), 6, Proquest (Order No. 9615222).

49. Natan M. Meir, *Kiev: Jewish Metropolis, A History, 1859–1914* (Bloomington: Indiana University Press, 2010), 212, 219.

50. Dovid Pinski, "Sholem-Aleykhems yubileum," *Der arbayter*, October 3, 1908, 5.

51. "Siḥot," *Hed ha-zeman*, November 11, 1908, 2.

52. Sh. Tshernovitsh, "Le-yovel ha-sifruti shel Shalom-Alekhem," *Hed ha-zeman*, September 20, 1908, 1.

53. Talent: "Azav ha-yehudi," *Ha-tsevi*, February 19, 1909, 1. Health: Y. Ug, "Tsu Sholem-Alekhems yubileum," *Lodzher tageblat*, October 8 [21], 1908, 2. Blood: Ug, "Tsu Sholem-Alekhems yubileum," 2.

54. For this line of argument, see "Ḥogege-ha-yovelim shelanu," *Hed ha-zeman*, November 5, 1908, 1; Yitsḥak Dov Berkowitz, "Sholem Aleykhems yubileum," *Der morgn-zhurnal*, November 16, 1908, 4; B"N [Re'uven Brainen], "Tsum yubileum fun Sholem-Aleykhem," *Unzer lebn*, October 12 [25], 1908, 2. This is also a point of reference in hindsight for Sholem Aleichem's daughter. See Goldberg, *My Father, Sholom Aleichem*, 240. Specifically, there was interest in purchasing Sholem Aleichem a property in Palestine, which Sholem Aleichem mentions in a letter to Gershn Levin. It also was publicly mentioned in the press. See Sholem Aleichem, "Letter to Gershn Levin (January 15, 1909)," in *Briv fun Sholem-Aleykhem, 1879–1916*, ed. Avrom Lis (Tel Aviv: Beys Sholem-Aleykhem & Perets Farlag, 1995), 489; "Shalom Alekhem be-Erets Yisra'el," *Ha-tsevi*, January 31, 1909, 2.

55. The majority of Yiddish articles concerned with Tolstoy's jubilee mention this ban. For example, see Yankl Gelm, "Tolstoys yubileum un di rusishe regirung," *Der amerikaner*, September 18, 1908, 7.

56. Ban: "Gzeyres af Tolstoy," *Varhayt*, August 5, 1908, 1; "The Tolstoi Celebration," *Jewish Chronicle*, September 25, 1908, 11; "Yidn af der ufname bay shvartsn: Tolstoys hayntiker yubileum," *Haynt*, August 28 [September 10], 1908, 1; Gelm, "Tolstoys yubileum un di rusishe regirung," 7. Health: "Di Krankhayt fun L. Tolstoy," *Haynt*, August 15 [28], 1908, 1; "Graf Tolstoy baym shtarbn," *Der morgn-zhurnal*, August 27, 1908, 1; "Liyev Tolstoy 80 yor alt," *Fraye arbayter shtime*, August 29, 1908, 1. Jubilee: "Fun der letster minut: Graf Tolstoys yubiley," *Haynt*, August 26 [September 8], 1908, 1; "Gantse velt git koved Tolstoyen," *Varhayt*, September 11, 1908, 1; "Leo Tolstoy: Zayn lebn, shriftn un tetikayten (tsum hayntikn yubileum)," *Varhayt* , September 10, 1908, 1; B"N [Re'uven Brainen], "Tsum yubileum fun Sholem-Aleykhem," 2. Literature: "Yidn af der ufname bay shvartsn," 1; V. Edlin, "Tolstoy iber kunst," *Der amerikaner*, September 18, 1908, 13; Izidor Lazar, "Kinstler un verk: Tolstoy in poeziye un filosofiye," *Roman-*

tsaytung 32 (September 4 [17], 1908): 1059–66. Ideology: M. L. R., "Tsu akhtsikyor-iken yubileum fun'm Graf Leo Tolstoy, 1828–1908," *Di naye tsayt: Zamlbukh* 4 (1908): 65–76; A. Tanenboym, "Lev Tolstoy: Zayn lebn un zayn virkn," *Der morgn-zhurnal*, September 13, 1908, 4; H. Zolotarov, "Tolstoy," *Di tsukunft* 13, no. 10 (1908): 3–8. Importance for humanity: "Graf Tolstoy: Tsu zayn akhtsikn yubileum," *Der arbayter*, September 5, 1908, 5; "Tsu Lev Tolstoys akhtsikyerikes yubileum," *Roman-tsaytung* 33 (August 28 [September 10], 1908): 1027–28; "Liyev Tolstoy," *D"r Birnboyms vokhenblat*, September 13, 1908, 1–4.

57. This occurred in the *Jewish Chronicle*. See "Help Needed for 'Shalom Aleichem,'" *Jewish Chronicle*, September 25, 1908, 11; "The Tolstoi Celebration," 11. It also occurred in the Warsaw-based *Unzer lebn*. See B"N [Re'uven Brainen], "Tsum yubileum fun Sholem-Aleykhem," 2; Mordkhe Spektor, "Sholem-Aleykhem (tsu zayn 25-yerign yubileum)," *Unzer lebn*, October 12 [25], 1908, 2.

58. B"N [Re'uven Brainen], "Tsum yubileum fun Sholem-Aleykhem," 2.

59. "Sholem-Aleykhems yubileum," *Der arbayter*, November 21, 1908, 5.

60. Sh. Frug, "Der royter gelekhter," *Der fraynd*, September 4 [17], 1908, 1. The text was reprinted at least twice. See Sh. Frug, "Der royter gelekhter," *Haynt*, September 7 [20], 1908, 2; Sh. Frug, "Der royter gelekhter," *Der arbayter*, October 10, 1908, 6.

61. Hillel Zeitlin, "Sholem-Aleykhem: Etlekhe verter fun zayn yubileum," *Haynt*, September 11 [24], 1908, 2.

62. Goethe is one of many cases explored by Ebstein in his sketches of tubercular geniuses. Erich Ebstein, *Tuberkulose als Schicksal: Eine Sammling pathographischer Skizzen von Calvin bis Klabund, 1509–1928* (Stuttgart: Ferdinand Enke Verlag, 1932), 74–76.

63. For a discussion of Keats's tubercular history and legacy, see René J. Dubos and Jean Dubos, *The White Plague: Tuberculosis, Man, and Society* (New Brunswick, NJ: Rutgers University Press, 1996), 11–17; Lawlor, *Consumption and Literature*, esp. chaps. 5, 7. For a discussion of the aesthetic idealization of the female consumptive in the English context, see Katherine Byrne, *Tuberculosis and the Victorian Literary Imagination* (New York: Cambridge University Press, 2011), 74, esp. chap. 4; Lawlor, *Consumption and Literature*, esp. chap. 6. For a discussion of the aesthetic idealization of the female consumptive in the French context, see David S. Barnes, *The Making of a Social Disease: Tuberculosis in Nineteenth-Century France* (Berkeley: University of California Press, 1995), 50. For a discussion of the aestheticization of the female consumptive as it relates to the feminized image of the Jewish male, see Sander L. Gilman, *Franz Kafka: The Jewish Patient* (New York: Routledge, 1995), 54.

64. Dubos and Dubos, *The White Plague*, 100–110. For an English-language biography of Koch, see Thomas D. Brock, *Robert Koch: A Life in Medicine and Bacteriology* (Madison, WI: Science Tech Publishers, 1988).

65. For example, see the September 30, 1908, edition of *Der morgn-zhurnal*. The

edition features an article about the implications of the World Tuberculosis Congress, Weizmann's letter, and an article about the number of deaths reported that were caused by tuberculosis. "Yubileum far Sholem Aleykhem," 1; "Der alveltlikher kampf gegn shvindzukht," *Der morgn-zhurnal*, September 30, 1908, 4; "Shvindzukht toytet milyonen mentshn," *Der morgn-zhurnal*, September 30, 1908, 1.

66. All references to this story refer to the 1937 reprint. Sholem Aleichem, "Shmuel Shmelkes un zayn yubileum," in *Fun Kasrilevke*, vol. 19, *Ale verk fun Sholem-Aleykhem* (New York: Morgn-Frayhayt, 1937), 203–37.

67. "In Boyberik" was later renamed "Goles datshe" (Diaspora Summer Hut). There are multiple passages about the air quality, local sanatoria, and the kefir that the patients are forced to imbibe—an experience Sholem Aleichem would one day share. Sholem Aleichem, "Goles datshe," in *Zumer-lebn*, vol. 11, *Ale verk fun Sholem-Aleykhem* (New York: Morgn-Frayhayt, 1937), 7–72. For an English translation, see Sholom Aleichem, "Home Away from Home," in *Stories and Satires*, trans. Curt Leviant (New York: T. Yoseloff, 1959), 308–49. In "To the Hot Springs," readers encounter guests seeking all types of therapy in Boyberik (hydrotherapy, massages, etc.) as well as other characters on their way to the more fashionable west European spas of Marienbad and Baden-Baden. Sholem Aleichem, "In di varembeder," in *Zumer-lebn*, vol. 11, *Ale verk fun Sholem-Aleykhem* (New York: Morgn-Frayhayt, 1937), 73–118. For an English translation, see Sholom Aleichem, "To the Hot Springs," in *Stories and Satires*, trans. Curt Leviant (New York: T. Yoseloff, 1959), 350–78. One could also add here the consumptive references in two of Sholem Aleichem's most famous monologues, "The Pot" of 1901 and "Geese" of 1902. In the former, though consumption is never named, it is the ominous health threat that hovers over the widow who narrates the story. Her husband coughed himself into the grave, and her son, dangerously flirting with secular studies, is currently sick with that very same ominous cough. We find another educated, consumptive son of an impoverished market woman who coughs and coughs throughout the monologue, "Geese." Sholem Aleichem, "Dos tepl," in *Monologn*, vol. 25, *Ale verk fun Sholem-Aleykhem* (New York: Morgn-Frayhayt, 1937), 7–26; Sholem Aleichem, "Genz," in *Monologn*, vol. 25, *Ale verk fun Sholem-Aleykhem* (New York: Morgn-Frayhayt, 1937), 27–44. For English translations, see Sholom Aleichem, "Geese," in *My First Love Affair and Other Stories*, trans. Curt Leviant (Mineola, NY: Dover Publications, 2002), 116–28; Sholem Aleichem, "The Pot," in *The Best of Sholem Aleichem*, ed. Irving Howe and Ruth Wisse (Northvale, NJ: Jason Aronson, 1989), 71–81.

68. Sholem Aleichem, "Fun der Rivyere," in *Monologn*, vol. 25, *Ale verk fun Sholem-Aleykhem* (New York: Morgn-Frayhayt, 1937), 215. For an English translation, see Sholom Aleichem, "From the Riviera," in *My First Love Affair and Other Stories*, trans. Curt Leviant (Mineola, NY: Dover Publications, 2002), 303.

69. Sholem Aleichem, *Maryenbad*, in *Zumer-lebn*, vol. 11, *Ale verk fun Sholem-Aleykhem* (New York: Morgn-Frayhayt, 1937), 119–292. For an English translation, see

Sholem Aleichem, *Marienbad*, trans. Aliza Shevrin (New York: Putnam, 1982). Alongside *Marienbad*, Sholem Aleichem also invoked tuberculosis in several short stories of the period. For example, written in a Swiss sanatorium in 1909, the short story "The Happiest Man in Kodne" describes the pathetic joy of a father who succeeds in securing a doctor's visit for his son who is spitting up blood. See Sholem Aleichem, "Der gliklekhster in Kodne," in *Ayznban-geshikhtes*, vol. 26, *Ale verk fun Sholem-Aleykhem* (New York: Morgn-Frayhayt, 1937), 23–38 For an English translation, see Sholem Aleichem, "The Happiest Man in Kodny," in *Tevye the Dairyman and the Railroad Stories*, trans. Hillel Halkin (New York: Schocken Books, 1987), 143–52. Sholem Aleichem followed this in 1911 with a short text titled "Call Me a Nutcracker." There the protagonist has difficulty procuring a residence permit in the city of Yehupetz, Sholem Aleichem's fictional stand-in for Kiev. He had come to Yehupetz, as we later learn, to seek treatment for his cough, his asthma, and what is later described as "a touch of tuberculosis." Sholem Aleichem, "Ruf mikh knaknisl," in *Ayznban-geshikhtes*, vol. 26, *Ale verk fun Sholem-Aleykhem* (New York: Morgn-Frayhayt, 1937), 277. For an English translation, see Sholem Aleichem, "Go Climb a Tree If You Don't Like It," in *Tevye the Dairyman and the Railroad Stories*, trans. Hillel Halkin (New York: Schocken Books, 1987), 269–74. Following his own diagnosis, Sholem also completed his serialized novel *Wandering Stars* (1909–10), which features his most fully articulated tubercular character, Hotsmakh. He is a miserable actor and manipulative leader of a Yiddish acting troupe who is told, as was Sholem Aleichem himself, to travel to Italy to recuperate. Hotsmakh refuses to do so and ultimately dies sick and alone in London. Sholem Aleichem, *Blondzhende shtern, I*, vol. 10, *Ale verk fun Sholem-Aleykhem* (Warsaw: Tsentral, 1914); Sholem Aleichem, *Blondzhende shtern, II*, vol. 11, *Ale verk fun Sholem-Aleykhem* (Warsaw: Tsentral, 1914). For an English translation of the text, see Sholem Aleichem, *Wandering Stars*, trans. Aliza Shevrin (New York: Viking, 2009).

70. On the history of bathing, taking the cure, and health tourism among central and eastern European Jewry, see Miriam Zadoff, *Next Year in Marienbad: The Lost Worlds of Jewish Spa Culture*, trans. William Templer (Philadelphia: University of Pennsylvania Press, 2012).

71. "Sholem-Aleykhems yubileum," *Der arbayter*, December 12, 1908, 1; "Sholem-Aleykhems yubileum," *Der arbayter*, December 19, 1908, 1; "Sholem-Aleykhems yubileum," *Der arbayter*, December 26, 1908, 1; "Sholem-Aleykhems yubileum," *Der arbayter*, January 2, 1909, 1.

72. The text was published in the New York Yiddish weekly *Der amerikaner* from January 8, 1909, to January 15, 1909; in the Vilna-based Hebrew weekly *Hed ha-zeman* from January 14, 1909, to February 9, 1909; and in the Warsaw-based Yiddish daily *Der fraynd* from December 7 [20] 1908, to December 18 [31], 1908. A Hebrew booklet also appeared. Sholem Aleichem, *Shmuel Shmelḳis ve-ḥag-yovlo* (Vilna: Zaldaski Dfus, 1909). An English translation of the introduction also was printed in the *Jewish Chron-*

icle. Sholem Aleichem, "Shmuel Shmelkess and His Jubilee," trans. Israel Cohen, *Jewish Chronicle*, November 27, 1908, 34.

73. This is related in an unpublished letter from Dubnow to Sholem Aleichem. It appears that there were plans to have it translated into Russian for Sh. Anski's journal, *Evreiskii mir*. However, it was not printed in the journal. See Simon Dubnow, "Letter to S. Rabinovitsh," November 24, 1908, Box 10, Folder lamed-dalet 7/19, Beth Shalom Aleichem Archive.

74. This "literary transmutation," writes Casanova, "is achieved by crossing a magic frontier that allows a text composed in an unprestigious language—or even a non-literary language, which is to say one that either does not exist or is unrecognized in the verbal marketplace—to pass into a literary language." Pascale Casanova, *The World Republic of Letters* (Cambridge, MA: Harvard University Press, 2004), 136.

75. In the New York newspaper *Der morgn-zhurnal*, an anonymous author declared the story the "gem of all that this great humorist has written until now." "Shmuel Shmelkes un zayn yubileum," *Der morgn-zhurnal*, January 4, 1909, 2.

76. Berkowitz, *Ha-rishonim ki-vene adam*, 631.

77. Sholem Aleichem, "Letter to Gershn Levin (November 12, 1908)," in *Briv fun Sholem-Aleykhem, 1879–1916*, ed. Avrom Lis (Tel Aviv: Beys Sholem-Aleykhem & Perets Farlag, 1995), 477.

78. Sholem Aleichem, "Letter to Yitskhok Yampolski (n.d.)," in *Briv fun Sholem-Aleykhem, 1879–1916*, ed. Avrom Lis (Tel Aviv: Beys Sholem-Aleykhem & Perets Farlag, 1995), 486.

79. Sholem Aleichem, "Letter to Y. D. Berkovits," October 14, 1908, Folder mem-bet 32/85, Beth Shalom Aleichem Archive. As Gérard Genette reminds us, a preface serves as the forum in which an author "offer[s] the reader an advance commentary on a text the reader has not yet become familiar with." Gérard Genette, *Paratexts: Thresholds of Interpretation*, trans. Jane E. Lewin (Cambridge: Cambridge University Press, 1997), 237, 197. Emphasis in original.

80. Sholem Aleichem, "Shmuel Shmelkes un zayn yubileum," 1937, 205.

81. Ibid.

82. Ibid., 203, 203–4.

83. Ibid., 205.

84. There exists in Yiddish the phrase *zayn mit emetsn a shmelke*, which might be translated "to be intimate with someone," referring to being on close terms with someone rather than connoting any sexual relation. A *shmelke* is an intimate, a friend, someone whom you know well. Shmuel Shmelkes might be translated to "My buddy Sam." Rabinovitsh has created here another friendly everyman for his readers. *Shmelke* also has a secondary meaning. The phrase *er iz a gantser shmelke* translates to "he is quite a prominent figure," which can be stated both sincerely and sarcastically. *Shmelke* actually means both "your buddy Joe" and "big man on campus." And Sholem Aleichem's

Shmuel Shmelkes embodies these characteristics. He is both the average poor Kasrilevke resident, trying each day to avoid the muddy streets, and the Yiddish writer being celebrated from afar. He is both relatable and incomprehensible. On "Shmelke," see Alexander Harkavy, "Shmelke," *Yiddish-English-Hebrew Dictionary* (New Haven, CT: Yale University Press in Cooperation with YIVO Institute for Jewish Research, 2006), 510.

85. Sholem Aleichem, "Shmuel Shmelkes un zayn yubileum," 1937, 226–28.

86. Ibid., 227.

87. Ibid.

88. Ibid., 228.

89. Yasnaya Polyana was Tolstoy's estate. Sholem Aleichem, "Tsu Mendele Moykher-Sforims yubileum," *Der veg*, January 19, 1906, 1.

90. Sholem Aleichem, "Shmuel Shmelkes un zayn yubileum," 1937, 233.

91. *A gut oyg*, literally, "a good eye." This is an example of an antiphrasis in Yiddish. The phrase "a good eye" connotes "an evil eye," which I have rendered "bad luck." The letter is misattributed and misdated in the collected letters of Sholem Aleichem to Mordkhe Spektor. See Sholem Aleichem, "Letter to Mordkhe Spektor (October–November 1908) [*sic*]," in *Briv fun Sholem-Aleykhem, 1879–1916*, ed. Avrom Lis (Tel Aviv: Beys Sholem-Aleykhem & Perets Farlag, 1995), 475. I have consulted the original letter addressed to Yankev Dinezon in the Beit Sholem Aleichem Archive. See Sholem Aleichem, "Letter to Yankev Dinezon," October 18 [31], 1908, Folder mem-dalet 4/45, Beth Shalom Aleichem Archive.

92. Sholem Aleichem, "Letter to Gershn Levin (November 23, 1908)," in *Briv fun Sholem-Aleykhem, 1879–1916*, ed. Avrom Lis (Tel Aviv: Beys Sholem-Aleykhem & Perets Farlag, 1995), 478.

93. Ibid. In a letter dated November 22, 1908, Sholem Aleichem wrote Sharira a florid letter narrating the scarcity of patrons in Jewish history and advocating that Sharira become "the first Jewish patron [*der ershter yidisher metsenant*]." The letter was in response to one Sharira had written Sholem Aleichem on the occasion of his jubilee. See Sholem Aleichem, "Letter to Shmuel Sharira," November 22, 1908, 4, Folder mem-shin 12/1, Beth Shalom Aleichem Archive.

94. Bialistok: "Khronik: Sholem-Aleykhems yubileum," *Teatr velt* 3 (October 16, 1908): 10. Łódź: "Der Sholem-Aleykhem-ovent," *Lodzher tageblat*, November 9 [22], 1908, 3. Odessa: It was difficult to get official permission to hold the events planned in Odessa. Despite these administrative difficulties, a letter was sent to Sholem Aleichem from the Hebrew literary elite of Odessa. See "Ḥogege-ha-yovelim shelanu," 1; "Khronikah ivrit," *Hed ha-zeman*, November 8, 1908, 3; Salem, "Me-are ha-medinah: Odessa," *Hed ha-zeman*, December 28, 1908, 3. Vilna: "Le-ḥag yovelo shel Shalom Alekhem," *Hed ha-zeman*, October 22, 1908, 3. Warsaw: For one article advertising an event in Warsaw, see "Sholem-Aleykhem ovent," *Haynt* (Warsaw), November 18 [December 1], 1908, 1. Kiev: The celebrations in Kiev had trouble acquiring the proper permission

from the authorities to conduct the jubilee ceremonies in Yiddish. Eventually, a celebration was held in Russian. The Kiev committee was also particularly interested in raising funds to purchase a plot of land for Sholem Aleichem in Palestine and raised money to that end. For difficulties dealing with the government authorities, see "Be-Rusiyah," *Ha-tsevi*, November 26, 1908, 2; "Khronikah ha-ir," *Hed ha-zeman*, November 10, 1908, 3; "Tsu Sholem-Aleykhems yubileum: A spetsiele telegrame tsum 'fraynd,'" *Der fraynd*, September 26 [October 9], 1908, 4; Matarah, "Me-are ha-medinah: Kiev," *Hed ha-zeman*, December 8, 1908, 3; Meir, *Kiev*, 184. For information on the committee's intention to purchase land in Palestine, see "Shalom Alekhem be-Erets Yisra'el," 2. St. Petersburg: See, for example, "Tsu Sholem Aleykhems yubileum," *Der fraynd*, September 17 [30], 1908, 2. London: "Shalom Aleichem," *Jewish Chronicle*, December 11, 1908, 34. Geneva: Weizmann signs his letter, "Chairman of the Geneva Committee for the Celebration of Sholem Aleichem's Jubilee [*Forzitsender fun Zhenever komitet af fayern Sholem-Aleykhem's yubileum*]." See, for example, Weizmann, "Sholem Aleykhems yubileum," *Der morgn-zhurnal*, October 15, 1908, 5. South Africa: This was reported by Berkowitz. Berkowitz, *Ha-rishonim ki-vene adam*, 620. Buenos Aires: Sholem Aleichem, "Cedars of Lebanon: Sholem Aleichem in Sickness, Letter from Sholom Aleichem to Israel Cohen (November 19, 1909)," trans. Israel Cohen, *Commentary*, October 1950, 383. In this letter, Sholem Aleichem also mentions that jubilee events are taking place in Chicago, Cleveland, St. Louis, and Montreal. Jerusalem: "Yafo," *Ha-tsevi*, June 15, 1909, 2. Alexandria: Sholem Aleichem," Letter to Natashe Mazor (January 25 [February 7], 1909)," in *Briv fun Sholem-Aleykhem, 1879–1916*, ed. Avrom Lis (Tel Aviv: Beys Sholem-Aleykhem & Perets Farlag, 1995), 91. Toronto: Yoysef Rozenfeld, "Sholem Aleykhems yubileum in Toronto, Kenede," *Der arbayter*, November 14, 1908, 1. New York: "Advertisement for Sholem Aleichem Jubilee Evening," *Der morgn-zhurnal*, December 28, 1908, 7. Philadelphia: Dovid Pinski, "Sholem Aleykhems yubileum," *Der arbayter*, October 10, 1908, 6. Jersey City: "Vaytere baytrage tsu Sholem Aleykhem fond," *Der morgn-zhurnal*, January 7, 1909, 5. Denver: "Sholem Aleykhem oventn in Denver, Kol.," *Der morgn-zhurnal*, January 10, 1909, 4. South Bend: "Vaytere baytrage tsum Sholem-Aleykhem fond," *Der morgn-zhurnal*, December 15, 1908, 8. Waco: "Der Sholem Aleykhem fond," *Der morgn-zhurnal*, January 15, 1909, 2. On Vilna and Irkutsk, see Sholem Aleichem, "Letter to Gershn Levin (November 23, 1908)," in *Briv fun Sholem-Aleykhem, 1879–1916*, ed. Avrom Lis (Tel Aviv: Beys Sholem-Aleykhem & Perets Farlag, 1995), 478.

95. This committee headed by Pinski would soon send the ailing Sholem Aleichem a Yiddish typewriter. Unable to write while standing at a desk, Sholem Aleichem initially embraced the typewriter. For his praise, see Sholem Aleichem, "Letter to Mendele Moykher-Sforim (February 20 to March 5, 1909)," in *Briv fun Sholem-Aleykhem, 1879–1916*, ed. Avrom Lis (Tel Aviv: Beys Sholem-Aleykhem & Perets Farlag, 1995), 491. This sentiment was echoed in a letter to Israel Cohen in England. Sholem Aleichem

wrote to Cohen, "My American colleagues in New York have presented me—may their hands never ache—on the occasion of my literary jubilee, with a typewriter, so I am no longer writing with a pen. And this is the best thing I could wish for in the interest of my health." See Sholem Aleichem, "Cedars of Lebanon: Sholem Aleichem in Sickness, Letter from Sholom Aleichem to Israel Cohen (March 6, 1909)," trans. Israel Cohen, *Commentary*, October 1950, 381.

96. For a description in anticipation of the evening, see "Sholem Aleykhem's yuibileum haynt in Thalia," *Der morgn-zhurnal*, December 28, 1908, 8. For a description of the evening after the fact, see "Groyser oylem bay'm Sholem Aleykhem ovent," 7.

97. "A vikhtike 'Sholem Aleykhehm' komitet," *Der morgn-zhurnal*, December 11, 1908, 5.

98. Along with writing for the Yiddish press, Selikovitch is most famous for writing a Palestinian Arabic textbook with Yiddish explanations. Rachel Simon, "Teach Yourself Arabic—in Yiddish!," *MELA*, no. 82 (2009): 1–15.

99. Israel Cohen, "Cedars of Lebanon: Sholem Aleichem in Sickness," *Commentary*, October 1950, 379.

100. Levin, "Sholem-Aleykhems krankhayt un zayn 25-yeriker yoyvl," 6.

101. "Khronikah ivrit," 3.

102. Tsivyon (pseudonym of Ben-Tsien Hofman), "Vider vegn Sholem-Aleykhem," *Yidishe arbayter velt*, December 25, 1908, 4. For the previous, critical article, see Tsivyon, "Eyn ernst vort tsu Sholem-Aleykhems yubileum," *Yidishe arbayter velt*, December 4, 1908, 5.

103. Authors of several articles write of disappointing turnouts to evening celebrations in London, New York, and Vilna. See "Khronikah mekomit," *Hed ha-zeman*, November 10, 1908, 3; "Sholem-Aleykhems yubileum," *Der arbayter*, January 2, 1909, 1; Israel Cohen, "To the Editor of the *Jewish Chronicle*," *Jewish Chronicle*, November 27, 1908, 34. In New York, an author blames the small audience on the socialist newspaper *Forverts*, which planned an evening with Samuel Gompers the same night as that for Sholem Aleichem. Perhaps the most interesting critique of the fund-raising efforts was the comedic sketch included in the Warsaw periodical *Der humorist*. There, a scene is described in which a group of armed men attack Sholem Aleichem's hotel room to steal all the money from the jubilee. However, all that they find are telegrams.

104. Vilnai, "Al-yad mitato shel Shalom Alekhem," 1.

105. For Dinezon's account, see Dinezon, "Letter to Sholem Aleichem," August 21, 1908, Box 10, Folder lamed-dalet 10/52, Beth Shalom Aleichem Archive; Yankev Dinezon, "A briv in redaktsiye," *Unzer Lebn*, September 11, 1908, 2–3; Yankev Dinezon, "Letter to Sholem Aleichem," October 9, 1908, Box 10, Folder lamed-dalet 10/54, Beth Shalom Aleichem Archive.

106. Percy Bysshe Shelley, *Adonais, An Elegy on the Death of John Keats (1821)* (London: Publication for the Shelley Society by Reeves and Turner, 1886), 4.

107. For a general account of these negotiations, see Levin, "Mayne zikhroynes vegn Sholem-Aleykhem," 263–71.

108. The committee included the author and literary advocate Yankev Dinezon, the writer and doctor Gershn Levin, the Zionist activist Avrom Podlishevski, and the editor Noyekh Finkelshteyn. On the committee, see Gershn Levin and Avrom Podlishevski, "Tsu Sholem-Aleykhems fererer," *Unzer lebn*, September 16 [October 9], 1908, 1; Gershn Levin and Avrom Podlishevski, "Tsu Sholem-Aleykhems ferehrer," *Unzer lebn* (Warsaw), September 26 [October 9], 1908, 2–3.

109. Sh., "Le-yovelo shel Shalom Alekhem," 1. See also B"N [Re'uven Brainen], "Tsum yubileum fun Sholem-Aleykhem," 2.

110. Sholem Aleichem, "Letter to Yankev Dinezon (March 27, 1909)," in *Briv fun Sholem-Aleykhem, 1879–1916*, ed. Avrom Lis (Tel Aviv: Beys Sholem-Aleykhem & Perets Farlag, 1995), 501.

111. "Fun der letster minut: Tsum Sholem-Aleykhem yubileum," *Haynt* (Warsaw), October 14 [27], 1908, 1.

112. "Fun der letster minut: Afn mayontik far Sholem-Aleykhem," *Haynt*, October 16 [29], 1908, 1. Additional donations were documented in *Haynt* throughout October and November.

113. Yankev Dinezon was particularly impressed with Olga Rabinovitsh's negotiating skills and the influence of her presence. In his letter from May 1909, Dinezon declared Olga Rabinovitsh to be "a great diplomat." See Yankev Dinezon, "Letter to Sholem Aleichem," March 28, 1908, Box 10, Folder lamed-dalet 10/62, Beth Shalom Aleichem Archive; Yankev Dinezon, "Letter to Sholem Aleichem," May 17, 1909, Box 10, Folder lamed-dalet 10/64, Beth Shalom Aleichem Archive; Yankev Dinezon, "Letter to Sholem Aleichem," May 4, 1909, Box 10, Folder lamed-dalet 10/63, Beth Shalom Aleichem Archive. For Berkowitz's account, see Berkowitz, *Ha-rishonim ki-vene adam*, 681–83. See also Levin, "Mayne zikhroynes vegn Sholem-Aleykhem," 269.

114. Levin, "Mayne zikhroynes vegn Sholem-Aleykhem," 268.

115. In a letter read by Israel Cohen at the jubilee evening in London, Shalom Aleichem writes of his dream when someone will announce plans to publish all of his work in twenty volumes. "Tsvishn yidn in oysland: A Sholem-Aleykhem ovnt," *Unzer lebn*, December 25, 1908, 3.

116. He had not been able to do this since 1903. Dauber, *The Worlds of Sholem Aleichem*, 122.

117. See correspondence of Sholem Aleichem and Lidksi. Lidski wrote Sholem Aleichem a series of letters detailing the contract he was making in New York on his behalf to publish his collected work in three volumes in a print run of five thousand. For those letters, see Yankev Lidski, "Letter to Sholem Aleichem," August 19, 1909, Box 11, Folder lamed-lamed 46/11, Beth Shalom Aleichem Archive; Yankev Lidski, "Letter to Sholem Aleichem," October 24, 1909, Box 11, Folder lamed-lamed 46/14, Beth Shalom

Aleichem Archive. For a copy of the contract, see "Contract between Lidski and Marinoff," October 17, 1909, Box 11, Folder lamed-lamed 46/13, Beth Shalom Aleichem Archive. Lidski also sent Sholem Aleichem detailed accounts of the number of pamphlets published and sold. See Yankev Lidski, "Accounts and Sales Records from Lidski to Sholem Aleichem," April 1909–September 1910, Box 11, Folder lamed-lamed 46/5, 6, 7, 9, 10, 15, 16, 17, 18, 19, 20, 21, Beth Shalom Aleichem Archive. A telling letter of July 1912 to the Yiddish critic Bal-Makshoves (pseudonym of Isidor Elyashev) also relates the financial stability that he enjoyed. Writing from a *Kurort* in Clarens, Switzerland, Sholem Aleichem responds to a recent article by Bal-Makhshoves that appears to criticize Yiddish writers who write only to make a living. Sholem Aleichem mocks the idea of "profit," noting that (1) there isn't much of a living to be made from Yiddish writing and (2) he wrote with all of his energy, his "blood and marrow"—again with the corporeal language!—even at times when he could not make a profit. He also admits that now, in the summer of 1912, he "can live, thank God, from my booklets alone, that are produced in the tens of thousands." Sholem Aleichem, "Letter to Bal-Makhshoves (July 28, 1912)," in *Briv fun Sholem-Aleykhem, 1879–1916*, ed. Avrom Lis (Tel Aviv: Beys Sholem Aleichem and Perets Farlag, 1995), 551.

118. Shmuel Werses, "Sholem-Alekhem: Ḥamishim shanot bikoret," in *Bikoret ha-bikoret: Ha'arakhot ve-gilgulehen* (Tel Aviv: Hotsa'at Yaḥdav, Iḥud Motsi'im La-Or, 1982), 169. Werses's article first appeared as Shmuel Werses, "Shalom Alekhem: Ha'arakhot ve-gilgulehen: Be-asplaklariyah shel ḥamishim shanot bikoret," *Molad* 17, no. 133–34 (1959): 404–21. All citations refer to the 1982 version in Werses's collected essays. David Roskies pairs the phenomenon of Sholem Aleichem criticism of 1908 with the occasional essays produced in the wake of Sholem Aleichem's death in 1916. David G. Roskies, "Introduction," *Prooftexts* 6, no. 1 (1986): 2.

119. Perceptive analyses by the now well-known Yiddish literary critics Shmuel Niger and Bal-Dimyen appeared in conjunction with the jubilee and remain pertinent to Sholem Aleichem scholarship until today. An article by Bal-Makhshoves was also printed to delineate a paradigm of Sholem Aleichem's literary "types," a key for future works of criticism. Shmuel Niger writes of Sholem Aleichem as a "happy pessimist." He writes with a humorous style but is not satiric. See Sh. Niger, "Tsu Sholem-Aleykhems yubiley (Part 1)," *Der tog*, October 9, 1908, 6–7; Sh. Niger, "Tsu Sholem-Aleykhems yubiley (Part 2)," *Der tog*, October 16, 1908, 7. Bal-Dimyen compares Sholem Aleichem both to Mendele and to Chekhov and describes Sholem Aleichem as a "democrat." He attends to a plurality of subject matter and includes a wide swath of the Jewish people in his literary purview. See Bal-Dimyen, "Sholem-Aleykhem, der folks-shrayber," *Dos naye lebn*, December 1, 1908, 38–49. Bal-Makhshoves produces a "typology" of Sholem Aleichem's characters, whom he describes as modeling national types. For an English translation of the article, see Bal-Makhshoves, "Sholem Aleichem [A Typology of His Characters] (1908)," *Prooftexts* 6, no. 1 (1986): 7–15. For Yiddish, see Bal-

Makhshoves, "Sholem Aleykhem," in *Geklibene shriftn* (Warsaw: Farlag Sh. Shreberk, 1929), 1:91–109. For the original publication see Bal-Makhshoves, "Notitsn fun a kritiker: Sholem-Aleykhem, I," *Der fraynd*, December 19 [January 1], 1908 [1909], 2–3; Bal-Makhshoves, "Notitsn fun a kritiker: Sholem-Aleykhem, II(a)," *Der fraynd*, January 23 [February 5], 1909, 2; Bal-Makhshoves, "Notitsn fun a kritiker: Sholem-Aleykhem, II(b)," *Der fraynd*, January 25 [February 7], 1909, 2; Bal-Makhshoves, "Notitsn fun a kritiker: Sholem-Aleykhem, III," *Der fraynd*, February 16 [March 1], 1909, 2.

120. Sholem Aleichem, "Letter to Yankev Dinezon," October 18 [31], 1908.

121. Sholem Aleichem, "Letter to Gershn Levin (March 27, 1909)," in *Briv fun Sholem-Aleykhem, 1879–1916*, ed. Avrom Lis (Tel Aviv: Beys Sholem-Aleykhem & Perets Farlag, 1995), 500.

122. "Vast Crowds Honor Sholem Aleichem," *New York Times*, May 16, 1916, 13. For a historical analysis, see Ellen D. Kellman, "Sholem Aleichem's Funeral (New York, 1916): The Making of a National Pageant," *YIVO Annual* 20 (1991): 277–304.

123. On the politics and poetics of Sholem Aleichem's grave, see David G. Roskies, *The Jewish Search for a Usable Past* (Bloomington: Indiana University Press, 1999), chap. 7.

124. My punctuation here follows the gravestone version. Sholem Aleichem, "Di epitafiye fun Sholem-Aleykhem," vol. 16, *Ale verk fun Sholem-Aleykhem* (New York: Morgn-Frayhayt, 1937), 293.

125. "Shalom Alekhem," *Ha-tsevi*, July 2, 1909, 2; "Le-matsavo shel Shalom Alekhem," *Ha-tsevi*, November 12, 1909, 2; "Sholem-Aleykhem in Nervi (Italiyen)," *Der shtrahl* 1, no. 2 (1910): 7–9. The article in *Der shtrahl* featured four photographs of Sholem Aleichem in Italy, including one of him by the sea and one of him in bed surrounded by journals.

126. Gershn Levin, "Sholem-Aleykhem un der toyt," *Haynt*, April 23, 1926, 5. This version was also written down in a letter from Sholem Aleichem to his son-in-law, Berkowitz. Sholem Aleichem, "Letter to Y. D. Berkowitz (November 23, 1905)," 50–51.

127. On the Americanization of the novel, see Seth L. Wolitz, "The Americanization of Tevye or Boarding the Jewish 'Mayflower,'" *American Quarterly* 40, no. 4 (1988): 514–36.

Chapter 2

1. Jane Austen, *Persuasion* (London: J. M. Dent & Sons, 1992), 131.

2. Muki Tsur, "Ke-ḥakot Raḥel: Kavim biyografiyim," in *Ha-shirim*, by Raḥel (Bene Barak: Ha-Kibuts Ha-Me'uḥad, 2011), 19.

3. This fermented dairy product derived from mare's milk was frequently prescribed in the nineteenth century to consumptives and those suffering from lung infections. Chekhov received the same instruction while taking the cure in Ufa in 1901. Richard Carter, "Anton P. Chekhov, MD (1860–1904): Dual Medical and Literary Careers," *Annals of Thoracic Surgery* 61, no. 5 (1996): 1561.

4. Uri Milstein, "Dodati Raḥel," in *Raḥel: Shirim, mikhtavim, reshimot, korot ḥayeha*, by Raḥel (Tel Aviv: Zemorah Bitan, 1985), 29.

5. Throughout this book, I refer to the poet by her first name, Raḥel. Like Sholem Aleichem, part of the poet's public allure stemmed from the accessibility and deceptively generic resonances of her name. At the time of her death, her full name was Raḥel Bluvshtein Sela. In the notes, I reference the poet as Raḥel to reflect common bibliographic practices. Also, while there is scant research on Raḥel's time in Toulouse, one creative resource is Nurith Gertz's recently published biographical novel that reimagines Raḥel's time in France as well as her love affair with a fellow student. Nurith Gertz, *Yam beni le-venekh* (Or Yehudah: Devir, 2015).

6. Now called Sukhumi or Sokhumi, capital of Abkhazia in western Georgia.

7. Raḥel, "I Live High Up in a Sanatorium [IA zhivu vysoko v sanatorii]," in *Lakh ve-alayikh: Ahavat Raḥel u-Mikha'el: Mikhtavim, shirim, divre hesber*, ed. Binyamin Ḥakhlili (Tel Aviv: Ha-Kibuts Ha-Me'uḥad, 1987), 79.

8. Ibid., lines 13–16.

9. A notable exception was the work of Tamar Dolzhinski, who compared Raḥel's early Russian poetry with her later work. Tamar Dolzhinski, "Al shireha ha-rusi'im," *Davar*, April 11, 1937.

10. Amos Ron, "A Rachel for Everyone: The Kinneret Cemetery as a Site of Civil Pilgrimage," in *Sanctity of Time and Space in Traditions and Modernity*, ed. Alberdina Houtman, Marcel Poorthuis, and Joshua Schwartz (Boston: Brill, 1998), 349–59.

11. Raḥel's exit from Degania became the subject of much controversy. Her literary executor and great nephew, Uri Milstein, caused a stir in 1985. In an introduction to a collection of his great-aunt's work, he argued that Raḥel "was forced to leave [*hukhraḥah la'azov*] Degania and the Galilee" as a result of her illness. He then accused "those of the second and third *aliyah*" of having "felt ashamed" of their behavior toward Raḥel and for "having abandoned her [*hizniḥuhah*]." Milstein argued that the ensuing sense of guilt caused "the labor movement [to cultivate] the myth of Raḥel following her death." Many former residents of Degania as well as labor movement activists responded harshly to Milstein's claims. They argued that Raḥel understood that she had to leave Degania. They contended that she understood the community could not properly care for her. The tension heightened to the point that Milstein brought one of the most vocal respondents, Raḥel Savurai, to court in a defamation suit. He won the suit and was rewarded eighty-seven hundred shekels. The anecdote emphasizes that Raḥel's tubercular capital continued to be mobilized long after her death. For Milstein's claims, see Milstein, "Dodati Raḥel," 41, 51. For charged reactions, see Arnon Lapid, "Ba-layla ba ha-mevaser," *Ha-daf ha-yarok*, August 27, 1985, Folder: Raḥel, Degania Archive; Raḥel Savurai, "Morashtah Shel Raḥel," *Ha-daf ha-yarok*, September 10, 1985, Folder: Raḥel, Degania Archive. For the court's ruling, see Natan Ro'i, "Bet-hamishpat: Uri Milshteyn lo neheneh mi-tamluge Raḥel ha-meshoreret," *Davar*, February 27, 1987, Folder: Raḥel, Degania Archive.

12. For example, see Shmu'el Dayan, "Im Raḥel ba-Kineret," *Davar*, April 24, 1936, 5.

13. Ḥamutal Tsamir, "Ha-korban he-ḥalutsi, ha-arets ha-kedoshah ve-hofa'atah shel shirat ha-nashim be-shnot ha-esrim," in *Rega shel huledet: Meḥkarim me-sifrut ivrit uve-sifrut yidish li-khevod Dan Miron*, ed. Ḥannan Ḥever (Jerusalem: Bialik Institute, 2007), esp. 666.

14. Dan Miron may be credited for initiating what continues to be a lively scholarly discussion about the nature of Raḥel's writing, her style, and the influence of her gender on her literary career. See Dan Miron, *Imahot meyasdot, aḥayot ḥorgot: Al reshit shirat ha-nashim ha-ivrit* (Tel Aviv: Ha-Kibuts Ha-Me'uḥad, 2004), 14–20, 90–150. On issues concerning the intersection of Raḥel's modernist style and gender, see Naomi Brenner, "Slippery Selves: Rachel Bluvstein and Anna Margolin in Poetry and Public," *Nashim* 19 (2010): 100–133; Michael Gluzman, *The Politics of Canonicity: Lines of Resistance in Modernist Hebrew Poetry* (Stanford, CA: Stanford University Press, 2003), 100–140; Dana Olmert, *Bi-tenu'at safah ikeshet: Ketivah ve-ahavah be-shirat ha-meshorerot ha-ivriyot ha-rishonot* (Haifa: University of Haifa Press, 2012), 43–90; Miryam Segal, "Rachel Bluwstein's 'Aftergrowth' Poetics," *Prooftexts* 25, no. 2 (2005): 319–61. On issues concerning Raḥel's modernist style and invocation of a female biblical namesake, see Susan Starr Sered, "A Tale of Three Rachels, or the Cultural *Her*story of a Symbol," *Nashim* 1 (1998): 5–41; Wendy I. Zierler, *And Rachel Stole the Idols: The Emergence of Modern Hebrew Women's Writing* (Detroit, MI: Wayne State University Press, 2004), 75–90. On the importance of gender in Raḥel's posthumous hagiography, see Ḥamutal Tsamir, "Ha-korban he-ḥalutsi."

15. "Tuberculosis Sufferers," *Palestine Post*, March 8, 1935 On the history of the hospital in Tsefat, see Merav Gertz-Ronen, *Me'ah shanah le-vet ha-ḥolim bi-Tsefat, 1910–2010* (Zichron-Ya'akov: Itay Bahur, 2010).

16. Sheila M. Rothman, *Living in the Shadow of Death: Tuberculosis and the Social Experience of Illness in America* (Baltimore: Johns Hopkins University Press, 1995), 7, 77.

17. While the term "invalid" has fallen out of use in medical discourse, I invoke the term as it was commonly used throughout the nineteenth century to describe a category of ailing bodies. As Diane Price Herndl has demonstrated, especially with respect to women, "invalidism" as a mode "referred to a lack or power as well as a tendency toward illness." Diane Price Herndl, *Invalid Women: Figuring Feminine Illness in American Fiction and Culture, 1840–1940* (Chapel Hill: University of North Carolina Press, 1993), 1.

18. Miriam Bailin, *The Sickroom in Victorian Fiction: The Art of Being Ill* (Cambridge: Cambridge University Press, 1994), 15, 17.

19. Ibid., 32.

20. Ibid., 34.

21. Maria H. Frawley, *Invalidism and Identity in Nineteenth-Century Britain* (Chicago: University of Chicago Press, 2004), 1.

22. Harriet Martineau, *Life in the Sick-Room*, ed. Maria H. Frawley (Orchard Park, NY: Broadview Press, 2002), 129.

23. Michel Foucault, "Des espaces autres: Hétérotopies," *Architecture, Mouvement, Continuité* 5 (1984): 46–49.

24. Nurit Govrin, *Ha-maḥatsit ha-rishonah: Dvora Baron—ḥayeha vi-yetsiratah (648–683)* (Jerusalem: Mosad Bialik, 1988), 270–73; Naomi Seidman, *A Marriage Made in Heaven* (Berkeley: University of California Press, 1997), chap. 3; Zierler, *And Rachel Stole the Idols.*

25. Amia Lieblich, *Rekamot: Siḥotai im Dvora Baron* (Jerusalem: Shoken, 1991), 271–90.

26. The promise of women's equality in the *yishuv*, as professed by leaders of the labor Zionist movement, more often than not led to little change in gendered hierarchies. Women, even in agricultural settlements, often lacked agency to assume roles beyond those of mother and caretaker. Deborah S. Bernstein, *Pioneers and Homemakers: Jewish Women in Pre-state Israel* (Albany: State University of New York, 1992); Margalit Shilo and Gid'on Kats, eds., *Migdar be-Yisra'el: Meḥkarim ḥadashim al migdar ba-yishuv uva-medinah* (Be'er Sheva: Universitat Ben Guryon Ba-Negev, 2011).

27. Dana Olmert has done significant work to assess how gender is deployed in Raḥel's poetry as a comment on the position of the woman in *yishuv* culture. Olmert notes that, because of her disease, Raḥel was unable to fully participate in the collective ideological identity of the *yishuv*. Rather, she had "to consolidate her identity, her poetic voice, and her position as a cultural critic, and the stays in Tel Aviv and Jerusalem allowed her to direct her energy to these tasks." I suggest in this chapter that we must attend not just to the fact of these stays but to the space of these stays and the space of the sickroom. Olmert, *Bi-tenu'at safah ikeshet*, 72–73.

28. Ḥayim Naḥman Bialik, "Al Raḥel," in *Raḥel ve-shiratah: Mivḥar divre zikhronot ve-he'arot*, ed. Mordekhai Snir and Shim'on Kushner (Tel Aviv: Davar, 1971), 91 (hereafter cited as *Raḥel ve-shiratah*).

29. On Gnessin's heart disease (*maḥalat ha-lev*), see Bentsiyon Benshalom, *Uri Nisan Genesin: Monografiyah* (Krakow: Miflat, 1934), 104; Sh. Bikhovsky, "Uri Nisan Genesin," in *Ha-tsidah: Kovets zikaron le-A. N. Genesin*, by Uri Nissan Gnessin (Jerusalem: Defus Aḥdut, 1913), 89–91; Zalman Shneur, "Al Uri Nisan Genesin," in *Ḥ. N. Bialik u-vene doro* (Tel Aviv: Devir, 1958), 405.

30. Mane himself acknowledged a link to his fellow tubercular Hebrew poets. Feeling death near, he called on Mikhal as a spiritual guide and sickly brother in arms. Mordecai Zevi Mane, "Letter to Koyfman 18 Av 1886 (#146)," in *Kol kitve Mordekhai Tsevi Maneh: Kovets shirav ma'amarav u-mikhtavav* (Warsaw: Tushiyah, 1897), 222–23.

31. "Nadson: The Poet of Despairing Hope," *Slavonic and East European Review* 15, no. 45 (1937): 681–83.

32. Throughout my analysis of Nadson, I draw heavily on Wessling's work. Robert Diedrich Wessling, "Semyon Nadson and the Cult of the Tubercular Poet" (PhD diss., University of California, Berkeley, 1988), 1–3, ProQuest (Order No. 9923103). Nadson spent nearly his entire life writing and recuperating in places such as Nice, Bern, and Boiarka.

33. Ibid., 36.

34. Nadson died in 1887, and the memory of his pathological poetic subject defined how generations of Russian critics—as well as Yiddish and Hebrew writers—would read his work and continually regenerate the so-called Nadson Cult. Ibid., 123–35. Nadson's disease interested his Yiddish readers, such as the poet Menakhem Boreysho. In 1912, on the occasion of the twenty-fifth anniversary of Nadson's death, Boreysho wrote a heartfelt account of Nadson's work and illness-plagued life. "There," wrote Boreysho, "on a table and in a closet, between the mighty Pushkin and even the lonely Lermentov, between the self-conscious Nekrasov and the folksy-sad Kozlov, is the sickly Nadson with his abstract aspirations." Menakhem [Boreysho], "S. Nadson (tsu zayn 25-tn yortsayt)," *Haynt*, January 31, 1912, 3.

35. Mordecai Zevi Mane, "Badad bi-me'oni," in *Kol kitve Mordekhai Tsevi Maneh: Kovets shirav ma'amarav u-mikhtavav* (Warsaw: Tushiyah, 1897), 122–23. "Hametsayer" was actually an acronym for "ha-baḥur Mordekhai Tsevi yalid Radoshkovits" (*the young man Mordekhai Tsevi, child of Radoshkovits*). Mane's work was also read with reference to his biographical experience of illness. Aleksandr Ziskind Rabinowitz, who would one day teach Hebrew to Raḥel comments that "the best of Mane's poems, in my opinion, are the lyric ones, in which he expressed his soul's private torture and the wonder of natural beauty." Joseph Klausner concurred. "In Mane's poetry," the Zionist literary critic writes, "besides the glory of nature, there is also the sadness of life." Specifically, he directs us to observe the photograph of Mane that accompanies his collected works and to "look at his gaunt face, which from want, suffering, and disease have left recognizable marks." What follows in Klausner's critique are extended expositions of tragedy in Mane's poetry. Avner Holtzman, "Mordekhai Tsevi Maneh: Meshorer vetsayar," in *Melekhet maḥashevet, teḥiyat ha-umah: Ha-sifrut ha-ivrit le- nokhaḥ ha-omanut ha-plastit* (Tel Aviv: Zemorah Bitan, 1999), 98, 101; Joseph Klausner, "Mordekhai Tsevi Mane," in *Yotsrim u-vonim: Ma'amre bikoret* (Tel Aviv: Devir, 1925), 1:264.

36. Raḥel, "Ḥadri he-ḥadash," in *Shirat Raḥel* (Tel Aviv: Davar, 1966), 53.

37. Walter Benjamin, "The Image of Proust," in *Illuminations: Essays and Reflections*, ed. Hannah Arendt, trans. Harry Zohn (New York: Schocken Books, 1968), 214. My emphasis.

38. Quoted in Tsur, "Ke-ḥakot Raḥel," 66.

39. Now known as Radashkovychi, Belarus.

40. Tsur, "Ke-ḥakot Raḥel," 51.

41. There is extensive writing on the concept of the "New Jew." For a general dis-

cussion, see S. Almog, *Zionism and History: The Rise of a New Jewish Consciousness* (New York: St. Martin's Press, 1987), chap. 2.

42. "Hegyone ha-magid," *Ha-magid* 30, no. 7 (1886): 51–52. Eliezer Ben-Yehudah, the so-called father of the modern Hebrew revival, arrived in Ottoman Palestine in 1881. He then sought respite in Algeria before ultimately succumbing to the disease in 1922. For mention of his disease and his time in Algeria, see Professor Denbi, "Eli'ezer Ben-Yehudah," *Do'ar Ha-yom*, December 26, 1922, 1; Daniel Perski, "Eli'ezer Ben-Yehudah," *Do'ar Ha-yom*, December 20, 1922, 4.

43. Mordecai Zevi Mane, "Letter to Parents 8 Iyar 1886 (#144)," in *Kol kitve Mordekhai Tsevi Maneh: Kovets shirav ma'amarav u-mikhtavav* (Warsaw: Tushiyah, 1897), 144. Mane went as far as to poeticize the idea of the land as salubrious in his 1886 poem, "My-Soul's Journey." There, the speaker exclaims that he longs for the air of the Holy Land, as it has the power to heal a corpse. Mordecai Zevi Mane, "Masa'at Nafshi," in *Kol kitve Mordekhai Tsevi Maneh: Kovets shirav ma'amarav u-mikhtavav* (Warsaw: Tushiyah, 1897), 147–50.

44. For information concerning the treatment of tuberculosis in British Mandate Palestine, see Gertz-Ronen, *Me'ah shanah le-vet ha-ḥolim bi-Tsefat*; Yaacov Khassis, *Shaḥefet be-Yisra'el: Uvdot, netunim u-megamot* (Tel Aviv: Merkaz Ha-Ligah La-Milḥamah Ba-Shaḥefet Uve-Maḥalot Re'ah Be-Yisra'el, 1964); Nisim Levi, *Perakim be-toldot ha-refu'ah be-Erets-Yisra'el, 1799–1948* (Tel Aviv: Ha-Kibuts Ha-Me'uḥad; Ha-Fakultah Li-Refu'ah al Shem Barukh Rapoport, Ha-Tekhniyon, 1998), 503–6. I have also drawn on the serial *Yedi'ot ha-ligah le-milḥamah ba-shaḥefet be-Yisra'el* (Tel Aviv: Ha-Ligah Le-Milḥamah Ba-Shaḥefet Uve-Maḥalot Re'ah Be-Yisra'el, 1958). See also "Ha-Ligah le-milḥamah ba -shaḥefet," *Davar*, October 10, 1930; Avigdor Mandelberg, "Ha-Shaḥefet ve-ha-po'alim (le-yom ha-peraḥ)," *Davar*, April 20, 1927; "Mikhtavim la-ma'arekhet: Azru la-milḥamah ba-shaḥefet," *Davar*, February 18, 1930.

45. "An Urgent Appeal: To the Editor of the Palestine Post," *Palestine Post*, January 31, 1933. In 1933 the efforts of the Anti-Tuberculosis League faced a complicated health landscape in which Jewish, Arab, and British doctors and patients competed for resources. The state of the Jewish health-care system was still in a relatively nascent form: The workers' General Health Fund (*kupat ḥolim klalit*) had only begun to take shape in 1911. After it was formally established in 1920, it functioned at a deficit for the next decade and was in a constant state of tension with Hadassah, the American-funded Zionist organization that began to exert managerial control over larger segments of medical care in Palestine. Shifra Shvarts, *The Workers' Health Fund in Eretz Israel: Kupat Holim, 1911–1937*, trans. Daniella Ashkenazy (Rochester, NY: University of Rochester Press, 2002).

46. Dr. Goldsmit, "Memorandum on the Question of Emigrants' Suffering from Tuberculosis with Recommendations for Treatment and Segregation by Dr. Goldsmit," June 1919, Z441685-lt, The Central Zionist Archives.

47. Sander L. Gilman, *Franz Kafka: The Jewish Patient* (New York: Routledge, 1995), chap. 4; Mitchell Bryan Hart, *The Healthy Jew: The Symbiosis of Judaism and Modern Medicine* (New York: Cambridge University Press, 2007), chap. 5.

48. This message was also communicated in literature. In the short story "At the End of Summer" (ca. 1920) by the Hebrew writer Dvora Baron, two consumptive characters are given the ghoulish task of accompanying a hearse filled with plague-ridden corpses to the cemetery. Walking with the corpses, they embody the ambiguous and ostracized position of the living dead. Dvora Baron, "Be-sof kayits," in *Parashiyot: Sipurim mekubatsim*, ed. Nurit Govrin and Avner Holtzman (Jerusalem: Mosad Byaliḳ, 2000), 631–35. For a discussion of this story, see Barbara E. Mann, *A Place in History: Modernism, Tel Aviv, and the Creation of Jewish Urban Space* (Stanford, CA: Stanford University Press, 2006), 31–32. Hebrew writing outside the *yishuv* also emphasized the stigma of the disease, such as in Baron's short story of 1907, "It Erupted." The tubercular protagonist, Ḥantshi, is a caretaker for a baby; she loses her job after she erupts in a bloody coughing fit in front of the baby's mother. Dvora Baron, "Hitparets . . . (reshimah)," in *Parashiyot mukdamot: Sipurim (1902–1921)*, ed. Avner Holtzman (Jerusalem: Mosad Bialik, 1988), 411–14.

49. Avraham Shlonsky, "Amal," in *Shirim* (Merḥavyah: Sifriyat Po'alim, 1954), 1:163–65.

50. A[vraham] Shlonsky, "Al 'ha-shalom,'" *Ketuvim*, May 11, 1927, 1. This quote is also of interest to Naomi Brenner. Naomi Rebecca Brenner, "Authorial Fictions: Literary and Public Personas in Modern Hebrew and Yiddish Literature" (PhD diss., University of California, Berkeley, 2008), 122, ProQuest (Order No. AA73331524).

51. Dan Miron, *From Continuity to Contiguity: Toward a New Jewish Literary Thinking* (Stanford, CA: Stanford University Press, 2010), 496.

52. Sandra Sufian has plotted how the efforts to eradicate malaria in Palestine dovetailed with the Zionist ideological agenda of healing the land and thereby healing the nation. Sandra M. Sufian, *Healing the Land and the Nation: Malaria and the Zionist Project in Palestine, 1920–1947* (Chicago: University of Chicago Press, 2007), 14.

53. Eric Zakim, *To Build and Be Built: Landscape, Literature, and the Construction of Zionist Identity* (Philadelphia: University of Pennsylvania Press, 2006), 65.

54. Ibid., 71.

55. Yosef Ḥayim Brenner, *Shekhol ve-kishalon* (Tel Aviv: Ha-Kibuts Ha-Me'uḥad, 2006).

56. The room was in the Tel Nordeau neighborhood. Raḥel, "Letter to Shulamit and Yitsḥak Klugai (n.d.)," in *Raḥel: Shirim, mikhtavim, reshimot, korot ḥayeha*, ed. Uri Milstein (Tel Aviv: Zemora Bitan, 1985), 98.

57. In a letter to Dvora Dayan, Raḥel describes herself as increasingly miserable but finds joy and relief in reading. Before closing the letter, she adds the postscript: "I should tell you that this letter was not written with *dam libi*. In our prosaic times, even

the poets use ink." Raḥel, "Letter to Dvora Dayan," ca. 1921, Zalman Shazar Collection 248, Document 92307/1, Machon Genazim. The letter was republished in *Davar*. See Raḥel "Yom ha-shanah ha-shishi lel-mot Raḥel," *Davar*, April 15, 1937, 28. On comparing herself to Chekhov, see Uri Milstein, "Einayim bo'arot," *Ḥadashot*, April 5, 1985.

58. Quoted in Tsur, "Ke-ḥakot Raḥel," 67. Raḥel also quotes the passage in Yiddish, "Lakhn iz gezunt. Doktoryrim heysn lakhn," in a letter to Shulamit Klugai. See Raḥel, "Letter to Shulamit Klugai (#12)," n.d., Arkhiyon ha-Medinah [Israel State Archives], accessed December 19, 2013, http://www.archives.gov.il/NR/rdonlyres/313D8E87-C7A0–4D83-B75D-85AD6F72DFC0/0/Rachel12.pdf.

59. Hebrew: "eyn zot ki eynkha ohevet et shiray." Rivkah Davidit, "Ba-me'uḥar," in *Raḥel ve-shiratah*, 45.

60. Miron, *Imahot meyasdot, aḥayot ḥorgot*, 118.

61. Herndl, *Invalid Women*, 9.

62. There is a long history of studying the salon as a place of cultural exchange, especially in the German- and Austrian-Jewish contexts. Deborah Hertz's study has been particularly helpful in mapping the boundaries of women's agency as participants—work that is indeed helpful in understanding the limits of Raḥel's power as a female host. I use the term here, however, not specifically to refer to the model of the German-Jewish salon but rather to delineate a domestic social space bounded by the proclivities of a female host and occupied with literary concerns that resonate with political consequence. Deborah Sadie Hertz, *Jewish High Society in Old Regime Berlin* (Syracuse, NY: Syracuse University Press, 2005).

63. Milstein, "Dodati Raḥel," 45.

64. Raḥel, "Letter to Shulamit Klugai (#23)," n.d., Arkhiyon ha-Medinah [Israel State Archives], accessed December 8, 2013, http://www.archives.gov.il/NR/rdonlyres/BB354F0B-0A8D-4A9F-803C-1EC96650B0C1/0/Rachel23.pdf.

65. Shulamit Lapid, "Taglit sifrutit-historit: Sefer yelado shel ha-meshoreret Raḥel nimtsa va-yetse la-or aḥare 43 shanot shivḥah u-genizah," *Ma'ariv*, June 7, 1974, 37. For additional historical background, see Muki Tsur, "'Ba-bayit uva-ḥuts'—gilgulo shel sefer," in *Ba-bayit uva-ḥuts*, by Raḥel (Tel Aviv: Tamuz, 2001), n.p.

66. Milstein, "Einayim bo'arot."

67. Shlomo Sheva, "Raḥel ba-aliyat-ha-gag," *Davar*, May 7, 1971, sec. Davar ha-shavu'a, 18–19.

68. On Gnessin's visit, see Ḥaim Be'er, "Raḥel: Safiyaḥ," *Davar*, April 26, 1985, sec. Davar ha-shavu'a, 5. On Bialik's visit, see Ḥayah Rutberg, "Raḥel ve-goralah," in *Raḥel ve-shiratah*, 28.

69. Avraham Broides, "Raḥel (sheloshim shanah le-motah)," *Ha-po'el ha-tsa'ir* 54, no. 30 (1961): 20.

70. Levi Ben-Amitai, "Be-meḥitsat Raḥel (20 shanah le-motah)," *Davar*, April 30, 1951, sec. Davar ha-shavu'a, 7; 10–11.

71. In her letters to Shulamit Klugai, her friend and fellow writer, Raḥel describes herself reciting poetry "out loud . . . in the emptiness of my room [*be-kol ram . . . be-shamemet ḥedri*]." She would go on to recount having recited poetry by Konstantin Balmont, adding that every sad song "seems to me like my own confession [*vidui*], like the story of my life, and I read it out loud to myself in the emptiness of my room [*shamemet ḥedri*], and my eyes fill with the tears." According to Rivkah Davidit, in the sickroom Raḥel would also "get drunk on the poetry" of the greats, such as Akhmatova, Pushkin, and Blok. On one occasion, Raḥel even asked her niece and caretaker, Sara Milstein, for feedback. Milstein had just read aloud a four stanza draft of what would later be titled "Spring" (Aviv). Milstein relates that she read the poem and found the final stanza to be wanting. Raḥel is said to have gotten angry, but she did eventually erase the stanza from the text. For letters to Klugai, see Raḥel, "Letter to Shulamit Klugai (#4)," n.d., Arkhiyon ha-Medinah [Israel State Archives], accessed December 8, 2013, http://www.archives.gov.il/NR/rdonlyres/B3713D18-FFC3–40CA-9BA7-BEE3CFD20C96/0/Rachel04.pdf; Raḥel, "Letter to Shulamit Klugai (#6)," n.d., Arkhiyon ha-Medinah [Israel State Archives], accessed December 8, 2013, http://www.archives.gov.il/NR/rdonlyres/D9D726A6-F674–4EC9–8B2A-85E9F9CB96E4/0/Rachel06.pdf. See also Davidit, "Ba-me'uḥar," 43. For the anecdote regarding Milstein, see Milstein, "Einayim bo'arot," 51.

72. Roberta Reeder, *Anna Akhmatova: Poet and Prophet* (New York: St. Martin's Press, 1994), 89.

73. For mention of the poet greeting her guests while bedridden or lying down, see Lapid, "Taglit sifrutit-historit," 37; Ḥayah Rutberg, "Zikhronot," in *Raḥel ve-shiratah,* 27; Gustah Rekhev, "Al Raḥel ha-meshoreret," in *Raḥel ve-shiratah*, 58. For mention of her eyes, see Davidit, "Ba-me'uḥar," 42; Brakhah Ḥabas, "Sirtutim li-dmutah," in *Raḥel ve-shiratah,* 54. On the sparse furnishings, see Rutberg, "Zikhronot," 27. On the presence of the Bible and flowers, as well as an insuppressible cough, see Avraham Broides, "Be-meḥitsatah," in *Raḥel ve-shiratah*, 101. For mention of her white dress, see Ben-Amitai, "Be-meḥitsat Raḥel," 7; Broides, "Raḥel (shloshim shanah le-motah)," 29; Brakhah Ḥabas, "Pegishah," in *Raḥel ve-shiratah*, 56. For additional general accounts of visits, see Itah Ig-Faktorit, "Raḥel ke-demut meḥanekhet," in *Raḥel ve-shiratah,* 62; Shmu'eli, "Ba-arov yomah," in *Raḥel ve-shiratah*, 50.

74. Raḥel, "Rak al atsmi," in *Shirat Raḥel* (Tel Aviv: Davar, 1966), 128.

75. Brenner, "Slippery Selves," 123.

76. Raḥel, "Ḥaye nemalim," in *Shirat Raḥel* (Tel Aviv: Davar, 1966), 228–29.

77. Raḥel, "Eni kovlah," in *Shirat Raḥel* (Tel Aviv: Davar, 1966), 63.

78. Sholem Aleichem, "Shmuel Shmelkes un zayn yubileum," vol. 19, *Ale verk fun Sholem-Aleykhem* (New York: Morgn-Frayhayt, 1937), 203.

79. Elaine Scarry, *The Body in Pain: The Making and Unmaking of the World* (New York: Oxford, 1985), 4.

80. My reading of Scarry here follows that of Ann Jurecic, who argues that the language of pain "cannot identify its object and thus it cannot confer a verifiable reality upon an internal experience." Yet she adds that Scarry herself "implies that language can be used to rebuild a shattered world or a shattered self." Here, Raḥel draws on the language-destroying pain as a literary and creative resource. Ann Jurecic, *Illness as Narrative* (Pittsburgh: University of Pittsburgh Press, 2012), 50.

81. Deuteronomy 34:1.

82. I am grateful here to the insights of the peer reviewer of this manuscript.

83. Zierler, *And Rachel Stole the Idols*, 239, 244.

84. Diana Postlethwaite has suggested that the art of seeing "transformed [Martineau's sickroom] from a cloistered retreat into a place of visionary perspective." Quoted in Frawley, *Invalidism and Identity in Nineteenth-Century Britain*, 226.

85. Martineau, *Life in the Sick-Room*, 67.

86. It is helpful to mention here the parallel to be found in Raḥel's poem "In the Hospital." Written from a hospital bed in Tsefat, the poem's speaker feels herself a captive in the space. She looks out the window and cries. Then, a doctor advises her to look beyond the mountain, and she smiles. It is unclear whether it is a smile of acceptance of her fate or actual joy. But it remains clear that the act of gazing out the window is, if only momentarily, liberating. See Raḥel, "Be-veit ha-ḥolim," in *Shirat Raḥel* (Tel Aviv: Davar, 1966), 32.

87. Raḥel, "Ets agas," in *Shirat Raḥel* (Tel Aviv: Davar, 1966), 30.

88. Raḥel, "Lo go'el—ve-karov kol kakh," in *Shirat Raḥel* (Tel Aviv: Davar, 1966), 91.

89. For example, see Z. Avigdori, "Ha-ḥevrah le-milḥamah ba-shaḥefet bi-Yerushalayim," *Do'ar ha-Yom*, September 29, 1931, 3. Z. Avigdori was also one of Raḥel's doctors. Asher Gilad, "Ha-rof'im: Raḥel u-maḥalat ha-sofrim (shaḥefet)," *Alon* 7 (June 2013): 16.

90. Clark Lawlor, *Consumption and Literature: The Making of the Romantic Disease* (New York: Palgrave Macmillan, 2006), 15–27; S. Gilman, *Franz Kafka*, 187–89.

91. Virginia Woolf, "A Room of One's Own," in *A Room of One's Own; and, Three Guineas*, ed. Morag Shiach (New York: Oxford University Press, 1992), 4.

92. Mandelberg, "Ha-shaḥefet ve-ha-po'alim (le-yom ha-peraḥ)," *Davar*, April 20, 1927, 3. For Mandelberg's brief account of his move to Palestine and involvement in the founding of the Anti-Tuberculosis League in Palestine, see Avigdor Mandelberg, *Me-ḥayai: Pirḳe zikhronot* (Tel Aviv: Yedidim, 1942), 111–16.

93. Raḥel, "Al ot ha-Zeman (1927)," in *Shirat Raḥel* (Tel Aviv: Davar, 1966), 204–5.

94. One exception in Sholem Aleichem's experience was his acquaintance with Daniel Charney in Bern, Switzerland, where both sought medical treatment. Daniel Charney, "Ikh shpil a 'zeks un zekhtsik' mit Sholem-Aleykhemen," in *Di velt iz kaylekhdik* (New York: CYCO-Bikher Farlag, 163), 248–52.

Chapter 3

1. Charles D. Spivak, "Letter to Zishe Landau," July 16, 1923, JCRS File 6361, Patient Record Morris Lune, JCRS Archive.

2. Shea Tenenbaum, "Rokhl—di tsarte dikhterin fun Yisroel (1890–1931)," *Di naye tsayt*, November 28, 1950.

3. Charles D. Spivak and Yehoash (S. Bloomgarden), *Yidish verterbukh: Enthalt ale hebreishe (un khaldeishe) verter, oysdruken un eygnemen, velkhe vern gebroykht in der yidisher shprukh, mit zeyer oysshprakh un aktsent, un mit bayshpilen fun vertlekh un shprikh-verter in ale velkhe zey kumen for* (New York: Farlag Yehoash, 1911).

4. Lune Mattes (M. Lune), "Light and Dreams," *Hatikvah* 1, no. 3 (1923): 5; Spivak, "Letter to Zishe Landau."

5. In the letter, Leivick refers to the poem as "The Ballad of Spivak Sanatorium." It first appeared in *Tsukunft* under the title "The Ballad of Denver Sanatorium." The poem was subsequently published under that same title in Leivick's 1937 collection, *Lider fun gan eyden: 1932-1936.* Throughout the chapter, I use the titles interchangeably. All references refer to the published version in *Lider fun gan eydn: 1932-1936.* H. Leivick, "Di balade fun Denver sanatoriyum," *Tsukunft* 40, no. 3 (1935): 131–34; "Di balade fun Denver Sanatoriyum," *Lider fun gan eyden: 1932–1936* (Chicago: Farlag Tseshinksi, 1937), 121–39.

6. Leivick, "Di balade fun Denver Sanatoriyum," 139, line 439.

7. Throughout this chapter, I focus on the JCRS as a space of literary production and the manner in which tubercular capital was mobilized on behalf of the Yiddish writer. Indeed, the JCRS would prove to be a center of a variety of crisscrossing Yiddish and Jewish literary networks. The JCRS also served as a hub of complementary scientific and cultural networks. For example, the in-house journal the *Sanatorium* publicized the latest medical treatments offered at the JCRS. In doing so, it disseminated contemporary medical best practices to fellow physicians, patients' families, and interested parties. In addition, the JCRS fostered the careers of its artist patients. Of particular interest may be the experience of the painter Max Lazarus. Born and raised in Trier, Lazarus came to America in 1938. After he entered the JCRS in 1942, he continued to paint and also began to teach art classes to his fellow patients. He continued to teach classes there after he was discharged in June 1944. He also continued to maintain a studio on the JCRS premises, often using the patients as his subjects. In 1945, an exhibition of his work was mounted at the Denver Art Museum. Lazarus's career was also supported by Sidney Bernstein, the director of Social Services and Public Relations at the JCRS. The JCRS continues to inspire visual artists and students at the Rocky Mountain College of Art and Design, which is housed in the former site of the sanatorium. As I learned while speaking to archivist Thyria Wilson, students at the college have been given the assignment to create art in response to research using the patient records of the JCRS. On Lazarus, see Bärbel Schulte, *Max Lazarus: Trier, St. Louis, Denver: Ein jüdisches Künstlerschiksal* (Trier: Stadtmuseum Simeonstift Trier, 2010), esp. chap. 11.

8. "Ten Leading Causes of Death in the United States, 1900, 1940, 1976," in *From Consumption to Tuberculosis: A Documentary History*, ed. Barbara Gutmann Rosenkrantz (New York: Garland Publishing, 1993), 3.

9. Jeanne Abrams, *Blazing the Tuberculosis Trail* (Denver: Colorado Historical Society, 1990); Jeanne Abrams, "Chasing the Cure: A History of the Jewish Consumptives' Relief Society of Denver" (PhD diss., University of Colorado at Boulder, 1983), ProQuest (Order No. 8408009); Jeanne Abrams, *Dr. Charles David Spivak: A Jewish Immigrant and the American Tuberculosis Movement* (Boulder: University Press of Colorado, 2009); Meindert Bosch, *Bridges across the Years: The Ninety-Year History of the Bethesda Hospital Association of Denver, Colorado* (Denver: Bethesda PsychHealth System, 1988); Charles Denison, *Rocky Mountain Health Resorts: An Analytical Study of High Altitudes in Relation to the Arrest of Chronic Pulmonary Disease* (Boston: Houghton, Osgood, 1880); Douglas R. McKay, *Asylum of the Gilded Pill: The Story of Cragmore Sanatorium* (Denver: State Historical Society of Colorado, 1983); Edwin S. Solly, *A Handbook of Medical Climatology: Embodying Its Principles and Therapeutic Application with Scientific Data of the Chief Health Reports of the World* (New York: Lea Brothers, 1897); Billy Mac Jones, *Health-Seekers in the Southwest, 1817–1900* (Norman: University of Oklahoma Press, 1967); Cynthia Kay Stout, "A Consumptives' Refuge: Colorado and Tuberculosis" (PhD diss., George Washington University, 1997), ProQuest (Order No. 9726673); Ida Libert Uchill, *Pioneers, Peddlers & Tsadikim: The Story of the Jews in Colorado* (Boulder: University Press of Colorado, 2000).

10. For a description of Dunbar's stay in Colorado, see Charles T. Davis, "Paul Laurence Dunbar," in *Black Is the Color of the Cosmos: Essays on Afro-American Literature and Culture, 1942–1981*, ed. Henry Louis Gates (New York: Garland Publishers, 1982), 66; Peter Revell, *Paul Laurence Dunbar* (Boston: Twayne Publishers, 1979), 53. On Pulitzer, see McKay, *Asylum of the Gilded Pill*, 66.

11. Thomas Crawford Galbreath, *Chasing the Cure* (Denver: Thomas Crawford Galbreath, 1908), 20.

12. "Maslianski bet rakhomim: Der groyser yidisher redner makht an ufruf far di korbones fun der blaser pest in Denver," *Yidishes tageblat*, May 23, 1909, JCRS Records, Box 198, JCRS—Newspaper Clippings, 1909–1912, JCRS Archive.

13. Charles D. Spivak, "The Genesis and Growth of the Jewish Consumptives Relief Society (Part I)," *The Sanatorium* 1, no. 1 (1907): 6. For the history of the institution, see Abrams, *Blazing the Tuberculosis Trail*; Abrams, "Chasing the Cure"; Abrams, *Dr. Charles David Spivak*; Uchill, *Pioneers, Peddlers & Tsadikim*. See also Jacob Marinoff, "Shtarbn fun hunger: 4 teg nit begrobn," *Yudishes tageblatt*, December 23, 1903.

14. Unlike the National Tuberculosis Association, also founded in 1904, the JCRS did not primarily seek to raise awareness about the disease or to agitate for government intervention. Rather, its concern was the free treatment of impoverished Jewish patients. For information about the National Tuberculosis Association, see Richard

Harrison Shryock, *National Tuberculosis Association, 1904–1954: A Study of the Voluntary Health Movement in the United States*, Public Health in America (New York: Arno Press, 1977); Michael E. Teller, *The Tuberculosis Movement: A Public Health Campaign in the Progressive Era* (New York: Greenwood Press, 1988). The National Tuberculosis Association also worked with the Red Cross and famously fund-raised using the Christmas Seal Campaign. The JCRS, though it treated non-Jews and did not deny non-Jews entrance into the sanatorium, primarily addressed the needs of Yiddish-speaking Jewish immigrants.

15. NJH also had a reputation of being a German-Jewish facility and accordingly hostile to the Yiddish-speaking Jewish immigrants arriving in the city. Abrams, "Chasing the Cure," 4; Abrams, *Dr. Charles David Spivak*, 78.

16. Charles D. Spivak, "The Jewish Press," in *First Annual Report of the Jewish Consumptives' Relief Society at Denver, Colo., 1905* (Denver: Smith-Brooks, 1905), 25–26. Additional calls were made in such English outlets as the *American Hebrew* and the *Reform Advocate*.

17. Morris Rosenfeld, "Di greste tsedoke," *Der teglikher herold*, n.d., JCRS Records, Box 197, JCRS—Newspaper Clippings, 1904–1906, JCRS Archive.

18. Another such field solicitor was the Hebrew and Yiddish poet M. M. Dolitzky, whose dramatic flair was evident in the appeals he published in the Yiddish press. Dolitzky also worked alongside Jacob Marinoff, the poet and future editor of the weekly Yiddish satirical magazine the *Big Prankster* (*Der groyser kundes*). See M. M. Dolitzky, "Eyn apil far Denver," *Yidishes tageblat*, March 2, 1906, JCRS Records, Box 197, JCRS—Newspaper Clippings, 1904–1906, JCRS Archive; M. M. Dolitzky, "Fun dem lebedikn beys-oylem" *Yudishes tageblat*, February 27, 1906. Dolitzky's time in Colorado also influenced his poetry. See, for example, M. M. Dolitzky, "In di Roki Berg," *Zunland*, June 1925, 19–20; Dolitzky, "Payks Pik," *Zunland*, July 1925, 14–15.

19. On Yehoash's life, see Evlin Yehoash Dworkin, "My Father Yehoash," in *Poems of Yehoash*, by Yehoash (London, Ontario, Canada: Canadian Yehoash Committee, 1952), 11–15; Chaim Leib Fox, "Yehoash," *Leksikon fun der nayer yidisher literatur* (New York: Congress for Jewish Culture, 1961), 4:233–44.

20. Yehoash, "Letter to Rose Cohen," June 16, 1899, Arc 116, Box 6, Folder: Cohen, Rose, Jewish Theological Seminary Archive. While in Denver, Yehoash tried his hand unsuccessfully at the liquor trade, worked in a saloon, and owned a garment business with Marinoff. He also spent some time in the National Jewish Hospital. Regarding his work in a saloon, see Yehoash, "Letter to Dr. Jacob Morris," March 23, 1907, Arc 116, Box 4, Folder: Dr. Morris, Jewish Theological Seminary Archive. Regarding his disappointing efforts in the liquor business, see Yehoash, "Letter to Rose Cohen," October 7, 1901, Arc 116, Box 6, Folder: Cohen, Rose, Jewish Theological Seminary Archive. For stationery listing him as a proprietor of a bespoke clothing company, see Yehoash, "Letter to Rose Cohen," August 12, 1903, Arc 116, Box 6, Folder: Cohen, Rose, Jewish

Theological Seminary Archive. For mention of his stay at NJH, see John Livingston, "Editor's Note," *Rocky Mountain Jewish Historical Notes*, Summer/Fall 1989, 1.

21. Yehoash, "Zununtergang in Kolerado," *Tsukunft* 1, no. 4 (1902): 186.

22. Although often cited as a single poem, "Amid the Colorado Mountains" is a translation of one poem and two parts of another poem. The first part of "Amid the Colorado Mountains" corresponds to Yehoash, "Abend-klangen, Part 3," in *Naye shriftn* (New York: Ferlag Yehoash, 1910), 1:111. The second part, to Yehoash, "Barg-geviter," in *Naye shriftn* (New York: Ferlag Yehoash, 1910), 1:107. The third part to Yehoash, "Abend-klangen, Part 2," in *Naye shriftn* (New York: Ferlag Yehoash, 1910), 1:110. The poem was collected and translated by Aaron Kramer. See Yehoash, "Amid the Colorado Mountains," in *A Century of Yiddish Poetry*, ed. and trans. Aaron Kramer (New York: Cornwall Books, 1989), 66–67.

23. George Byron, "Di gazel," trans. Yehoash, *Di yudishe bibliotek* 2 (1891): 203.

24. There is no record of Yehoash formally being admitted to the JCRS. It is possible that he received informal treatment from Spivak. Since the archival record does not specify his medical relationship to the institution, this chapter focuses solely on Yehoash's affiliation with the institution in his administrative and official capacity.

25. Charles D. Spivak, "Minutes of the JCRS Book 1," n.d., Box 299, Beck Archives Penrose Library.

26. In the following summer of 1909, it appears that Yehoash's wife did not want her husband to make the fund-raising rounds at the summer resorts in the Catskills because of his health; however, the JCRS board was confident that Yehoash would go anyway. "Board of Trustees Meeting Notes," JCRS Records, June 9, 1909, Box 298, JCRS Archive.

27. O. Leonard, "News and View," *Star*, April 30, 1909, JCRS Records, Box 198, JCRS—Newspaper Clippings, 1909–1912, JCRS Archive.

28. "The Jehoash Meeting in Philadelphia," *The Sanatorium*, 2, no. 6 (1908): 286.

29. The seventeenth-century French playwright and actor Jean-Baptiste Poquelin, known as Molière, remains one of the most famous consumptive performers and artists in theater and literary history. In what was to be his final performance, he played the lead role in *Le Malade imaginaire*. During the show, he erupted into a fit of coughing. Legend has it that Molière then died on the stage, having given his life in the name of art. As has been noted, Molière died shortly after the performance. On Molière's illness and death, see Virginia Scott, *Molière: A Theatrical Life* (New York: Cambridge University Press, 2000), 243–44, 256.

30. Charles D. Spivak, "Secretary's Report: Yehoash and His Jonathan," *The Sanatorium* 3, no. 2 (1909): 67.

31. "Der bezukh Fun 'Yehoash,'" *Der yidisher kuryer*, April 19, 1909, JCRS Records, Box 198, JCRS—Newspaper Clippings, 1909–1912, JCRS Archive.

32. Adolph Zederbaum, "Letter to Yehoash," September 22, 1908, Arc 116, Box 5, Folder: Dr. Tsederboyn, Jewish Theological Seminary Archive.

33. Jacob Marinoff, "Letter to Flora Bloomgarden," September 16, 1908, Arc 116, Box 4, Folder: Marinov, Y., Jewish Theological Seminary Archive.

34. "Advertisement for Sholem Aleichem Benefit Evening on 15 October 1908," *Varyhayt,* October 12, 1908; "Advertisement for Denver Sanatorium Benefit Evening on 14 October 1908," *Varyhayt,* October 12, 1908. The benefit for Sholem Aleichem was to be held on October 15 at Thomashefsky's People's Theatre. The benefit evening for the JCRS (here called the Denver Sanatorium) was to be held one day earlier, on October 14 at the New Star Theater.

35. Malcolm Andrews, *Charles Dickens and His Performing Selves: Dickens and the Public Readings* (New York: Oxford University Press, 2006), 131, 45.

36. "Der bezukh fun 'Yehoash.'"

37. Ben-Ishay, "Tsu Yehoash," *Der yidisher kuryer*, May 9, 1909; D. Pellman, "Letter to Yehoash," September 16, 1908, Arc 116, Box 5, Folder: D. Pellman, Jewish Theological Seminary Archive; "Jewish Poet Is Guest at Sanitarium Benefit," *Chicago Record*, May 10, 1909.

38. "Chicago Honors Yehoash," *The Sanatorium* 3, no. 4 (1909): 231. My emphasis.

39. Ernest Gilman, *Yiddish Poetry and the Tuberculosis Sanatorium, 1900–1970* (Syracuse, NY: Syracuse University Press, 2015), 7.

40. "Cough Drops," *The Sanatorium* 1, no. 3 (May 1907): 67.

41. The subtitle of *Tales of the Tents* was *Of the Patients, by the Patients, for the Patients.*

42. Editors of Hatikvah, "Literary and Dramatic Activities of Patients," *Hatikvah* 4, no. 3 (1926): 9.

43. Committee on Press and Propaganda, "Editorial," *The Sanatorium* 1, no. 1 (1907): 3.

44. Charles D. Spivak, "Minutes of the JCRS, Record of the Board of Trustees," March 6, 1907, Box 299, JCRS Archive.

45. Charles D. Spivak, "Sekreters berikht," *The Sanatorium* 3, no. 2 (1909): 145; "Advertisement: Advertise in the Sanatorium," *The Sanatorium* 3, no. 2 (1909): 158.

46. "The Scribe's Pinkes: Denver, Colorado," *The Sanatorium,* 1, no. 3 (1907): 58; "A Chat with the Publisher," *The Sanatorium,* 2, no. 3 (1908): 189.

47. "List of Subscriptions and Donations for 1908," *The Sanatorium* 3, no. 2 (1909): 127, 133.

48. I emphasize that what is rare is the decision of the journal to publish not only Yiddish translations but also material in Yiddish. For example, the patient-journal *Montefiore Echo* of the Montefiore Home and Hospital published some translations of Yiddish texts but not texts in Yiddish.

49. There were exceptions. The editor of the Yiddish daily *Forward*, Abe Cahan, attracted the attention of William Dean Howells, who ushered in the translation of Cahan's work. See Jules Chametzky, John Felstiner, Hilene Flanzbaum, and Kathryn Hell-

erstein, eds., *Jewish American Literature: A Norton Anthology* (New York: W. W. Norton, 2001); Aviva Taubenfeld, "'Only an L': Linguistic Borders and the Immigrant Author in Abraham Cahan's *Yekl* and *Yankel Der Yankee*," in *Multilingual America: Transnationalism, Ethnicity, and the Languages of American Literature*, ed. Werner Sollors (New York: New York University Press, 1998), 144–65.

50. One Yiddish writer to contribute material in the first year of the *Sanatorium* was Dovid Pinski. See Dovid Pinski, "Gasn-bilder," *The Sanatorium* 2, no. 4 (1908): 225–26.

51. Yehoash, "Letter to Jacob Gordin," April 26, 1908, Arc 116, Box 1, Folder: Gordin, Jacob, Jewish Theological Seminary Archive. My emphasis.

52. Jacob Gordin, "A briv fun Her Yankev Gordin," *The Sanatorium* 2, no. 4 (1908): 224.

53. Barbara Henry, *Rewriting Russia: Jacob Gordin's Yiddish Drama* (Seattle: University of Washington Press, 2011), 162.

54. "Our Bilingual Bi-monthly," *The Sanatorium* 3, no. 2 (1909): 68; Charles D. Spivak, "Sekreters berikht: Unzer baredevdiker meshulekh—der sanatoriyum," *The Sanatorium* 3, no. 2 (1909): 146.

55. "Mr. Jacob Gordin," *The Sanatorium* 3, no. 4 (1909): 228. The letter follows the note.

56. Leon Kobrin, "Di retung," *The Sanatorium* 2, no. 3 (1908): 173–86; Leon Kobrin, "The Rescue: A Drama, Part 1," *The Sanatorium* 2, no. 5 (1908), 247–50; Leon Kobrin, "The Rescue: A Drama, Part 2," *The Sanatorium* 2, no. 6 (1908), 298–302. Kobrin had been treated by Spivak while both were living in Philadelphia. See Abrams, *Dr. Charles David Spivak*, 47.

57. "Editorial: Leon Kobrin's Drama," *The Sanatorium* 2, no. 3 (1908): 130.

58. Joel Berkowitz, *Shakespeare on the American Yiddish Stage* (Iowa City: University of Iowa Press, 2002), 121–29.

59. Sh. Niger, *Dertseylers un romanistn* (New York: CYCO-Bikher Farlag, 1946), 218, quoted in J. Berkowitz, *Shakespeare on the American Yiddish Stage*, 123.

60. Kobrin, "The Rescue: A Drama, Part 1," 248; Kobrin, "The Rescue: A Drama, Part 2," 299, 301.

61. Morris Winchcvsky, "Der alter krenk Ayk," trans. Annie Goldstein, *The Sanatorium* 2, no. 4 (1908): 219–22.

62. Morris Winchevsky, "Cranky Old Ike," *The Social-Democrat* 4, no. 8 (1900): 253–56. All subsequent citations refer to this edition.

63. Ibid., 254.

64. "A New Poet–Solomon Bloomgarden," *The Maccabaean* 4, no. 6 (1903): 303.

65. Yehoash (Solomon Bloomgarden), "At Quarantine," *The Maccabaean* 4, no. 6 (1903): 304; Yehoash (Solomon Bloomgarden), "The Phantom of Death," *The Maccabaean* 4, no. 6 (1903): 304.

66. Daniel Charney, "Fun Eyrope keyn Elis Aylend un tsurik (Part 1)," *Der tog*, November 15, 1925, 6. Charney wrote of his experiences in a series of articles for *Der tog*. See ibid.; Daniel Charney, "Fun Eyrope keyn Elis Aylend un tsurik (Part 2)," *Der tog*, November 22, 1925; Daniel Charney, "Fun Eyrope keyn Elis Aylend un tsurik (Part 3)," *Der tog*, November 29, 1925; Daniel Charney, "Fun Eyrope keyn Elis Aylend un tsurik (Part 4)," *Der tog*, December 6, 1925; Daniel Charney, "Fun Eyrope keyn Elis Aylend un tsurik (Part 5)," *Der tog*, December 14, 1925; Daniel Charney, "Fun Eyrope keyn Elis Aylend un tsurik (Part 6)," *Der tog*, December 21, 1925.

67. Henry Wadsworth Longfellow, *Dos lid fun Hayavata*, trans. Yehoash (New York: Ferlag Yehoash, 1910).

68. In this vein, Rachel Rubinstein argues that "identification with Native Americans made it possible for the Yiddish writer to imaginatively inhabit the bodies both of Indians and aspirers to Indianness, natives and aliens, primitives and moderns, and in the process to both imitate and critique the racism and elitism of Anglo-American modernist literary practices." Rachel Rubinstein, *Members of the Tribe: Native America in the Jewish Imagination* (Detroit, MI: Wayne State University Press, 2010), 62. See also Stephen Katz, *Red, Black, and Jew: New Frontiers in Hebrew Literature* (Austin: University of Texas Press, 2009).

69. Alan Trachtenberg, "'Babe in the Yiddish Woods': Dos Lied Fun Hiavat'a," *Judaism* 50, no. 3 (2001): 332. See also Alan Trachtenberg, *Shades of Hiawatha: Staging Indians, Making Americans, 1880–1930* (New York: Hill & Wang, 2005), 140–69.

70. E. Gilman, *Yiddish Poetry and the Tuberculosis Sanatorium*, chap. 2. The tubercular Yiddish poet Reuben Ludwig, for example, had done just that after moving west for health reasons. For Ludwig's work, see "Indiyaner motivn," *Gezamelte lider* (New York: Y. L. Perets Shrayber-Farayn, 1927), 68–75.

71. For his insightful reading of Yehoash's poetry in light of the poet's stay in Denver, as well as his analysis of Yehoash's translation of *Hiawatha*, see Gilman, *Yiddish Poetry*.

72. John Keats, "Ode to a Nightingale," in *Poems of John Keats* (London: Lawrence & Bullen, 1896), 2:80, line 26.

73. C. Hillel Kauver, "A Plea for the Consumptive," *The Sanatorium* 1, no. 1 (1907): 8.

74. Yehoash, "The White Plague," *The Sanatorium* 1, no. 2 (1907): 30.

75. On the stigmatizing power of martial metaphors, see Susan Sontag, *Illness as Metaphor and AIDS and Its Metaphors* (New York: Picador USA, 2001).

76. "The Greatest Death Rate," *The Sanatorium* 1, no. 2 (1907): 30.

77. Yehoash, "The White Plague," *Colorado Medical Journal* 11 (1905): 434. The article followed "Jewish Consumptives' Relief Society Dedicates Three Tents," *Colorado Medical Journal* 11 (1905): 434.

78. James Barton Adams, *Some Letters and Writing of James Barton Adams* (Socorro, NM: Socorro County Historical Society, 1968).

79. James Barton Adams, "A Climate Worshipper," *The Sanatorium* 1, no. 2 (1907): 27.

80. Hannah Wirth-Nesher has commented on the phenomenon of linguistic passing in Jewish American literature, whereby an author suppresses any evidence of an accent. See Hana Wirth-Nesher, *Call It English: The Languages of Jewish American Literature* (Princeton, NJ: Princeton University Press, 2006), 56–60.

81. "Der Yehoash kontsert," *Der yidisher kuryer*, April 26, 1909, JCRS Records, Box 198, JCRS—Newspaper Clippings, 1909–1912, JCRS Archive.

82. Spivak, "Letter to Zishe Landau."

83. Lune Mattes, "Dem dikhter iz gut," in *Studya* (Los Angeles: Farlag "Palme," 1928), 24; Lune Mattes, "Kroyn fun zayn gnod," in *Studya* (Los Angeles: Farlag "Palme," 1928), 20. He also wrote the poem "Head Bent" (Kop geboygn) in honor of Spivak. See Lune Mattes, "Kop geboygn," in *Studya* (Los Angeles: Farlag "Palme," 1928), 20.

84. Mattes would also go on to fashion a poetic identity that was insistently tubercular, such as modeled by his 1928 collection *The White Prince of the White Plague*. His work was also translated into English in the pages of the JCRS publications and was also heavily influenced by the Coloradan landscape. See Lune Mattes, "Denver," trans. Abraham Wolftraub, *Hatikvah* 1, no. 2 (1923): 2; Lune Mattes, "Kolerade," in *Ofene toyren* (Denver: Literarishe Grupe (Dovid Edelsthat Branch 450 Arb. Ring) & Ladies Educational Club), 1923, 5–22; Lune Mattes, "The Song of Thanks and Love," trans. Deena Spivak Strauss, *Hatikvah* 1, no. 6 (1923): 15; Lune Mattes, *Der vayser prints fun der vayser plag* (Los Angeles: Farlag "Palme," 1928).

85. Shea Tenenbaum, "Nyu-York—Denver (reportazh-notitsn fun a rayze)," *Nyu-Yorker vokhenblat*, June 5, 1936, 11.

86. On Edelshtat, see Ori Kritz, *The Poetics of Anarchy: David Edelshtat's Revolutionary Poetry* (New York: Peter Lang, 1997). His contribution to communist-anarchist politics even garnered the attention of Emma Goldman. Emma Goldman, *Living My Life* (New York: Alfred A. Knopf, 1931), 1:55.

87. While in the sanatorium, Leivick learned that his play, *The Golem*, was being performed in English in Los Angeles. It had been performed in Hebrew in Moscow by the HaBimah group in 1925. See Freddie Rokem, "Hebrew Theater from 1889 to 1948," in *Theater in Israel*, ed. Linda Ben-Zvi (Ann Arbor: University of Michigan Press, 1996), 75. For his reflections on the occasion of the English performance, see H. Leivick, "Letter to Daniel and Samuel Leivick," November 4, 1932, RG 315, Folder 32, YIVO.

88. Leivick's patient record at the JCRS archives contains clippings from multiple newspapers and periodicals concerning his journey, including *Morgen Zhurnal* (New York), *Hebrew Journal* (Toronto), *Jewish World* (Philadelphia), *Yidish* (New York), *Eagle* (Montreal), and *Forverts* (Chicago). Gossip was also stirred when the New York communist paper, *Morgn-Frayhayt*, published an article in the summer of 1932 accusing

Leivick of being alienated from the workers and feeling himself above the patients of the JCRS. The JCRS patients, in turn, published a retort in the New York periodical *Yidish*, ensuring that he maintained close relations with them. For these clippings, see "Clippings pertaining to 1932 Leivick Affair," JCRS File 9698, Patient Record Halpern Leivick, JCRS Archive.

89. Ralph Radetsky, "Denver Patient World Famous Playwright," *Post*, August 11, 1935, 3, JCRS File 9698, Patient Record Halpern Leivick, JCRS Archive.

90. Chas. Miller, "Letter to H. Leyvik," n.d., RG 315, Box 65, Folder 74, YIVO; "Ticket for Mr. and Mrs. H. Leivick as Delegates to the 37th Annual National Convention of the Jewish Consumptives' Relief Society of Denver, CO," March 29, 1941, RG 315, Box 65, Folder 74, YIVO.

91. For basic biographical information on Tenenbaum, see Chaim Leib Fox, "Shiye Tenenboym," *Leksikon fun der nayer yidisher literatur* (New York: Congress for Jewish Culture, 1961), 4:98–99.

92. Shea Tenenbaum, "Letter to H. Leivick," n.d. (ca. 1934–35), RG 315, Box 29, Folder 54, YIVO.

93. Shea Tenenbaum, "Letter to H. Leivick," March 11, 1935, RG 315, Box 29, Folder 54, YIVO.

94. Shea Tenenbaum, "H. Leyvik—der mentsh," *Tshernovitser bleter*, June 24, 1936.

95. H. Leivick, "Volkns ahintern vald," in *Lider* (New York: Farlag "Fraynt," 1932), 300.

96. Shea Tenenbaum, "Friling in Denver," *Tshernovitser bleter*, August 6, 1936.

97. Shea Tenenbaum, "Tuberkuloze," in *Bay der velt tsugast: Dertseyln un reportazhn* (Warsaw: Literarishe Bleter, 1937), 10–12.

98. H. Leivick, "Di balade fun Denver Sanatoriyum," in *Lider fun gan eyden: 1932–1936* (Chicago: Farlag Tseshinksi, 1937), 121–39.

99. Leivick, "Di balade fun Denver Sanatoriyum," 125, line 85.

100. Gilman, *Yiddish Poetry and the Tuberculosis Sanatorium*, 100.

101. During his time in the JCRS, Leivick demonstrated interest in Spinoza. While there, he read Spinoza's *Ethics*. He also wrote an eleven-part poem named for the philosopher, in which he examines Spinoza's philosophy by rendering the Amsterdam legend the tubercular roommate of an ailing speaker. H. Leivick, "Shpinoze," in *Lider fun gan eyden: 1932–1936* (Chicago: Farlag Tseshinski, 1937), 101–11. Leivick also sent a letter to his wife requesting that she send him the translation of Spinoza's *Ethics*. H. Leivick, "Letter to Sarah Leivick," January 30, 1933, RG 315, Folder 32, YIVO; Benedictus de Spinoza, *Barukh Shpinoza: Di etik*, trans. William Nathanson (Chicago: Naye Gezelshaft, 1923). On the cultural importance of Spinoza, see Daniel B. Schwartz, *The First Modern Jew: Spinoza and the History of an Image* (Princeton, NJ: Princeton University Press, 2012).

102. David Edelshtat, "Mayn tsevoe," in *Shriftn* (New York: Arbayter Fraynd, Fraye Arbeter Shtime, 1925), 230, lines 1–4.

103. Leivick, "Di balade fun Denver Sanatoriyum," 131, line 234.

104. Ibid., 139, line 439.

105. Shea Tenenbaum, "Lider fun gan-eydn," *Der Yidisher kuryer*, June 16, 1940.

106. Shea Tenenbaum, "Letter to H. Leivick," May 1937, RG 315, Box 29, Folder 54, YIVO.

107. Shea Tenenbaum, "Letter to H. Leivick," April 25, 1936, RG 315, Box 29, Folder 54, YIVO.

108. He writes in a letter to Leivick that Abraham Reisen had expressed some interest in publishing a book about "life in Spivak Sanatorium." In his 1937 work, *Bay der velt tsugast*, Tenenbaum published several items related to his experience of tuberculosis. However, a full volume does not appear to have ever been published. For a description of the publishing possibility, see Shea Tenenbaum, "Letter to H. Leivick," July 1936, RG 315, Box 29, Folder 54, YIVO.

109. Tenenbaum, "H. Leyvik—der mentsh."

110. Shea Tenenbaum, "Baynakht baym keyver fun Dovid Edelshtat," in *Hunger tsum vort: Miniyaturn* (New York: CYCO-Bikher Farlag, 1971), 412.

111. Ibid., 413.

112. Now known as Chernivitsi, Ukraine.

113. Indeed, he and Charney had already corresponded about his sanatorium poetry as early as September 1932, when Charney was serving as a Yiddish correspondent in Berlin. In this earlier exchange, Charney had directed Leivick's attention to a sanatorium poem "Toward Death," which he had written while hospitalized in Bern, Switzerland. Daniel Charney, "Letter to H. Leivick," September 21, 1932, RG 315, Box 29, Folder 54, YIVO; Daniel Charney, "Tsum Toyt," in *Oyfn shvel fun yener velt: Tipn, bilder, epizodn* (New York: n.p., 1947), 184.

114. One of the more curious documents in Charney's generally curious archival collection is a list of writers and cultural activists who visited him at the WCS as well as the number of times each visited. See Daniel Charney, "Reshime fun shrayber un klal-tuer, vos hobn mikh bazukht in sanatoriye far di 2 yor 1948–1949," n.d., RG 421, Box 23, Folder 285, YIVO.

115. Daniel Charney, *Oyfn shvel fun yener velt: Tipn, bilder, epizodn* (New York: n.p., 1947), 77.

116. H. Leivick, "Februar in Liberti," in *Lider fun gan eyden: 1932–1936* (Chicago: Farlag Tseshinski, 1937), 150–52.

117. An explicit engagement can be found in an article written for the journal of the Workmen's Circle, *Der fraynd*, in 1947. There, Charney opens an article celebrating the thirty-sixth year of the WCS by quoting from a poem Leivick wrote while in Liberty. In the remainder of the article, Charney once again invokes the tubercular literary tradition of Sholem Aleichem, Yehoash, and Edelshtat into which he has entered. Daniel Charney, "Ikh zing tsu aykh fun der Liberti-Sanatoriye," *Der fraynd* 3, no. 3 (June 1946): 14.

118. Charney, *Oyfn shvel fun yener*, 5; Leivick, *Mit der sheyres hapleyte* (New York: H. Leyvik Yubiley-Komitet durkhn Tsiko-Farlag, 1947), 184–85.

119. Leivick, *Mit der sheyres hapleyte*, 181.

120. Ibid., 183.

121. "Editorial: The Consumptive in Literature," *The Sanatorium* 5, no. 1 (1911): 3, 4.

Chapter 4

1. David Vogel, "Y. Kh. Brener: A por verter tsu zayn 4th yortsayt," *Literarishe bleter*, no. 52 (April 30, 1925): 1.

2. As told to Eli Mohar in an interview. See Eli Mohar, "Ke-shemesh be-yom-kevisah," *Davar*, February 12, 1971, sec. Davar ha-shavu'a, 9.

3. Yitsḥak Dov Berkowitz, *Unzere rishonim: Zikhroynes-dertseylungen vegn Sholem-Aleykhem un zayn dor* (Tel Aviv: Menorah, 1966), 4:89–90.

4. For an analysis of the versions of this death scene, including that of Chekhov's wife, Olga Knipper, see Janet Malcolm, *Reading Chekhov: A Critical Journey* (New York: Random House, 2001), esp. 62–72.

5. Uri Milstein, "Einayim bo'arot," *Ḥadashot*, April 5, 1985.

6. Quoted in Muki Tsur, "Ke-ḥakot Raḥel: Kavim biyografiyim," in *Ha-shirim*, by Raḥel (Bene Barak: Ha-Kibuts Ha-Meuḥad, 2011), 67. Raḥel also quotes the passage in Yiddish, "*Lakhn iz gezunt. Doktoryrim heysn lakhn,*" in a letter to Shulamit Klugai. See Raḥel, "Letter to Shulamit Klugai (#12)," n.d., Arkhiyon ha-Medinah [Israel State Archives], accessed December 19, 2013, http://www.archives.gov.il/NR/rdonlyres/313D8E87-C7A0-4D83-B75D-85AD6F72DFC0/0/Rachel12.pdf, accessed December 19, 2013.

7. Daniel Charney, *Oyfn shvel fun yener velt: Tipn, bilder, epizodn* (New York: n.p., 1947), 77.

8. One could also mention here Schnitzler's novella *Fräulein Else* (1924) as well as Zofia Nałkowska's 1927 Polish novella, *Choucas*. Arthur Schnitzler, *Fräulein Else*, trans. F. Y. Lyon (London: Pushkin Press, 2013); Zofia Nałkowska, *Choucas: An International Novel*, trans. Ursula Philips (DeKalb: Northern Illinois University Press, 2014).

9. On Klabund's experiences in Davos as well as a biographical description of his tubercular experience, see Paul Raabe, *Klabund in Davos: Texte, Bilder, Dokumente* (Zurich: Arche Verlag, 1990).

10. Mann visited his wife, Katja, in Davos in 1912. On Davos as well as Mann's realist literary relation to it, see Thomas Sprecher, *Auf dem Weg zum "Zauberberg": Die Davoser Literaturtage 1996*, Thomas-Mann-Studien (Frankfurt am Main: V. Klostermann, 1997), 16:11–19.

11. The novella was first published in 1927. All citations in this book refer to the 2008 edition of the text. David Vogel, *Be-vet ha-marpe: Sipur*, ed. Asher Barash (Jerusa-

lem: Mitspeh, 1927); David Vogel, *Be-vet ha-marpe* (Tel Aviv: Ha-Kibuts Ha-Me'uḥad, 2008).

12. Now known as Sataniv, Ukraine.

13. At the outset of World War I, he was imprisoned for living as a Russian subject in Austria. For Vogel's general biography, see Dan Pagis, "David Vogel," in *Mi-ḥuts la-shurah: Masot ve-reshimot al ha-shirah ha-ivrit ha-modernit* (Jerusalem: Keshev, 2003), 9–29.

14. Glenda Abramson, "Poet of the Dark Gate: The Poetry of David Vogel," *Jewish Book Annual* 50 (1992): 128–42; Glenda Abramson, "Vogel and the City," in *The Russian Jewish Diaspora and European Culture, 1917–1937*, ed. Jörg Schulte, Olga Tabachnikova, and Peter Wagstaff (Boston: Brill, 2012), 37–54; Robert Alter, "Fogel and the Forging of the Hebrew Self," *Prooftexts* 13, no. 1 (1993): 2–13; Robert Alter, *The Invention of Hebrew Prose: Modern Fiction and the Language of Realism* (Seattle: University of Washington Press, 1988), 76–91; Yoram Baranovski, "Misḥake ahavah ve-mavet," *Davar*, January 9, 1975, sec. Masa: Musaf le-Davar; Chana Kronfeld, "Fogel and Modernism: A Liminal Moment in Hebrew Literary History," *Prooftexts* 13, no. 1 (1993): 45–63; Dan Miron, "Ahavah teluyah ba-davar: Toldot hitkablutah shel shirat David Fogel," in *Aderet le-Vinyamin: Sefer ha-yovel li-Vinyamin Harshav*, ed. Ziva Ben-Porat (Tel Aviv: Ha-Kibuts Ha-Meʾuḥad, 1999), esp. 1:54; Shachar M. Pinsker, *Literary Passports: The Making of Modernist Hebrew Fiction in Europe* (Stanford, CA: Stanford University Press, 2011); Gershon Shaked, "David Fogel," in *Ha-siporet ha-ivrit, 1880–1980* (Tel Aviv: Ha-Kibuts Ha-Meʾuḥad and Keter, 1988), 93–101; Shimon Sandbank, "David Fogel, Georg Trakl—veha-tsevaʿim," in *Shete berekhot ba-yaʿar: Kesharim u-makbilot ben ha-shirah ha-ivrit veha-shirah ha-eropit* (Tel Aviv: Ha-Kibuts Ha-Meʾuḥad, 1976), 70–92; Harold Shimel, "Ha-tsad shelanu—hayam shelanu," *Davar*, July 19, 1974.

15. On Vogel's different approach to writing than Trakl's, see Sandbank, "David Fogel, Georg Trakl." On Vogel and Goethe, see Michael Gluzman, "Unmasking the Politics of Simplicity in Modernist Hebrew Poetry: Rereading David Fogel," *Prooftexts* 13, no. 1 (1993): 35–36. On Vogel and Mann, see most recently Orna Mondschein, *Sifrut ha-sanaṭoryum: Keri'ah Be-Tomas Man, David Fogel, Bruno Shults* (Tel Aviv: Resling, 2016), 10.

16. Shaked, "David Fogel," 95.

17. Alter, *The Invention of Hebrew Prose*, 91; Shaked, "David Fogel," 95.

18. On the notion of the minor and the simple, see Gluzman, "Unmasking the Politics of Simplicity in Modernist Hebrew Poetry"; Chana Kronfeld, *On the Margins of Modernism: Decentering Literary Dynamics* (Berkeley: University of California Press, 1996), 7. See also Miron's response in Miron, "Ahavah teluyah ba-davar," 55.

19. David Vogel, "Letter to Sh. Pollack," May 21, 1923, 4–5, David Vogel Collection 231, Document 19227/1, Machon Genazim.

20. Yoḥanan Arnon, *Uri Tsevi Grinberg: Taḥahnot be-ḥayav* (Tel Aviv: Eked, 1991), 79–80.

21. On their reception in Palestine, see Menaḥem Poznanski, "Letter #126 to G. Shofman (31 May 1930)," in *Igrot tar'at-tashtaz* (Tel Aviv: M. Z. Volfovski, 1960), 135. On their illness in Palestine, see Arnon, *Uri Tsevi Grinberg*, 80.

22. Ibid., 84. My emphasis.

23. Although it was his mother tongue, Vogel may have struggled to write in Yiddish. According to the Yiddish poet Melech Ravitch, Vogel had the idea in 1919 to publish a Yiddish literary pamphlet on the theme of death but had trouble writing in Yiddish. Though the pamphlet *Death Cycle (Toyt-tsiklus)* was eventually published, Vogel's Hebrew poems appear there only in Yiddish translation. On the initiation of the journal, see Melech Ravitch, "David Fogel," in *Mayn leksikon* (Montreal: Aroysgegebn fun a Komitet, 1958), 5:333. See also Melech Ravitch, ed., *Toyt-Tsiklus* (Vienna: Der Kval, 1920).

24. For an investigation into various psychological motivations prompting Vogel to write his final prose work in Yiddish, see Shiri Goren, "Writing on the Verge of Catastrophe: David Vogel's Last Work of Prose," in *Choosing Yiddish: New Frontiers of Language and Culture*, ed. Lara Rabinovich, Shiri Goren, and Hannah S. Pressman (Detroit, MI: Wayne State University Press, 2013), 29–45.

25. Alter, "Fogel and the Forging of the Hebrew Self," 5. Alter continues his claim as follows: "Indeed, his incorrigible Europeanness is no less determinative of his identity than that of his exact Germanophone coeval, Walter Benjamin: both men in the end perished because they could not manage to extricate themselves, even as the clouds of destruction gathered, from the European setting they had made their only conceivable theater of operation" (ibid.). I note here my discomfort with this contention made by Alter and often repeated throughout Hebrew and English criticism of Vogel's work. His attachment to European aesthetics, so the argument goes, blinded him to the fact that he would ultimately be killed by Nazis. His belief in the idea of Europe, accordingly, was naïve and misplaced. The logic of this critique, however, is fundamentally flawed and insists on blaming the victim for his own death as a result of political myopia rather than Nazi aggression. It also frequently assumes migration—and, more often than not, migration to Palestine—would have been a better solution, as if alternative solutions were readily available. I must note my displeasure with this line of argumentation that accuses Vogel, Benjamin, and others as having placed aesthetic idealism above political realism, an accusation that can only be made in hindsight and that judges aesthetics to be less important than nationalism.

26. On the evolution of Hebrew into a language of modern culture at the end of the nineteenth century, see Benjamin Harshav, *Language in Time of Revolution* (Berkeley: University of California Press, 1993).

27. David Vogel, *Ketsot ha-yamim*, in *Taḥanot kavot: Novelot, roman, sipur, yoman* ([Tel Aviv]: Ha-Kibuts Ha-Me'uḥad, 1990), 280–81.

28. First published in Berlin in 1902, the translation would go on to sell more than one hundred thousand copies. As Mordekhai Eran and Ya'akov Shavit have written, the Bible was particularly successful due to its use of popular German language. It also incorporated certain Protestant nomenclature, such as referring to the Tetragammaton as "der Herr" rather than "der Ewige." The latter had been customary in German renderings of the Bible by Jewish translators since Moses Mendelssohn's *Biur*. Bernfeld's translation also had a subtle assimilatory agenda that sought to homogenize Jewish and Christian scriptural vocabulary. Mordekhai Eran and Ya'akov Shavit, "'Tanakh yehudi be-germanit': Tirgum ha-tana'kh le-germanit al-yade Shim'on Bernfeld (1903): Ben meḥkar 'kofer' le-tirgum 'shomrani,'" *Bet mikra* 54, no. 2 (2008): 127–28, 142.

29. Vogel, *Ketsot ha-yamim*, 283.

30. I am grateful to Na'ama Rokem for alerting me to this trend in metaphoric language. Ḥaim Naḥman Bialik, "Ḥevlei lashon," in *Kol kitve Ḥayim Naḥman Bialik* (Tel Aviv: Dvir, 1956), 196; Dan Miron, *From Continuity to Contiguity: Toward a New Jewish Literary Thinking* (Stanford, CA: Stanford University Press, 2010), 423.

31. Vogel, *Ketsot ha-yamim*, 310.

32. Ibid., 289.

33. Ibid., 295.

34. Ibid., 310.

35. For this run-through of the relationship between illness and creativity in German intellectual history, I have relied on the efficient narrative account of Dietrich von Engelhardt, which itself follows the classic projection plotted by Hermann J. Weigand in his chapter "Disease" in his study of *Der Zauberberg*. Dietrich von Engelhardt, "Tuberkulose und Kultur um 1900. Arzt, Patient und Sanatorium in Thomas Manns *Zauberberg* aus Medizinihistorischer Sicht," in *Auf dem Weg zum "Zauberberg": Die Davoser Literaturtage, 1996*, ed. Thomas Sprecher (Frankfurt am Main: Vittorio Klostermann, 1997), 340–41; Hermann J. Weigand, *Thomas Mann's Novel, "Der Zauberberg": A Study* (New York: D. Appleton-Century, 1933), 39–58. For Weigand's comments on Goethe, see p. 40.

36. On Novalis, see Clark Lawlor, *Consumption and Literature: The Making of the Romantic Disease* (New York: Palgrave Macmillan, 2006), 119. For mention of Novalis's relationship to disease as it pertains to the perception of disease among and following German Romantic writers, see Stephen C. Meredith, "Mortal Illness on the Magic Mountain," in *A Companion to Thomas Mann's "Magic Mountain,"* ed. Stephen D. Dowden (Columbia, SC: Camden House, 1999), 117; Weigand, *Thomas Mann's Novel, "Der Zauberber,"* 40.

37. Friedrich Nietzsche, *The Will to Power*, trans. Anthony M. Ludovici (London:

George Allen & Unwin, 1924), 2:811, http://archive.org/stream/completeworksthe15nietuoft/completeworksthe15nietuoft_djvu.txt.

38. Thomas Mann, *Reflections of a Nonpolitical Man*, trans. Walter D. Morris (New York: Frederick Ungar Publishing, 1983), 13.

39. Thomas Mann, "Introduction," in *The Short Novels of Dostoevsky* (New York: Dial Press, 1945), xiv. See also Thomas Mann, "Goethe and Tolstoy," in *Three Essays*, trans. H. T. Lowe-Porter (New York: Alfred A. Knopf, 1929), 3–140.

40. Vogel, *Ketsot ha-yamim*, 294.

41. Ibid., 299.

42. Alter, "Fogel and the Forging of the Hebrew Self," 5–6.

43. David Vogel, "Letter to Sh. Pollack," February 18, 1924, David Vogel Collection 231, Document 19243/1, Machon Genazim; Vogel, "Letter to Sh. Pollack," July 17, 1924, David Vogel Collection 231, Document 19293/1, Machon Genazim.

44. David Vogel, "Letter to Sh. Pollack," June 9, 1924, David Vogel Collection 231, Document 19241/1, Machon Genazim; Vogel, "Letter to Sh. Pollack," July 17, 1924; David Vogel, "Letter to Sh. Pollack," August 31, 1924, David Vogel Collection 231, Document 19242/1, Machon Genazim.

45. David Vogel, "Letter to Sh. Pollack," December 3, 1924, David Vogel Collection 231, Document 19240/1, Machon Genazim.

46. Raphael Hausmann, *Die Weintraubenkur: Mit Rücksicht auf Erfahrungen in Meran* (Meran: Fridolin Plant, 1905).

47. On the history of Merano as a space of Jewish health tourism as well as an analysis of the often hostile environment of the conservative, Catholic region, see Sabine Mayr's work, *Südtirol und seine jüdischen AutorInnen* (Innsbruck: Studienverlag, forthcoming). I am grateful to Mayr for sharing an earlier version of her work with me. On the Jewish social history of Marienbad and Carlsbad, see Miriam Zadoff, *Next Year in Marienbad: The Lost Worlds of Jewish Spa Culture*, trans. William Templer (Philadelphia: University of Pennsylvania Press, 2012).

48. For an analysis of Schnitzler's love letters to Olga Waissnix from Meran, to which he traveled for health reasons in 1886, see Bettina Marxer, "Die Liebesbegegnung in Meran," in *Liebesbriefe, und was nun einmal so gennant wird: Korrespondenzen zwischen Arthur Schnitlzer, Olga Waissnix und Mare Reinhard: Eine literatur- und kulturwissenschaftliche Lektüre* (Würzberg: Königshausen & Neumann, 2001), 57–75. On evidence of Zweig's time in Meran, see Stefan Zweig and Friderike Zweig, *Briefwechsel: 1912–1942* (Berlin: Alfred Scherz Verlag, 1951), 45. For Kafka's letters to his family from Meran, see Franz Kafka, *Letters to Ottla and the Family*, ed. Nahum N. Glatzer, trans. Richard Winston and Clara Winston (New York: Schocken Books, 1982), 42–52.

49. Re'uven Brainin, *Perets ben Mosheh Smolenskin: Ḥayav u-sefarav* (Warsaw: Tushiyah, 1896), 152.

50. David Vogel, "Letter to Sh. Pollack," December 15, 1925, David Vogel Collection 231, Document 19247/1, Machon Genazim.

51. David Vogel, "Letter 3 (Vienna, December 15, 1925)," trans. Mikhail Krutikov, *Jews and Slavs* 17 (2006): 100.

52. For biographical information and archival material related to Knöpfmacher, see *Guide to the Papers of Hugo Knoepfmacher (1890–1980), 1865–1979, AR7172*, accessed October 30, 2014, http://digifindingaids.cjh.org/?pID=256143.

53. I am grateful to Eugenio Valentini of the Merano historical archive for finding records of Vogel's stay in the *Meraner Kurzeitung*. For Vogel's records of his stay in 1925, see also David Vogel, "Letter to Sh. Pollack," February 28, 1925, David Vogel Collection 231, Document 19244/1, Machon Genazim. For 1926, see David Vogel, "Letter to Sh. Pollack," February 18, 1926, David Vogel Collection 231, Document 19248/1, Machon Genazim; David Vogel, "Letter to Sh. Pollack," March 18, 1926, David Vogel Collection 231, Document 19249/1, Machon Genazim.

54. Hugo Knöpfmacher, "Der hebräische Dichter David Vogel," *Jüddische Rundschau*, December 11, 1925, 811.

55. David Vogel, "Degalim sheḥorim mefarperim," in *Kol ha-shirim*, ed. Aharon Komem (Tel Aviv: Ha-Kibuts Ha-Meʾuḥad, 1998), 80.

56. Ibid.; Knöpfmacher, "Der hebräische Dichter David Vogel," 811. My emphasis.

57. David Vogel, "Letter to A. Broides," October 29, 1937, David Vogel Collection 231, Document 43957/1, Machon Genazim.

58. We know from correspondence that Vogel had begun to try his hand at prose by the winter of 1925, and it is possible that he drafted the novella while he recuperated in Merano in 1926. Accordingly, the novella may read as a form of patient life writing. Alternatively, the manuscript that remains in the archive is dated "Paris 1926" and may indicate that Vogel drafted the entirety of the text after his return to Paris in the summer of 1926. We must also note here that although *In the Sanatorium* is Vogel's first published novella, it was not his first attempt at prose. After leaving the sanatorium the first time in 1925, Vogel made his way to Paris. Along the way, he began to experiment with prose writing, which admittedly did not come easily. In 1925, he published a Yiddish article on the occasion of the fourth anniversary of the death of Y. Ḥ. Brenner in the Warsaw weekly *Literarishe bleter*. And in 1925–26, he drafted though did not publish a short text titled "The Inhabitant" (Ha-dayar), in which the erotic and the sickly make uncomfortable bedfellows. Moshe, a male boarder, sleeps with his landlady, Beile. When her children discover a man in her bed the next morning and threaten to squeal, Beile yells at them to "let a sick man rest," attempting to cover up her affair under the guise of illness. Having felt well up to that point, Moshe then begins to feel sick to his stomach. David Vogel, "Dayar," in *Taḥanot kavot: Novelot, roman, sipur, yoman* ([Tel Aviv]: Ha-Kibuts Ha-Meʾuḥad, 1990), 265–68.

59. Irme is a nickname for men named "Yirmiyahu," the Hebrew equivalent of Jeremiah.

60. Sabine Mayr has explored the multiple valences of the term "Asyl," reminding us that it refers to those who seek shelter in an "asylum" because they need protection. It is not a neutral space of healing but an active institution for the desperate. See Mayr, *Südtirol und seine jüdischen AutorInnen.*

61. On the early history of the sanatorium and influence of the Königswarter family on the region, see Rosanna Pruccoli, "Un cimetero, un sanatorio per indigenti e una sinagoga: Storia di un patto di solidarietà," in *Storie di ebrei: Contributi storici sulla presenza ebraica in Alto Adige e in Trentino = Jüdische Schicksale: Beiträge zu einer Geschichtsforschung über die jüdische Ansässigkeit in Südtirol und im Trentino*, ed. Federico Steinhaus and Rosanna Pruccoli ([Merano] (Bolzano): Comunità ebraica di Merano/Jüdische Kultusgemeinde Meran, 2004), 47–76.

62. Ostrau is the present-day city of Ostrava, Czech Republic. Vogel, *Be-vet ha-marpe*, 22.

63. The novel was completed in 1916 and published the next year. Klabund, *Die Krankheit*, ed. Christian V. Zimmerman, vol. 2, *Werke in Acht Bänden* (Heidelberg: Elfenbeing Verlag, 1999), http://gutenberg.spiegel.de/buch/die-krankheit-2549/1.

64. Katrin Max, *Liegekur und Bakterienrausch: Literarische Deutungen der Tuberkulose im Zauberberg und Anderswo* (Würzberg: Verlag Köningshausen & Neumann GmbH, 2013), 103–4.

65. Aharon Komem, *Ha-ofel veha-pele: Iyunim bi-yetsirato shel David Fogel* (Haifa: Universitet Ḥefah & Zemorah-Bitan, 2001), 123.

66. Vogel, *Be-vet ha-marpe*, 56.

67. Sh[lomo] Ts[emaḥ], "Be-vet ha-marpe," *Moznayim*, 1929, 12.

68. Shaked, "David Fogel," 95.

69. Menachem Perry, "Ibud Fogel et Fogel: Aḥarit-davar le'taḥanot kavot," in *Taḥanot kavot: Novelot, roman, sipur, yoman*, by David Vogel (Tel Aviv: Ha-Kibuts Ha-Me'uḥad, 1990), 332.

70. Max, *Liegekur und Bakterienrausch*, 132–38.

71. Orna Mondschein has similarly noticed that the religious profile of the sanatorium distinguishes it from Mann's Berghof. Mondschein, *Sifrut ha-sanatoryum*, 9. In contrast, Sabine Mayr has also investigated the ways in which Vogel's text works to marginalize the specifically Jewish cultural references of the sanatorium experience. For example, Vogel does not mention the existence of a synagogue next to the historical sanatorium. By overlooking the Jewish built environment, Vogel's characters further assert themselves as assimilating, bourgeois, German-speaking Jews. For Mayr's extended analysis of the novella as a Foucauldian heterotopia, see Mayr, *Südtirol und seine jüdischen AutorInnen.*

72. In a discussion with Castorp regarding Naphta, Joachim Ziemmsen comments on

Naphta's nose: "And that nose is too Jewish, too—take a good look at him." Thomas Mann, *The Magic Mountain*, trans. John E. Woods (New York: Alfred A. Knopf, 1995), 379.

73. Ruth HaCohen, "Sounds of Revelation: Aesthetic-Political Theology in Schoenberg's Moses and Aron," *Modernist Cultures* 1, no. 2 (2005): 112.

74. Ibid., 133n23. See also Ghil 'ad Zuckerman, *Language Contact and Lexical Enrichment in Israeli Hebrew* (New York: Palgrave Macmillan, 2003).

75. Maya Barzilai, "S. Y. Agnon's German Consecration and the 'Miracle' of Hebrew Letters," *Prooftexts* 33, no. 1 (2013): 58–75; Amir Eshel and Na'ama Rokem, "German and Hebrew: Histories of a Conversation," *Prooftexts* 33, no. 1 (2013): 1–8; Na'ama Rokem, "German-Hebrew Encounters in the Poetry and Correspondence of Yehuda Amichai and Paul Celan," *Prooftexts* 30, no. 1 (2010): 97–127; Rachel Seelig, *Strangers in Berlin: Modern Jewish Literature between East and West, 1919–1933* (Ann Arbor: University of Michigan Press, 2016).

76. Seelig, *Strangers in Berlin*, 77.

77. Vogel, *Be-vet ha-marpe*, 10. Mann's novel has been read as a critique of the moneymaking agenda of health resorts that promote expensive treatments that have no demonstrable effect. Vogel's novella may also be read as a critique of the contemporary health infrastructure in which indigent Jewish tuberculars were completely dependent on charities for health care. On Mann, see Thomas Sprecher, "Kur-, Kultur- und Kapitalismuskritik im Zauberberg," in *Literatur und Krankheit im Fin-de-Siècle (1890–1914): Thomas Mann im europäischen Kontext* (Frankfurt am Main: Vittorio Klostermann, 2002), 187–249.

78. Vogel, *Be-vet ha-marpe*, 47.

79. Ibid., 44.

80. David Vogel, "Im Sanatorium," in *Im Sanatorium, An der See: Zwei Novellen*, trans. Ruth Achlama (Munich: List Verlag, 2013), 11.

81. Mani Leib, "Mayn lebn in tsoybertol," in *Tsuzamen*, ed. S. L. Shneiderman (Tel Aviv: Y. L. Perets, 1974), 494.

82. My translation follows that of Ruth Wisse. For her commentary on the letter, see Ruth R. Wisse, *A Little Love in Big Manhattan* (Cambridge, MA: Harvard University Press, 1988), 210.

83. Vogel, *Ketsot ha-yamim*, 283.

84. Komem, *Ha-ofel veha-pele*, 131.

85. Vogel, *Be-vet ha-marpe*, 19.

86. Ibid., 24.

87. Ibid., 47.

88. Vogel is likely referring to a variant of the following folk poem: "Der / Rebensaft / Gibt uns Kraft, / Ist gut, / Schafft Muth / Und Gluth / Dem Bluth." Joh. Hehl, ed., "Die Weinflasche," in *Blüthen der Musen für das Jahr 1816* (Vienna: Jos. Riedl, 1816), 14.

89. This is further emphasized by the footnote that Vogel appends to the scene, where he translates the German phrase as follows: *Asis ananim / noten lanu koaḥ, / meorer damenu / u-mosif omets la-lev* (Juice of grapes / gives us strength / arouses our blood / and gives courage to the heart). In the Hebrew, Vogel specifically directs readers' attention to this link between *Rebensaft* and the *lev* (heart, chest). The former works to help those afflicted with chest diseases. Yet here, the German "juice of the grapes" is not being deployed for the health benefits of the Hebrew tubercular but, rather, in the name of romantic exploits. Vogel, *Be-vet ha-marpe*, 78.

90. Ibid., 81.

91. Ibid., 79.

92. Ibid., 10.

93. Ibid.

94. Maureen Quilligan, *The Language of Allegory: Defining the Genre* (Ithaca, NY: Cornell University Press, 1979), 26.

95. My translation follows that of Ruth Wisse. Wisse, *A Little Love in Big Manhattan*, 210.

96. David Vogel, "Letter to Melech Ravitch," January 16, 1925, ARC. 40 1540, Folder D. Vogel, National Library of Israel Archives.

97. Vogel, *Be-vet ha-marpe*, 30.

98. Haun Saussy, "In the Workshop of Equivalences: Translation, Institutions, Media in the Jesuit Re-formation of China," in *Great Walls of Discourse and Other Adventures in Cultural China* (Cambridge, MA: Harvard University Asia Center, 2001), 32.

99. Vogel, *Be-vet ha-marpe*, 42.

100. Elisheva Carlebach, *Palaces of Time: Jewish Calendar and Culture in Early Modern Europe* (Cambridge, MA: The Belknap Press of Harvard University Press, 2011), 4.

101. Vogel, *Ketsot ha-yamim*, 286.

102. Mann, *The Magic Mountain*, 7.

103. Ibid., 221.

104. Russell A. Berman, "Modernism and the Bildungsroman: Thomas Mann's *Magic Mountain*," in *The Cambridge Companion to the Modern German Novel*, ed. Graham Bartram (Cambridge: Cambridge University Press, 2004), 74. See also T. J. Reed, *Thomas Mann: The Uses of Tradition* (Oxford: Clarendon Press, 1996), 226–74.

105. Vogel, *Be-vet ha-marpe*, 48.

Epilogue

1. Aharon Appelfeld, "Badenhaim, ir nofesh," in *Shanim ve-sha'ot* (Tel Aviv: Ha-Kibuts Ha-Me'uḥad, 1975), 81; Aharon Appelfeld, *Badenheim 1939*, trans. Dalya Bilu (Boston: D. R. Godine, 1980), 117. I draw on Bilu's translation throughout this chapter. It should also be noted that Appelfeld's novella was an expansion on an earlier short

story (1972) simply titled "Badenheim," without the additional reference to *ir nofesh* (resort town). I restrict my reading here to the 1975 novella.

2. On Vogel's time in Paris, see Yeshurun Keshet, "Rishme masa be-Eyrope," *Hado'ar* 39 (October 13, 1967): 738–40.

3. On David and Ada Vogel's time in France during World War II, see Dan Laor, "Le-an huvelu ha-otsrim? Al ha-perek he-ḥaser bakhronikat ha-milḥamah shel David Fogel," in *Mimerkazim la-merkaz: Sefer Nurit Govrin*, ed. Avner Holtzman, Mikhal Oron, and Zivah Shamir (Tel Aviv: Mekhon Kats Le-Ḥeker Ha-Sifrut Ha-Ivrit, Bet Ha-Sefer Le-Mada'e Ha-Yahadut al Shem Ḥayim Rozenberg, Universitat Tel-Aviv, 2005), 385–411.

4. Henry W. Paul, *Henri de Rothschild, 1872–1947: Medicine and Theater* (Burlington, VT: Ashgate Publishing, 2011), 25.

5. The Yiddish text remains in manuscript form and has been published only in Hebrew translation. David Vogel, *Kulam yats'u la-krav*, in *Taḥanot kavot: Novelot, roman, sipur, yoman*, ed. Menachem Perry ([Tel Aviv]: Ha-Kibuts Ha-Me'uḥad, 1990), 72.

6. Ibid., 116.

7. Thomas Dormandy, *The White Death: A History of Tuberculosis* (London : Hambledon Press, 1999), 362–69.

8. It is interesting to note that tuberculosis would continue to play a role in the Jewish history of Merano immediately following World War II. After the war, Merano served as a common stopping point for Jewish émigrés on their way to Palestine, as it was the headquarters of the local *Bricha* unit that facilitated illegal immigration to Palestine. Many Jewish refugees, moreover, arrived in Merano under the guise of being tuberculosis patients and from there continued on their path to immigration. In addition, a Merano sanatorium was established specifically to provide mental health care to the Jewish victims of the Auschwitz concentration camp. See Jack Adler, "Therapeutic Group Work with Tuberculosis Displaced Persons," *International Journal of Group Psychotherapy* 3, no. 1 (1953): 302–8; Yehuda Bauer, *Flight and Rescue: Brichah* (New York: Random House, 1971), 174; Jacob Markovizky, "The Italian Government's Response to the Problem of Jewish Refugees 1945–1948," *Journal of Israeli History: Politics, Society, Culture* 19, no. 1 (1998): 23–39; and Eva Pfanzelter, "Between Brenner and Bari: Jewish Refugees in Italy 1945 to 1948," *Journal of Israeli History: Politics, Society, Culture* 19, no. 3 (1998): 83–104.

9. Ernest Gilman, *Yiddish Poetry and the Tuberculosis Sanatorium, 1900–1970* (Syracuse, NY: Syracuse University Press, 2015), xvii.

10. Abba Kovner, for example, draws on his experience of cancer as the source of his collection, *Sloan Kettering*. In a complementary manner, Yotam Reuveny's *Night Diary*, published in three volumes, draws not on the author's experience of illness but on his experience of gay culture in Tel Aviv in the 1980s to posit AIDS as "a philosophical tool that allows [characters] to transcend not only their 'disease' but also the 'mundane.'"

Abba Kovner, *Slon Ketering: Po'emah* (Tel Aviv: Ha-Kibuts Ha-Me'uhad, 1987); Yotam Reuveny, *Yomam lailah* (Tel Aviv: Kadim, 1987); Yotam Reuveny, *Yomam lailah 2* (Tel Aviv: Modan, 1988); Yotam Reuveny, *Yomam lailah 3* (Tel Aviv: Nimrod, 1989); Oren Segal, "Sisyphus in Tel Aviv: AIDS in Yotam Reuveny's Night Diary," *Prooftexts* 32 (2012): 116.

11. Yankev Glatshteyn, "Tsuriktrakhtungen," in *Gezangen fun rekhts tsu links* (New York: Bikher Farlag, 1971), 12.

12. Sharon L. Snyder, Brenda Jo Brueggmann, and Rosemarie Garland-Thomson, eds., *Disability Studies: Enabling the Humanities* (New York: Modern Language Association of America, 2002). Disability studies has also become more prominent in scholarship concerning Hebrew literature. For one recent example, see Dror Harari, "Performing the Un-chosen Israeli Body: Nataly Zukerman's *Haguf Ha'acher*," *TDR: The Drama Review* 60, no. 1 (2016), 157–64.

13. Chava Rosenfarb, "Te-be-tse balade," in *Di balade fun nekhtikhn vald* (London: Narod Press, 1947), 19–24.

14. Chava Rosenfarb, *Briv tsu Abrashen* (Tel Aviv: Y. L. Perets Farlag, 1992).

15. At the end of the novel, the protagonist learns that, in fact, she has been writing to Abrashe's paralyzed cousin. The Abrashe of the title had perished.

16. This is especially noticeable in memoirs, such as that of Inge Auerbacher. Auerbacher developed tuberculosis as a young child in the Theresienstadt concentration camp, where she was imprisoned at the age of seven. In her memoir, written for an adolescent audience, she recalls that she had prayed for tuberculosis while in Theresienstadt because children with the disease were given a small amount of additional food. She, too, eventually tests positive. Her symptoms begin to manifest while on the ship to America. After landing, her family did not speak of the disease by name because of the stigma associated with it. She is hospitalized for the disease in America and suffers from reoccurring episodes for the next decade. Inge Auerbacher, *Beyond the Yellow Star to America* (Unionville, NY: Royal Fireworks Press, 1995).

17. H. Leivick, *Mit der sheyres hapleyte* (New York: H. Leyvik Yubiley-Komitet durkhn Tsiko-Farlag, 1947). The Machon Lavon archive also contains a letter written in Yiddish by the patients of the Gauting Sanatorium from 1953. They are writing because they are considering moving en masse to Israel, yet they want to make sure that they will be met with the necessary accommodations once they arrive. They have heard that other tubercular immigrants were thrown into transit camps (*ma'abarot*), where they only become sicker. They write that they are aware that the economic situation in Israel is not good, but they claim a moral right to demand appropriate funds, as they are the last "remaining victims [*di letste farblibene korboynes*] of Hitler's regime." Yidishe Patsiantn Komitet (Sanatorium Gauting), "Tazkir shel va'ad ḥole shaḥefet be-maḥane Fernvald-Germaniyah," October 1, 1952, VII-126–876, Machon Lavon.

18. He was born in the Bukovina region of Romania, now in Ukraine.

19. Gila Ramras-Rauch, *Aharon Appelfeld: The Holocaust and Beyond* (Bloomington: Indiana University Press, 1994), 3–12.

20. I draw here on Jeffrey Green's translation. Aharon Appelfeld, *Ad she-ya'aleh amud ha-shaḥar* (Jerusalem: Keter, 1995), 21, 57; Aharon Appelfeld, *Until the Dawn's Light*, trans. Jeffrey M. Green (New York: Schocken Books, 2011), 23, 69.

21. Appelfeld, "Badenhaim, ir nofesh," 103; Appelfeld, *Badenheim 1939*, 148.

22. Yigal Schwartz, *The Zionist Paradox: Hebrew Literature and Israeli Identity*, trans. Michal Sapir (Waltham, MA: Brandeis University Press, 2014), 96; Ramras-Rauch, *Aharon Appelfeld*, 14.

23. In an interview with Philip Roth, Appelfeld reflected on his memories of spa towns from his childhood. In hindsight, he recalls that the resorts were "shockingly petit bourgeois and idiotic in their formalities. Even as a child," he explains, "I saw how ridiculous they were." As quoted in "A Conversation with Philip Roth," in *Beyond Despair: Three Lectures and a Conversation with Philip Roth* (New York: Fromm International, 1994), 66.

24. Ruth Wisse includes the novella in her list of recommended reading in "Literature of the Holocaust [*Shoah, Khurbn*]." Ruth R. Wisse, *The Modern Jewish Canon* (New York: Free Press, 2000), 383.

BIBLIOGRAPHY

Abel, Emily K. *Tuberculosis and the Politics of Exclusion: A History of Public Health and Migration to Los Angeles*. New Brunswick, NJ: Rutgers University Press, 2007.

Abrams, Jeanne. *Blazing the Tuberculosis Trail*. Denver: Colorado Historical Society, 1990.

———. "Chasing the Cure: A History of the Jewish Consumptives' Relief Society of Denver." PhD diss., University of Colorado at Boulder, 1983. ProQuest (Order No. 8408009).

———. *Dr. Charles David Spivak: A Jewish Immigrant and the American Tuberculosis Movement*. Boulder: University Press of Colorado, 2009.

Abramson, Glenda. "Poet of the Dark Gate: The Poetry of David Vogel." *Jewish Book Annual* 50 (1992): 128–42.

———. "Vogel and the City." In *The Russian Jewish Diaspora and European Culture, 1917–1937*, edited by Jörg Schulte, Olga Tabachnikova, and Peter Wagstaff, 37–54. Boston: Brill, 2012.

Adams, James Barton. "A Climate Worshipper." *The Sanatorium* 1, no. 2 (1907): 27.

Adler, Jack. "Therapeutic Group Work with Tuberculosis Displaced Persons." *International Journal of Group Psychotherapy* 3, no. 1 (1953): 302–8.

"Advertisement: Advertise in the Sanatorium." *The Sanatorium* 3, no. 2 (1909): 158.

"Advertisement: $100.00: Four Prizes for Short Stories." *The Sanatorium* 5, no. 1 (1911): 32.

"Advertisement for Denver Sanatorium Benefit Evening on 14 October 1908." *Varhayt*, October 12, 1908.

"Advertisement for Sholem Aleichem Benefit Evening on 15 October 1908." *Varhayt*, October 12, 1908.

"Advertisement for Sholem Aleichem Jubilee Evening." *Der morgn-zhurnal*, December 28, 1908.

Aleksadrov, Kh. "Amerike un Mendeles yubileum (a briv fun Nu-York)." *Der fraynd*, February 12 [25], 1906.

Almog, S. *Zionism and History: The Rise of a New Jewish Consciousness*. New York: St. Martin's Press, 1987.

Alter, Robert. "Fogel and the Forging of the Hebrew Self." *Prooftexts* 13, no. 1 (1993): 2–13.

———. *The Invention of Hebrew Prose: Modern Fiction and the Language of Realism*. Seattle: University of Washington Press, 1988.

"Der alveltlikher kampf gegn shvindzukht." *Der morgn-zhurnal*, September 30, 1908.

Andrews, Malcolm. *Charles Dickens and His Performing Selves: Dickens and the Public Readings*. New York: Oxford University Press, 2006.

Appelfeld, Aharon. *Ad she-ya'aleh amud ha-shaḥar*. Jerusalem: Keter, 1995.

———. "Badenhaim, ir nofesh." In *Shanim ve-sha'ot*, 5–103. Tel Aviv: Ha-Kibuts Ha-Meʾuḥad, 1975.

———. *Badenheim 1939*. Translated by Dalya Bilu. Boston: D. R. Godine, 1980.

———. "A Conversation with Philip Roth." In *Beyond Despair: Three Lectures and a Conversation with Philip Roth*, 59–80. New York: Fromm International, 1994.

———. *Until the Dawn's Light*. Translated by Jeffrey M. Green. New York: Schocken Books, 2011.

Arnon, Yoḥanan. *Uri Tsevi Grinberg: Taḥahnot be-ḥayav*. Tel Aviv: Eked, 1991.

Asch, Sholem. *Ist river: Roman*. New York: Elias Laub, 1946.

Auerbacher, Inge. *Beyond the Yellow Star to America*. Unionville, NY: Royal Fireworks Press, 1995.

Austen, Jane. *Persuasion*. London: J. M. Dent & Sons, 1992.

Avigdori, Z. "Ha-ḥevrah le-milḥamah ba-shaḥefet bi-Yerushalayim." *Do'ar ha-yom*, September 29, 1931.

"Azav ha-yehudi." *Ha-tsevi*, February 19, 1909.

Bailin, Miriam. *The Sickroom in Victorian Fiction: The Art of Being Ill*. Cambridge: Cambridge University Press, 1994.

Bal-Dimyen. "A briv in redaktsiye." *Der fraynd*, September 24 [October 7], 1908.

———. "Sholem-Aleykhem, der folks-shrayber." *Dos naye lebn*, December 1, 1908.

Bal-Makhshoves. "Notitsn fun a kritiker: Sholem-Aleykhem, I." *Der fraynd*, December 19, 1908 [January 1, 1909].

———. "Notitsn fun a kritiker: Sholem-Aleykhem, II(a)." *Der fraynd*, January 23 [February 5], 1909.

———. "Notitsn fun a kritiker: Sholem-Aleykhem, II(b)." *Der fraynd*, January 25 [February 7], 1909.

———. “Notitsn fun a kritiker: Sholem-Aleykhem, III.” *Der fraynd*, February 16 [March 1], 1909.

———. “Sholem Aleichem [A Typology of His Characters] (1908).” *Prooftexts* 6, no. 1 (1986): 7–15.

———. “Sholem Aleykhem.” In *Geklibene shriftn*, 1:91–109. Warsaw: Farlag Sh. Shreberk, 1929.

“Baranovitshi.” *Hed ha-zeman*, August 17, 1908.

Baranovski, Yoram. “Misḥake ahavah ve-mavet.” *Davar*, January 9, 1975, sec. Masa: Musaf le-Davar.

Barnes, David S. *The Making of a Social Disease: Tuberculosis in Nineteenth-Century France*. Berkeley: University of California Press, 1995.

Baron, Dvora. “Be-sof kayits.” In *Parashiyot: Sipurim mekubatsim*, edited by Nurit Govrin and Avner Holtzman, 631–35. Jerusalem: Mosad Bialik, 2000.

———. “Hitparets . . . (reshimah).” In *Parashiyot mukdamot: Sipurim (1902–1921)*, edited by Avner Holtzman, 411–14. Jerusalem: Mosad Bialik, 1988.

Barzilai, Maya. “S. Y. Agnon’s German Consecration and the ‘Miracle’ of Hebrew Letters.” *Prooftexts* 33, no. 1 (2013): 58–75.

Bauer, Yehuda. *Flight and Rescue: Brichah*. New York: Random House, 1970.

Be’er, Ḥaim. “Raḥel: Safiyaḥ.” *Davar*, April 26, 1985, sec. Davar ha-shavu’a.

Ben-Amitai, Levi. “Be-meḥitsat Raḥel (20 shanah le-motah).” *Davar*, April 30, 1951, sec. Davar ha-shavu’a.

Ben-Ishay. “Tsu Yehoash.” *Der yidisher kuryer*, May 9, 1909.

Benjamin, Walter. “The Image of Proust.” In *Illuminations: Essays and Reflections*, edited by Hannah Arendt, translated by Harry Zohn, 201–15. New York: Schocken Books, 1968.

Benshalom, Bentsiyon. *Uri Nisan Genesin: Monografiyah*. Krakow: Miflat, 1934.

Berkowitz, Joel. *Shakespeare on the American Yiddish Stage*. Iowa City: University of Iowa Press, 2002.

Berkowitz, Yitsḥak Dov. *Ha-rishonim ki-vene adam: Sipure zikhronot al Shalom Alekhem u-vene doro*. Tel Aviv: Devir, 1975.

———. “Mit der mishpokhe fun shriftshteler.” In *Dos Sholem-Aleykhem-bukh*, by Sholem Aleichem, edited by Yitsḥak Dov Berkowitz, 153–89. New York: Ikuf, 1958.

———. “Sholem Aleykhems yubileum.” *Der morgn-zhurnal*, November 16, 1908.

———. *Unzere rishonim: Zikhroynes-dertseylungen vegn Sholem-Aleykhem un zayn dor*. 5 vols. Tel Aviv: Menorah, 1966.

Berman, Russell A. “Modernism and the Bildungsroman: Thomas Mann’s *Magic Mountain*.” In *The Cambridge Companion to the Modern German Novel*, edited by Graham Bartram, 77–92. Cambridge: Cambridge University Press, 2004.

Bernstein, Deborah S. *Pioneers and Homemakers: Jewish Women in Pre-state Israel.* Albany: State University of New York, 1992.

"Be-Rusiyah." *Hashkafah,* September 4, 1908.

"Be-Rusiyah." *Ha-tsevi,* November 26, 1908.

"Der bezukh fun 'Yehoash.'" *Der yidisher kuryer,* April 19, 1909. JCRS Records, Box 198, JCRS—Newspaper Clippings, 1909–1912. JCRS Archive.

Bialik, Ḥayim Naḥman. "Al Raḥel." In *Raḥel ve-shiratah: Mivḥar divre zikhronot ve-he'arot,* edited by Mordekhai Snir and Shim'on Kushner, 91. Tel Aviv: Davar, 1971.

———. "Ḥevlei lashon." In *Kol kitve Ḥayim Naḥman Bialik,* 185–90. Tel Aviv: Dvir, 1956.

Bikhovsky, Sh. "Uri Nisan Genesin." In *Ha-tsidah: Kovets zikaron le-A. N. Genesin,* by Uri Nissan Gnessin, 88–95. Jerusalem: Defus Aḥdut, 1913.

Bikhovsky, Z. "Forvort." In *Higeniye bay iden amol un atsind,* by Gershn Levin, 5–6. Warsaw: TOZ, 1925.

Blake, Ben K., dir. *Two Sisters: Tsvey shvester* (1938). Waltham, MA: National Center for Jewish Film, Brandeis University, ca. 2006. DVD, 82 min.

B"N [Re'uven Brainin]. "Tsum yubileum fun Sholem-Aleykhem." *Unzer lebn,* October 12 [25], 1908.

"Board of Trustees Meeting Notes," June 9, 1909. JCRS Records, Box 298. JCRS Archive.

[Boreysho], Menakhem. "S. Nadson (tsu zayn 25-tn yortsayt)." *Haynt,* January 31, 1912.

Bosch, Meindert. *Bridges across the Years: The Ninety-Year History of the Bethesda Hospital Association of Denver, Colorado.* Denver: Bethesda PsychHealth System, 1988.

Bourdieu, Pierre. *The Field of Cultural Production: Essays on Art and Literature.* Edited by Randal Johnson. New York: Columbia University Press, 1993.

———. "The Forms of Capital." In *Handbook of Theory and Research for the Sociology of Education,* edited by John G. Richardson, 241–58. New York: Greenwood Press, 1996.

Brainin, Re'uven. *Perets ben Mosheh Smolenskin: Ḥayav u-sefarav.* Warsaw: Tushiyah, 1896.

Brainin, Re'uven, and *Der veg.* "Letter to Sholem Aleichem," Erev Yom Kippur 1908. Box 11, Folder lamed-vov 31/1. Beth Shalom Aleichem Archive.

Brenner, Naomi Rebecca. "Authorial Fictions: Literary and Public Personas in Modern Hebrew and Yiddish Literature." PhD diss., University of California, Berkeley, 2008. ProQuest (Order No. AAT3331524).

———. "Slippery Selves: Rachel Bluvstein and Anna Margolin in Poetry and Public." *Nashim* 19 (2010): 100–133.

Brenner, Yosef Ḥayim. *Shekhol ve-kishalon.* Tel Aviv: Ha-Kibuts Ha-Me'uhad, 2006.

Brock, Thomas D. *Robert Koch: A Life in Medicine and Bacteriology*. Madison, WI: Science Tech Publishers, 1988.

Broides, Avraham. "Be-meḥitsatah." In *Raḥel ve-shiratah: Mivḥar divre zikhronot ve-he'arot*, edited by Mordekhai Snir and Shim'on Kushner, 101–3. Tel Aviv: Davar, 1971.

———. "Raḥel (sheloshim shanah le-motah)." *Ha-po'el ha-tsa'ir* 54, no. 30 (1961): 20.

Burgess, Thomas Henry. *Climate of Italy in Relation to Pulmonary Consumption with Remarks on the Influence of Foreign Climates upon Invalids*. London: Longman, Brown, Green & Longmans, 1852.

Buzelin, Hélène. "Unexpected Allies: How Latour's Network Theory Could Complement Bourdieusian Analyses in Translation Studies." *The Translator* 11, no. 2 (2005): 193–218.

Byrne, Katherine. *Tuberculosis and the Victorian Literary Imagination*. New York: Cambridge University Press, 2011.

Byron, George. "Di gazel." Translated by Yehoash. *Di yudishe bibliotek* 2 (1891): 203.

Callon, Michel. "Some Elements of Translation: Domestication of the Scallops and the Fisherman of St. Brieuc Bay." In *Power, Action and Belief: A New Sociology of Knowledge*, edited by John Law, 196–223. Boston: Routledge & Kegan Paul, 1986.

Cammy, Justin. "Judging *The Judgment of Shomer*: Jewish Literature versus Jewish Reading." In *Arguing the Modern Jewish Canon: Essays on Literature and Culture in Honor of Ruth R. Wisse*, edited by Justin Cammy, Dara Horn, Alyssa Quint, and Rachel Rubinstein, 85–128. Cambridge, MA: Harvard University Press, 2008.

Carlebach, Elisheva. *Palaces of Time: Jewish Calendar and Culture in Early Modern Europe*. Cambridge, MA: The Belknap Press of Harvard University Press, 2011.

Carter, Richard. "Anton P. Chekhov, MD (1860–1904): Dual Medical and Literary Careers." *Annals of Thoracic Surgery* 61, no. 5 (1996): 1557–63.

Casanova, Pascale. *The World Republic of Letters*. Cambridge, MA: Harvard University Press, 2004.

Centers for Disease Control and Prevention. "Tuberculosis (TB)." Accessed December 26, 2014. http://www.cdc.gov/tb/.

Chametzky, Jules, John Felstiner, Hilene Flanzbaum, and Kathryn Hellerstein, eds. *Jewish American Literature: A Norton Anthology*. New York: W. W. Norton, 2001.

Charney, Daniel. *Bargaroyf: Bletlekh fun a lebn*. Warsaw: Literarishe Bleter, 1934.

———. "Fun Eyrope keyn Elis Aylend un tsurik (Part 1)." *Der tog*, November 15, 1925.

———. "Fun Eyrope keyn Elis Aylend un tsurik (Part 2)." *Der tog*, November 22, 1925.

———. "Fun Eyrope keyn Elis Aylend un tsurik (Part 3)." *Der tog*, November 29, 1925.

———. "Fun Eyrope keyn Elis Aylend un tsurik (Part 4)." *Der tog*, December 6, 1925.

———. "Fun Eyrope keyn Elis Aylend un tsurik (Part 5)." *Der tog*, December 14, 1925.

———. "Fun Eyrope keyn Elis Aylend un tsurik (Part 6)." *Der tog*, December 21, 1925.

———. "Ikh shpil a 'zeks un zekhtsik' mit Sholem-Aleykhemen." In *Di velt iz kaylekhdik*, 248–52. New York: CYCO-Bikher Farlag, 1963.

———. "Ikh zing tsu aykh fun der Liberti-Sanatoriye." *Der fraynd* 3, no. 3 (June 1946): 14.

———. "Letter to H. Leivick," September 21, 1932. RG 315, Box 29, Folder 54. YIVO.

———. *Oyfn shvel fun yener velt: Tipn, bilder, epizodn*. New York: n.p., 1947.

———. "Reshime fun shrayber un klal-tuer, vos hobn mikh bazukht in sanatoriye far di 2 yor 1948–1949," n.d. RG 421, Box 23, Folder 285. YIVO.

———. "Tsum toyt." In *Oyfn shvel fun yener velt: Tipn, bilder, epizodn*, 184. New York: n.p., 1947.

"A Chat with the Publisher." *The Sanatorium* 2, no. 3 (1908): 189.

"Chicago Honors Yehoash." *The Sanatorium* 3, no. 4 (1909): 230–32.

"Clippings pertaining to 1932 Leivick Affair." JCRS File 9698, Patient Record Halpern Leivick. JCRS Archive.

Cohen, Israel. "Cedars of Lebanon: Sholem Aleichem in Sickness." *Commentary*, October 1950, 379–83.

———. "Shalom Aleichem: Letter from Israel Cohen." *Jewish Chronicle*, November 20, 1908.

———. "To the Editor of the *Jewish Chronicle*." *Jewish Chronicle*, November 27, 1908.

Committee on Press and Propaganda. "Editorial." *The Sanatorium* 1, no. 1 (1907): 3–4.

"Contract between Lidski and Marinoff." New York, October 17, 1909. Box 11, Folder lamed-lamed 46/13. Beth Shalom Aleichem Archive.

"Cough Drops." *The Sanatorium* 1, no. 3 (May 1907): 67.

Damesek, Shlomo. *Be-gorali*. New York: Hotsa'at Bitsaron, 1945.

Dauber, Jeremy. *The Worlds of Sholem Aleichem*. New York: Nextbook & Schocken Books, 2013.

David, Michael Zdenek. "The White Plague in the Red Capital: The Control of Tuberculosis in Russia, 1900–1941." PhD diss., University of Chicago, 2007. ProQuest/UMI (Publication No. 3287026).

Davidit, Rivkah. "Ba-me'uḥar." In *Raḥel ve-shiratah: Mivḥar divre zikhronot ve-he'arot*, edited by Mordekhai Snir and Shim'on Kushner, 42–46. Tel Aviv: Davar, 1971.

Davis, Charles T. "Paul Laurence Dunbar." In *Black Is the Color of the Cosmos: Essays on Afro-American Literature and Culture, 1942–1981*, edited by Henry Louis Gates, 121–65. New York: Garland Publishers, 1982.

Dayan, Shmu'el. "Im Raḥel ba-Kineret." *Davar*, April 24, 1936.

Denbi. "Eli'ezer Ben-Yehudah." *Do'ar Ha-yom*, December 26, 1922.

Denison, Charles. *Rocky Mountain Health Resorts: An Analytical Study of High Altitudes in Relation to the Arrest of Chronic Pulmonary Disease*. Boston: Houghton, Osgood, 1880.

Dinezon, Yankev. "A briv in redaktsiye." *Unzer lebn*, September 11, 1908.

———. "Letter to Sholem Aleichem," March 28, 1908. Box 10, Folder lamed-dalet 10/62. Beth Shalom Aleichem Archive.

———. "Letter to Sholem Aleichem," August 12, 1908. Box 10, Folder lamed-dalet 10/52. Beth Shalom Aleichem Archive.

———. "Letter to Sholem Aleichem," August 21, 1908. Box 10, Folder lamed-dalet 10/52. Beth Shalom Aleichem Archive.

———. "Letter to Sholem Aleichem," October 9, 1908. Box 10, Folder lamed-dalet 10/54. Beth Shalom Aleichem Archive.

———. "Letter to Sholem Aleichem," May 4, 1909. Box 10, Folder lamed-dalet 10/63. Beth Shalom Aleichem Archive.

———. "Letter to Sholem Aleichem," May 17, 1909. Box 10, Folder lamed-dalet 10/64. Beth Shalom Aleichem Archive.

Dolitzky, M. M. "Eyn apil far Denver." *Yidishes tageblat*, March 2, 1906. JCRS Records, Box 197, JCRS—Newspaper Clippings, 1904–1906. JCRS Archive.

———. "Fun dem lebedikn beys-oylem." *Yidishes tageblat*, February 27, 1906.

———. "In di Roki Berg." *Zunland*, June 1925, 19–20.

———. "Payks Pik." *Zunland*, July 1925, 14–15.

Dolzhinski, Tamar. "Al shireha ha-rusi'im." *Davar*, April 11, 1937.

Dormandy, Thomas. *The White Death: A History of Tuberculosis*. London: Hambledon Press, 1999.

Dubnow, Simon. "Letter to S. Rabinovitsh," November 24, 1908. Box 10, Folder lamed-dalet 7/19. Beth Shalom Aleichem Archive.

Dubos, René J., and Jean Dubos. *The White Plague: Tuberculosis, Man, and Society*. New Brunswick, NJ: Rutgers University Press, 1996.

Dworkin, Evlin Yehoash. "My Father Yehoash." In *Poems of Yehoash*, by Yehoash, 11–15. London, Ontario, Canada: Canadian Yehoash Committee, 1952.

Ebstein, Erich. *Tuberkulose als Schicksal: Eine Sammlung pathographischer Skizzen von Calvin bis Klabund, 1509–1928*. Stuttgart: Ferdinand Enke Verlag, 1932.

Edelshtat, David. "Mayn tsevoe." In *Shriftn*, 230. New York: Arbayter Fraynd, Fraye Arbeyter Shtime, 1925.

"Editorial: Leon Kobrin's Drama." *The Sanatorium* 2, no. 3 (1908): 130.

"Editorial: The Consumptive in Literature." *The Sanatorium* 5, no. 1 (1911): 3–4.

Editors of *Hatikvah*. "Literary and Dramatic Activities of Patients." *Hatikvah* 4, no. 3 (1926): 9.

Edlin, V. "Tolstoy iber kunst." *Der amerikaner*, September 18, 1908.

Efron, John M. *Defenders of the Race: Jewish Doctors and Race Science in Fin-de-Siècle Europe*. New Haven, CT: Yale University Press, 1994.

———. *Medicine and the German Jews: A History*. New Haven, CT: Yale University Press, 2001.

"Endlikh a monument tsu ere fun Dovid Edelshtat." *Fraye arbayter shtime*, December 18, 1915.

Epelberg, H. "A yontef vokh: Tsu Sholem Aleykhems 25 yorikn yubileum." *Teatr velt* 3 (October 16, 1908): 4.

Epstein, Lisa Rae. "Caring for the Soul's House: The Jews of Russia and Health Care, 1860–1914." PhD diss., Yale University, 1995. ProQuest/UMI (Publication No. AAT9615222).

Eran, Mordekhai, and Ya'akov Shavit. "'Tanakh yehudi be-germanit': Tirgum ha-tana'kh le-germanit al-yade Shim'on Bernfeld (1903): Ben meḥkar 'kofer' le-tirgum 'shomrani.'" *Bet mikra* 54, no. 2 (2008): 121–52.

"Der ershter Sholem-Aleykhem ovnt in Lodzh." *Lodzher tageblat*, May 29 [June 11], 1908.

Eshel, Amir, and Na'ama Rokem. "German and Hebrew: Histories of a Conversation." *Prooftexts* 33, no. 1 (2013): 1–8.

Fassin, Didier. "Another Politics of Life Is Possible." *Theory, Culture & Society* 26 (2009): 44–60.

———. "Ethics of Survival: A Democratic Approach to the Politics of Life." *Humanity: An International Journal of Human Rights, Humanitarianism, and Development* 1, no. 1 (2010): 81–95.

Foucault, Michel. "Des espaces autres: Hétérotopies." *Architecture, Mouvement, Continuité* 5 (1984): 46–49.

Fox, Chaim Leib. "Shiye Tenenboym." In *Leksikon fun der nayer yidisher literatur*, 4:98–99. New York: Congress for Jewish Culture, 1961.

———. "Yehoash." In *Leksikon fun der nayer yidisher literatur*, 4:233–44. New York: Congress for Jewish Culture, 1961.

Frawley, Maria H. *Invalidism and Identity in Nineteenth-Century Britain*. Chicago: University of Chicago Press, 2004.

Frieden, Ken. *Classic Yiddish Fiction: Abramovitsh, Sholem Aleichem, and Peretz*. Albany: State University of New York Press, 1995.

Frug, Sh. "Der royter gelekhter." *Der fraynd*, September 4 [17], 1908.

———. "Der royter gelekhter." *Haynt*, September 7 [20], 1908.

———. "Der royter gelekhter." *Der arbayter*, October 10, 1908.

"Fun der letster minut: Afn mayontik far Sholem-Aleykhem." *Haynt*, October 16 [29], 1908.
"Fun der letster minut: Graf Tolstoys yubiley." *Haynt*, August 26 [September 8], 1908.
"Fun der letster minut: Tsum Sholem-Aleykhem yubileum. *Haynt*, October 14 [27], 1908.
"Fun varshever lebn: Sholem-Aleykhem in Varshe." *Unzer lebn*, May 18 [31], 1908.
"Fun varshever lebn: Yudishes." *Unzer lebn*, May 30 [June 12], 1908.
Galbreath, Thomas Crawford. *Chasing the Cure*. Denver: Thomas Crawford Galbreath, 1908.
"Gantse velt git koved Tolstoyen." *Varhayt*, September 11, 1908.
Gelm, Yankl. "Tolstoys yubileum un di rusishe regirung." *Der amerikaner*, September 18, 1908.
Genette, Gérard. *Paratexts: Thresholds of Interpretation*. Translated by Jane E. Lewin. Cambridge: Cambridge University Press, 1997.
Gertz, Nurith. *Yam beni le-venekh*. Or Yehudah: Devir, 2015.
Gertz-Ronen, Merav. *Me'ah shanah le-vet ha-ḥolim bi-Tsefat, 1910–2010*. Zichron-Ya'akov: Itay Bahur, 2010.
Gilad, Asher. "Ha-rof'im: Raḥel u-maḥalat ha-sofrim (shaḥefet)." *Alon* 7 (June 2013): 16–19.
Gilman, Ernest. *Yiddish Poetry and the Tuberculosis Sanatorium, 1900–1970*. Syracuse, NY: Syracuse University Press, 2015.
Gilman, Sander L. *Franz Kafka: The Jewish Patient*. New York: Routledge, 1995.
———. *The Jew's Body*. New York: Routledge, 1991.
Glaser, Amelia. *Jews and Ukrainians in Russia's Literary Borderlands: From the Shtetl Fair to the Petersburg Bookshop*. Evanston, IL: Northwestern University Press, 2012.
Glatshteyn, Yankev. "Tsuriktrakhtungen." In *Gezangen fun rekhts tsu links*, 9–18. New York: Bikher Farlag, 1971.
Gluzman, Michael. *Ha-guf ha-tsiyoni: Le'umiyut, migdar u-miniyut ba-sifrut ha-ivrit ha-ḥadashah*. Tel Aviv: Ha-Kibuts Ha-Me'uḥad, 2007.
———. *The Politics of Canonicity: Lines of Resistance in Modernist Hebrew Poetry*. Stanford, CA: Stanford University Press, 2003.
———. "Unmasking the Politics of Simplicity in Modernist Hebrew Poetry: Rereading David Fogel." *Prooftexts* 13, no. 1 (1993): 21–41.
Gnessin, Uri Nissan. *Etsel*. Tel Aviv: Yaḥdav, 1965.
Goethe, Johann Wolfgang von. *Wilhelm Meister's Apprenticeship*. In *Goethe: The Collected Works*, vol. 9, edited and translated by Eric A. Blackall. New York: Suhrkamp Publishers, 1983.
Gogol, Nikolai Vasilevich. "Dead Souls." In *Dead Souls: The Reavey Translation, Backgrounds and Sources, Essays in Criticism*, translated by George Reavey, 1–408. New York: W. W. Norton, 1985.

Goldberg, Marie Waife. *My Father, Sholom Aleichem*. New York: Simon & Schuster, 1968.
Goldman, Emma. *Living My Life*. 2 vols. New York: Alfred A. Knopf, 1931.
Goldsmit, Dr. "Memorandum on the Question of Emigrants' Suffering from Tuberculosis with Recommendations for Treatment and Segregation by Dr. Goldsmit," June 1919. Z441685-lt. The Central Zionist Archives.
Gordin, Jacob. "A briv fun Her Yankev Gordin." *The Sanatorium* 2, no. 4 (1908): 224.
Goren, Shiri. "Writing on the Verge of Catastrophe: David Vogel's Last Work of Prose." In *Choosing Yiddish: New Frontiers of Language and Culture*, edited by Lara Rabinovich, Shiri Goren, and Hannah S. Pressman, 29–45. Detroit, MI: Wayne State University Press, 2013.
Gotlieb, M. *Zayt gezund*. Warsaw: Tsukermans Folksbibliotek, 1899–1900.
Govrin, Nurit. *Ha-maḥatsit ha-rishonah: Dvora Baron—ḥayeha vi-yetsiratah (648–683)*. Jerusalem: Mosad Bialik, 1988.
"Graf Tolstoy baym shtarbn." *Der morgn-zhurnal*, August 27, 1908.
"Graf Tolstoy: Tsu zayn akhtsikn yubileum." *Der arbayter*, September 5, 1908.
"The Greatest Death Rate." *The Sanatorium* 1, no. 2 (1907): 30.
Greenblatt, Stephen. *Renaissance Self-Fashioning: From More to Shakespeare*. Chicago: University of Chicago Press, 2005.
"Groyser Oylem bay'm Sholem Aleykhem ovent." *Der morgn-zhurnal*, December 29, 1908.
Guide to the Papers of Hugo Knoepfmacher (1890–1980), 1865–1979, AR7172. Leo Baeck Institute. Accessed October 30, 2014. http://digifindingaids.cjh.org/?pID=256143.
"Gzeyres af Tolstoy." *Varhayt*, August 5, 1908.
Ḥabas, Brakhah. "Pegishah." In *Raḥel ve-shiratah: Mivḥar divre zikhronot ve-he'arot*, edited by Mordekhai Snir and Shim'on Kushner, 56–57. Tel Aviv: Davar, 1971.
———. "Sirtutim li-dmutah." In *Raḥel ve-shiratah: Mivḥar divre zikhronot ve-he'arot*, edited by Mordekhai Snir and Shim'on Kushner, 54–55. Tel Aviv: Davar, 1971.
HaCohen, Ruth. "Sounds of Revelation: Aesthetic-Political Theology in Schoenberg's Moses and Aron." *Modernist Cultures* 1, no. 2 (2005): 110–40.
"Ha-ligah le-milḥamah ba-shaḥefet." *Davar*, October 10, 1930.
"Halpern Leivick Patient Record," n.d. File 9698. JCRS Archive.
Harari, Dror. "Performing the Un-chosen Israeli Body: Nataly Zukerman's *Haguf Ha'acher*." *TDR: The Drama Review* 60, no. 1 (2016): 157–64.
Harkavy, Alexander. "Shmelke." In *Yiddish-English-Hebrew Dictionary*. New Haven, CT: Yale University Press in Cooperation with YIVO Institute for Jewish Research, 2006.
Harshav, Benjamin. *Language in Time of Revolution*. Berkeley: University of California Press, 1993.

Hart, Mitchell Bryan. *The Healthy Jew: The Symbiosis of Judaism and Modern Medicine.* New York: Cambridge University Press, 2007.

Hausmann, Raphael. *Die Weintraubenkur: Mit Rücksicht auf Erfahrungen in Meran.* Meran: Fridolin Plant, 1905.

"Hegyone ha-magid." *Ha-magid* 30, no. 7 (1886): 51–52.

Hehl, Joh., ed. "Die Weinflasche." In *Blüthen der Musen für das Jahr 1816*, 14. Vienna: Jos. Riedl, 1816.

Hekkanen, Raila. "Fields, Networks and Finnish Prose: A Comparison of Bourdieusian Field Theory and Actor-Network Theory in Translation Sociology." In *Selected Papers of the CETRA Research Seminar in Translation Studies*, edited by Dries De Crom, 2009.

"Help Needed for 'Shalom Aleichem.'" *Jewish Chronicle*, September 25, 1908.

Henry, Barbara. *Rewriting Russia: Jacob Gordin's Yiddish Drama.* Seattle: University of Washington Press, 2011.

Herndl, Diane Price. *Invalid Women: Figuring Feminine Illness in American Fiction and Culture, 1840–1940.* Chapel Hill: University of North Carolina Press, 1993.

Hertz, Deborah Sadie. *Jewish High Society in Old Regime Berlin.* Syracuse, NY: Syracuse University Press, 2005.

Hillkowitz, Phillip, and C. D. Spivak, eds. "*The Sanatorium*: Index to Vol. I–Vol. V." In *The Sanatorium Vol. I–Vol. V: 1907–1911.* Denver, CO: n.p., 1911.

"Ḥogege-ha-yovelim shelanu." *Hed ha-zeman*, November 5, 1908.

Holtzman, Avner. "Mordekhai Tsevi Maneh: Meshorer ve-tsayar." In *Melekhet maḥashevet, teḥiyat ha-umah: Ha-sifrut ha-ivrit le-nokhaḥ ha-omanut ha-plastit*, 93–116. Tel Aviv: Zemorah Bitan, 1999.

Horowitz, Brian. *Jewish Philanthropy and Enlightenment in Late-Tsarist Russia.* Seattle: University of Washington Press, 2009.

Howe, Irving. *World of Our Fathers: The Journey of the East European Jews to America and the Life They Found and Made.* New York: Simon & Schuster, 1976.

Ig-Faktorit, Itah. "Raḥel ke-demut meḥanekhet." In *Raḥel ve-shiratah: Mivḥar divre zikhronot ve-he'arot*, edited by Mordekhai Snir and Shim'on Kushner, 60–63. Tel Aviv: Davar, 1971.

"The Jehoash Meeting in Philadelphia." *The Sanatorium* 2, no. 6 (1908): 286–87.

"The Jehoash Tour." *The Sanatorium* 3, no. 1 (1909): 20–22.

"Jewish Consumptives' Relief Society Dedicates Three Tents." *Colorado Medical Journal* 11 (1905): 434.

"Jewish Poet Is Guest at Sanitarium Benefit." *Chicago Record*, May 10, 1909.

Jones, Billy Mac. *Health-Seekers in the Southwest, 1817–1900.* Norman: University of Oklahoma Press, 1967.

Jurecic, Ann. *Illness as Narrative.* Pittsburgh: University of Pittsburgh Press, 2012.

Kafka, Franz. *Letters to Ottla and the Family*. Edited by Nahum N. Glatzer. Translated by Richard and Clara Winston. New York: Schocken Books, 1982.

Kants, Shimen. "Di geshikhte fun alt-un nay Otvotsk." In *Yizker-bukh tsu fareybiken dem ondenk fun di khorev-gevorene yidishe kehiles Otvotsk, Kartshev*, 70–92. Tel Aviv: Irgun Yotse Otvotsk Be-Yisra'el, 1968.

Kaplan, Marion A. *The Making of the Jewish Middle Class: Women, Family, and Identity in Imperial Germany*. New York: Oxford University Press, 1991.

Katz, Stephen. *Red, Black, and Jew: New Frontiers in Hebrew Literature*. Austin: University of Texas Press, 2009.

Kauver, C. Hillel. "A Plea for the Consumptive." *The Sanatorium* 1, no. 1 (1907): 8.

Keats, John. "Ode to a Nightingale." In *Poems of John Keats*, 2:79–82. London: Lawrence & Bullen, 1896.

Kellman, Ellen D. "Sholem Aleichem's Funeral (New York, 1916): The Making of a National Pageant." *YIVO Annual* 20 (1991): 277–304.

Keshet, Yeshurun. "Rishme masa be-Eyrope." *Ha-do'ar* 39 (October 13, 1967): 738–40.

Khassis, Yaacov. *Shaḥefet be-Yisra'el: Uvdot, netunim u-megamot*. Tel Aviv: Merkaz Ha-Ligah La-Milḥamah Ba-Shaḥefet Uve-Maḥalot Re'ah Be-Yisra'el, 1964.

"Khronik: Sholem-Aleykhems yubileum." *Teatr velt* 3 (October 16, 1908): 9–10.

"Khronikah ha-ir." *Hed ha-zeman*, November 10, 1908.

"Khronikah ivrit." *Hed ha-zeman*, November 8, 1908.

"Khronikah mekomit." *Hed ha-zeman*, November 10, 1908.

Klabund. *Die Krankheit*. Edited by Christian V. Zimmerman. Vol. 2, *Werke in Acht Bänden*. Heidelbern: Elfenbeing Verlag, 1999. http://gutenberg.spiegel.de/buch/die-krankheit-2549/1.

Klausner, Joseph. "Mordekhai Tsevi Mane." In *Yotsrim u-vonim: Ma'amre bikoret*, vol. 1. Tel Aviv: Devir, 1925.

Kleynman, Moyshe. "Di vokh fun Mendele Moykher Sforim: Der zeyde zol lebn, I." *Gut morgn*, December 22, 1910.

———. "Di vokh fun Mendele Moykher Sforim: Der zeyde zol lebn, II." *Gut morgn*, December 23, 1910.

———. "Di vokh fun Mendele Moykher Sforim: Der zeyde zol lebn, III." *Gut morgn*, December 24, 1908.

———. "Di vokh fun Mendele Moykher Sforim: Der zeyde zol lebn, IV." *Gut morgn*, December 26, 1908.

Knöpfmacher, Hugo. "Der hebräische Dichter David Vogel." *Jüddische Rundschau*, December 11, 1925, 811.

Kobrin, Leon. "Di retung." *The Sanatorium* 2, no. 3 (1908): 173–86.

———. "The Rescue: A Drama, Part I." *The Sanatorium* 2, no. 5 (1908): 247–50.

———. "The Rescue: A Drama, Part 2." *The Sanatorium* 2, no. 6 (1908): 298–302.

Koch, Robert. "Aetiology of Tuberculosis." Translated by Rev. F. Sause. In *From Consumption to Tuberculosis: A Documentary History*, edited by Barbara Gutmann Rosenkrantz, 197–224. New York: Garland Publishing, 1993.

Komem, Aharon. *Ha-ofel veha-pele: Iyunim bi-yetsirato shel David Fogel.* Haifa: Universitet Ḥefah & Zemorah-Bitan, 2001.

Kovner, Abba. *Slon Ketering: Po'emah.* Tel Aviv: Ha-Kibuts Ha-Me'uḥad, 1987.

"Di Krankhayt fun L. Tolstoy." *Haynt*, August 15 [28], 1908.

Kraut, Alan M. *Silent Travelers: Germs, Genes, and the "Immigrant Menace."* New York: Basic Books, 1994.

Kritz, Ori. *The Poetics of Anarchy: David Edelshtat's Revolutionary Poetry.* New York: Peter Lang, 1997.

Kronfeld, Chana. "Fogel and Modernism: A Liminal Moment in Hebrew Literary History." *Prooftexts* 13, no. 1 (1993): 45–63.

———. *On the Margins of Modernism: Decentering Literary Dynamics.* Berkeley: University of California Press, 1996.

Kung, Szu-Wen Cindy. "Translation Agents and Networks, with Reference to the Translation of Contemporary Taiwanese Novels." In *Translation Research Projects 2*, edited by Anthony Pym and Alexander Perekrestenko, 123–38. Tarragona, Spain: Intercultural Studies Group, 2009.

Laor, Dan. "Le-an huvelu ha-otsrim? Al ha-perek he-ḥaser bakhronikat ha-milḥamah shel David Fogel." In *Mimerkazim la-merkaz: Sefer Nurit Govrin*, edited by Avner Holtzman, Mikhal Oron, and Zivah Shamir, 385–411. Tel Aviv: Mekhon Kats Le-Ḥeker Ha-Sifrut Ha-Ivrit, Bet Ha-Sefer Le-Mada'e Ha-Yahadut al Shem Ḥayim Rozenberg, Universitat Tel-Aviv, 2005.

Lapid, Arnon. "Ba-layla ba ha-mevaser." *Ha-Daf ha-yarok*, August 27, 1985. Folder: Raḥel. Degania Archive.

Lapid, Shulamit. "Taglit sifrutit-historit: Sefer yelado shel ha-meshoreret Raḥel nimtsa va-yetse la-or aḥare 43 shanot shivḥah u-genizah." *Ma'ariv*, June 7, 1974.

Latour, Bruno. *Pandora's Hope: Essays on the Reality of Science Studies.* Cambridge, MA: Harvard University Press, 1999.

———. *Politics of Nature: How to Bring the Sciences into Democracy.* Cambridge, MA: Harvard University Press, 2004.

———. *Reassembling the Social: An Introduction to Actor-Network Theory.* Oxford: Oxford University Press, 2007.

Latour, Bruno, and Steve Woolgar. *Laboratory Life: The Construction of Scientific Facts.* Princeton, NJ: Princeton University Press, 1986.

Lawlor, Clark. *Consumption and Literature: The Making of the Romantic Disease.* New York: Palgrave Macmillan, 2006.

Lazar, Izidor. "Kinstler un verk: Tolstoy in poeziye un filosofiye." *Roman-tsaytung* 32 (September 4 [17], 1908): 1059–66.

———. "Sholem-Aleykhems 25 yoriker yubileum." *Lodzher tageblat*, October 10 [23], 1908.
"Le-ḥag yovelo shel Shalom Alekhem." *Hed ha-zeman*, October 22, 1908.
Leivick, H. "Di balade fun Denver Sanatoriyum." *Tsukunft* 40, no. 3 (1935): 131–34.
———. "Di balade fun Denver Sanatoriyum." In *Lider fun gan eyden: 1932–1936*, 121–39. Chicago: Farlag Tseshinksi, 1937.
———. "Februar in Liberti." In *Lider fun gan eyden: 1932–1936*, 150–52. Chicago: Farlag Tseshinski, 1937.
———. "Letter to Daniel and Samuel Leivick," November 4, 1932. RG 315, Folder 32. YIVO.
———. "Letter to Sarah Leivick," January 30, 1933. RG 315, Folder 32. YIVO.
———. "Letters from Denver Sanatorium," n.d. RG 315, Folder 74. YIVO.
———. "Letters to Wife and Children," n.d. RG 315, Folder 32. YIVO.
———. *Lider fun gan eyden: 1932–1936*. Chicago: Farlag Tseshinksi, 1937.
———. *Mit der sheyres hapleyte*. New York: H. Leyvik Yubiley-Komitet durkhn Tsiko-Farlag, 1947.
———. "Shpinoze." In *Lider fun gan eyden: 1932–1936*, 101–11. Chicago: Farlag Tseshinski, 1937.
———. "Volkns ahintern vald." In *Lider*, 292–300. New York: Farlag "Fraynt," 1932.
"Le-matsavo Shel Shalom Alekhem." *Ha-tsevi*, November 12, 1909.
Leonard, O. "News and View." *Star*, April 30, 1909. JCRS Records, Box 198, JCRS—Newspaper Clippings, 1909–1912. JCRS Archive.
"Leo Tolstoy: Zayn lebn, shriftn un tetikayten (tsum hayntikn yubileum)." *Varhayt*, September 10, 1908.
Levi, Nisim. *Peraḳim be-toldot ha-refu'ah be-Erets-Yisra'el, 1799–1948*. Tel Aviv: Ha-Kibuts Ha-Me'uḥad; Ha-Fakultah Li-Refu'ah al Shem Barukh Rapoport, Ha-Tekhniyon, 1998.
Levin, Gershn. "Der kamf mit der shvindzukht." *Haynt*, February 20 [March 5], 1909.
———. *Higeniye bay iden: Amol un atsind*. Warsaw: TOZ, 1925.
———. *Lungen-shvindukht iz heylbar!* Warsaw: TOZ, 1925.
———. "Mayne zikhroynes vegn Sholem-Aleykhem." In *Dos Sholem-Aleykhem-bukh*, edited by Yitsḥak Dov Berkowitz, 259–82. New York: Ikuf, 1958.
———. "Sholem-Aleykhems krankhayt un zayn 25-yeriker yoyvl: Fun der seriye, 'Varshe far der milkhome.'" *Haynt*, September 11, 1938.
———. "Sholem-Aleykhem un der toyt." *Haynt*, April 23, 1926.
———. "Tsu Sholem-Aleykhems yubileum." *Haynt*, September 10 [23], 1908.
Levin, Gershn, and Avrom Podlishevski. "Tsu Sholem-Aleykhems fererer." *Unzer lebn*, September 26 [October 9], 1908.
———. "Tsu Sholem-Aleykhems fererer." *Haynt*, September 25 [October 8], 1908.

Lidski, Yankev. "Accounts and Sales Records from Lidski to Sholem Aleichem," April 1909–September 1910. Box 11, Folder lamed-lamed 46/5, 6, 7, 9, 10, 15, 16, 17, 18, 19, 20, 21. Beth Shalom Aleichem Archive.

———. "Letter to Sholem Aleichem," August 19, 1909. Box 11, Folder lamed-lamed 46/11. Beth Shalom Aleichem Archive.

———. "Letter to Sholem Aleichem," October 24, 1909. Box 11, Folder lamed-lamed 46/14. Beth Shalom Aleichem Archive.

Lieblich, Amia. *Rekamot: Siḥotai im Dvora Baron.* Jerusalem: Shoken, 1991.

Ligah le-Milḥamah ba-Shaḥefet uve-Maḥalot Re'ah be-Yisra'el. *Yedi'ot ha-ligah le-milḥamah ba-shaḥefet be-Yisra'el.* Tel Aviv: Ha-Ligah Le-Milḥamah Ba-Shaḥefet Uve-Maḥalot Re'ah Be-Yisra'el, 1958.

"List of Subscriptions and Donations for 1908." *The Sanatorium* 3, no. 2 (1909): 127, 133.

"Literatur un kunst: Dem 11tn Oktober." *D"r Birnboyms vokhenblat.* September 18, 1908.

Livingston, John. "Editor's Note." *Rocky Mountain Jewish Historical Notes*, Summer/Fall 1989, 1–2.

"Liyev Tolstoy." *D"r Birnboyms vokhenblat*, September 13, 1908.

"Liyev Tolstoy 80 yor alt." *Fraye arbayter shtime*, August 29, 1908.

"Lodzher kronik: Sholem-Aleykhem in Lodzh." *Lodzher tageblat*, May 18 [31], 1908.

"Lodzher kronik: Tsum Sholem-Aleykhem." *Lodzher tageblat*, May 26 [June 8], 1908.

Longfellow, Henry Wadsworth. *Dos lid fun Hayavata.* Translated by Yehoash. New York: Ferlag Yehoash, 1910.

Ludwig, Reuben. "Indiyaner motivn." In *Gezamelte lider*, 68–75. New York: Y. L. Perets Shrayber-Farayn, 1927.

Luria, Yoysef. "Sholem Yankev Abramovitsh." *Dos yudishe folk*, December 25, 1906.

Luscombe, Richard. "Florida Closes Only Tuberculosis Hospital amid Worst US Outbreak in 20 Years." *The Guardian*, July 9, 2012, US edition. http://www.theguardian.com/world/2012/jul/09/florida-closes-tuberculosis-hospital-outbreak?newsfeed=true.

Malcolm, Janet. *Reading Chekhov: A Critical Journey.* New York: Random House, 2001.

Mandelberg, Avigdor. "Ha-shaḥefet ve-ha-po'alim (le-yom ha-peraḥ)." *Davar*, April 20, 1927.

———. *Me-ḥayai: Pirḳe zikhronot.* Tel Aviv: Yedidim, 1942.

Mane, Mordecai Zevi. "Badad bi-me'oni." In *Kol kitve Mordekhai Tsevi Maneh: Kovets shirav ma'amarav u-mikhtavav*, 122–23. Warsaw: Tushiyah, 1897.

———. "Letter to Koyfman 18 Av 1886 (#146)." In *Kol kitve Mordekhai Tsevi Maneh: Kovets shirav ma'amarav u-mikhtavav*, 222–23. Warsaw: Tushiyah, 1897.

———. "Letter to Parents 8 Iyar 1886 (#144)." In *Kol kitve Mordekhai Tsevi Maneh: Kovets shirav ma'amarav u-mikhtavav*. Warsaw: Tushiyah, 1897.

———. "Masa'at nafshi." In *Kol kitve Mordekhai Tsevi Maneh: Kovets shirav ma'amarav u-mikhtavav*, 147–50. Warsaw: Tushiyah, 1897.

Mani Leib. "Mayn lebn in tsoybertol." In *Tsuzamen*, edited by S. L. Shneiderman, 493–97. Tel Aviv: Y. L. Perets, 1974.

Mann, Barbara E. *A Place in History: Modernism, Tel Aviv, and the Creation of Jewish Urban Space*. Stanford, CA: Stanford University Press, 2006.

Mann, Thomas. "Goethe and Tolstoy." In *Three Essays*, translated by H. T. Lowe Porter, 3–140. New York: Alfred A. Knopf, 1929.

———. "Introduction." In *The Short Novels of Dostoevsky*, vii–xx. New York: Dial Press, 1945.

———. *The Magic Mountain*. Translated by John E. Woods. New York: Alfred A. Knopf, 1995.

———. *Reflections of a Nonpolitical Man*. Translated by Walter D. Morris. New York: Frederick Ungar Publishing, 1983.

———. *Tristan*. In *Death in Venice and Other Stories*, translated by H. T. Lowe-Porter, 317–57. New York: Alfred A. Knopf, 1947.

Marcus, Joseph. *Social and Political History of the Jews in Poland, 1919–1939*. Berlin: Walter de Gruyter, 1983.

Marinoff, Jacob. "Das schwindsüchtige Mädel (The Consumptive Maiden)." *The Sanatorium* 3, no. 1 (1909): 26.

———. "Letter to Flora Bloomgarden," September 16, 1908. Arc 116, Box 4, Folder: Marinov, Y. Jewish Theological Seminary Archive.

———. Shtarbn fun hunger: 4 teg nit begrobn." *Yudishes tageblatt*, December 23, 1903.

Markovizky, Jacob. "The Italian Government's Response to the Problem of Jewish Refugees 1945–1948." *Journal of Israeli History: Politics, Society, Culture* 19, no. 1 (1998): 23–39.

Martineau, Harriet. *Life in the Sick-Room*, edited by Maria H. Frawley. Orchard Park, NY: Broadview Press, 2002.

Marxer, Bettina. "Die Liebesbegegnung in Meran." In *Liebesbriefe, und was nun einmal so gennant wird: Korrespondenzen zwischen Arthur Schnitlzer, Olga Waissnix und Marie Reinhard: Eine literatur- und kulturwissenschaftliche Lektüre*. Würzberg: Königshausen & Neumann, 2001.

"Maslianski bet rakhomim: Der groyser yidisher redner makht an ufruf far di korbones fun der blaser pest in Denver." *Yidishes tageblat*, May 23, 1909. JCRS Records, Box 198, JCRS—Newspaper Clippings, 1909–1912. JCRS Archive.

Matarah. "Me-are ha-medinah: Kiev." *Hed ha-zeman*. December 8, 1908.

Mattes, Lune. "Dem dikhter iz gut." In *Studya*, 24. Los Angeles: Farlag "Palme," 1928.

———. "Denver." Translated by Abraham Wolftraub. *Hatikvah* 1, no. 2 (1923): 2.

———. "Kolerade." In *Ofene toyren*, 5–22. Denver: Literarishe Grupe (Dovid Edelsthat Branch 450 Arb. Ring) & Ladies Educational Club, 1923.

———. "Kop geboygn." In *Studya*, 20. Los Angeles: Farlag "Palme," 1928.

———. "Kroyn fun zayn gnod." In *Studya*, 20. Los Angeles: Farlag "Palme," 1928.

———. "Light and Dreams." *Hatikvah* 1, no. 3 (1923): 5–6.

———. *Ofene toyren*. Denver, CO: Literarishe Grupe (Dovid Edelsthat Branch 450 Arb. Ring) & Ladies Educational Club, 1923.

———. "The Song of Thanks and Love." Translated by Deena Spivak Strauss. *Hatikvah* 1, no. 6 (1923): 15.

———. *Der vayser prints fun der vayser plag*. Los Angeles: Farlag "Palme," 1927.

"Mattes Lune Patient Record," n.d. JCRS Folder 6361. JCRS Archive.

Max, Katrin. *Liegekur und Bakterienrausch: Literarische Deutungen der Tuberkulose im Zauberberg und anderswo*. Würzberg: Verlag Köningshausen & Neumann GmbH, 2013.

Mayr, Sabine. *Südtirol und seine jüdischen AutorInnen*. Innsbruck: Studienverlag, forthcoming.

McKay, Douglas R. *Asylum of the Gilded Pill: The Story of Cragmore Sanatorium*. Denver: State Historical Society of Colorado, 1983.

Meir, Natan M. *Kiev: Jewish Metropolis, A History, 1859–1914*. Bloomington: Indiana University Press, 2010.

"A Mendele-ovnt in Peterburg." *Der fraynd*, January 28 [February 10], 1911.

Meredith, Stephen C. "Mortal Illness on the Magic Mountain." In *A Companion to Thomas Mann's "Magic Mountain,"* edited by Stephen D. Dowden, 109–40. Columbia, SC: Camden House, 1999.

"Mikhtavim la-ma'arekhet: Azru la-milḥamah ba-shaḥefet." *Davar*, February 18, 1930.

Miller, Chas. "Letter to H. Leyvik," n.d. RG 315, Box 65, Folder 74. YIVO.

Miller, Marc. *Representing the Immigrant Experience: Morris Rosenfeld and the Emergence of Yiddish Literature in America*. Syracuse, NY: Syracuse University Press, 2007.

Milstein, Uri. "Dodati Raḥel." In *Raḥel: Shirim, mikhtavim, reshimot, korot ḥayeha*, by Raḥel, 25–51. Tel Aviv: Zemorah Bitan, 1985.

———. "Einayim bo'arot." *Ḥadashot*, April 5, 1985.

Miron, Dan. "Ahavah teluyah ba-davar: Toldot hitkablutah shel shirat David Fogel." In *Aderet le-Vinyamin: Sefer ha-yovel li-Vinyamin Harshav*, edited by Ziva Ben-Porat, 1:29–98. Tel Aviv: Ha-Kibuts Ha-Meʾuḥad, 1999.

———. *From Continuity to Contiguity: Toward a New Jewish Literary Thinking*. Stanford, CA: Stanford University Press, 2010.

———. *Imahot meyasdot, aḥayot ḥorgot: Al reshit shirat ha-nashim ha-ivrit*. Tel Aviv: Ha-Kibuts Ha-Me'uḥad, 2004.

———. "Sholem Aleichem: Person, Persona, Presence." In *The Image of the Shtetl and Other Studies of Modern Jewish Literary Imagination*, 128–56. Syracuse, NY: Syracuse University Press, 2000.

———. *A Traveler Disguised: The Rise of Modern Yiddish Fiction in the Nineteenth Century*. Syracuse, NY: Syracuse University Press, 1996.

M. L. R. "Tsu akhtsikyoriken yubileum fun'm Graf Leo Tolstoy, 1828–1908." *Di naye tsayt: Zamlbukh* 4 (1908): 65–76.

Mohar, Eli. "Ke-shemesh be-yom-kevisah." *Davar*, February 12, 1971, sec. Davar ha-shavu'a.

Mondschein, Orna. *Sifrut ha-sanaṭoryum: Keri'ah be-Tomas Man, David Fogel, Bruno Shults*. Tel Aviv: Resling, 2016.

Moore, Thomas. *The Life of Lord Byron*. London: John Murray, 1844.

Moorman, Lewis Jefferson. *Tuberculosis and Genius*. Chicago: University of Chicago Press, 1940.

"Mr. Jacob Gordin." *The Sanatorium* 3, no. 4 (1909): 228.

"Nadson: The Poet of Despairing Hope." *The Slavonic and East European Review* 15, no. 45 (1937): 680–87.

Nałkowska, Zofia. *Choucas: An International Novel*. Translated by Ursula Philips. DeKalb: Northern Illinois University Press, 2014.

Nepomniashtshi, Shloyme-Yankev. "Naye materialn vegn Sholem Aleykhem (1908–1909)." *Di royte velt* 6, no. 1–2 (1930): 170–92.

"A New Poet.—Solomon Bloomgarden." *The Maccabaean* 4, no. 6 (1903): 303–4.

Nietzsche, Friedrich. *The Will to Power*. Translated by Anthony M. Ludovici. Vol. 2. London: George Allen & Unwin, 1924. http://archive.org/stream/completeworksthe15nietuoft/completeworksthe15nietuoft_djvu.txt.

Niger, Sh. *Dertseylers un romanistn*. New York: CYCO-Bikher Farlag, 1946.

———. "Tsu Sholem-Aleykhems yubiley (Part 1)." *Der tog*, October 9, 1908.

———. "Tsu Sholem-Aleykhems yubiley (Part 2)." *Der tog*, October 16, 1908.

Niser-azl. "Sholem-Aleykhem (tsu zayn yubileum)." *Di tsukunft* 8, no. 12 (1908): 5–6.

O. Henry. "A Fog in Santone." In *The Complete Works of O. Henry*, 992–97. Garden City, NY: Doubleday, 1953.

Olmert, Dana. *Bi-tenu'at safah ikeshet: Ketivah ve-ahavah be-shirat ha-meshorerot ha-ivriyot ha-rishonot*. Haifa: University of Haifa Press, 2012.

Orenshteyn, Binyomen. *Khurbn: Otvotsk, Falenits, Kartshev*. Bamberg: Farvaltung fun Otvotsker, Falenitser un Kartshever Landslayt in der Amerikaner Zone in

Daytshland, Published under EUCOM Civil Affairs Division Authorization Number UNDP 219, 1948.

Otwock Sanatorium Patients. "Letter to Sholem Aleichem," May 30, 1908. Box 10, Folder lamed-alef 18/1. Beth Shalom Aleichem Archive.

"Our Bilingual Bi-monthly." *The Sanatorium* 3, no. 2 (1909): 68–69.

"Oysland: Berlin." *Di tsayt*, February 2, 1906.

Pagis, Dan. "David Vogel." In *Mi-ḥuts la-shurah: Masot ve-reshimot al ha-shirah ha-ivrit ha-modernit*, 9–67. Jerusalem: Keshev, 2003.

Paul, Henry W. *Henri de Rothschild, 1872–1947: Medicine and Theater*. Burlington, VT: Ashgate Publishing, 2011.

Pellman, D. "Letter to Yehoash," September 16, 1908. Arc 116, Box 5, Folder: D. Pellman. Jewish Theological Seminary Archive.

Peretz, I. L. "Mayses." In *Di tsayt*, vol. 2, *Ale verk fun Y. L. Perets*, 165–82. New York: Morgn-frayhayt with the Permission of B. Kletzkin Farlag, Poland, 1920.

Perry, Menachem. "Ibud Fogel et Fogel: Aḥarit-davar le'taḥanot kavot." In *Taḥanot kavot: Novelot, roman, sipur, yoman*, by David Vogel, 327–50. Tel Aviv: Ha-Kibuts Ha-Me'uḥad, 1990.

Perski, Daniel. "Eli'ezer Ben-Yehudah." *Do'ar Ha-yom*, December 20, 1922.

Pfanzelter, Eva. "Between Brenner and Bari: Jewish Refugees in Italy 1945 to 1948." *Journal of Israeli History: Politics, Society, Culture* 19, no. 3 (1998): 83–104.

Pinsker, Shachar M. *Literary Passports: The Making of Modernist Hebrew Fiction in Europe*. Stanford, CA: Stanford University Press, 2011.

Pinski, Dovid. "Gasn-bilder." *The Sanatorium* 2, no. 4 (1908): 225–26.

———. "Sholem-Aleykhems yubileum." *Der arbayter*, October 3, 1908.

———. "Sholem Aleykhems yubileum." *Der arbayter*, October 10, 1908.

Ployni ve-koyen. "Tsu Sholem-Aleykhems yubileum: Eynige algemeyne shtrikhen vegn dem literarishn verte fun dem grestn yidishn humorist." *Der amerikaner*, November 20, 1908.

Poznanski, Menaḥem. "Letter #126 to G. Shofman (31 May 1930)." In *Igrot tar'at-tashtaz*. Tel Aviv: M. Z. Volfovski, 1960.

Presner, Todd Samuel. *Muscular Judaism: The Jewish Body and the Politics of Regeneration*. Routledge Jewish Studies Series. New York: Routledge, 2007.

Pruccoli, Rosanna. "Un cimetero, un sanatorio per indigenti e una sinagoga: Storia di un patto di solidarietà." In *Storie di ebrei: Contributi storici sulla presenza ebraica in Alto Adige e in Trentino = Jüdische Schicksale: Beiträge zu einer Geschichtsforschung über die jüdische Ansässigkeit in Südtirol und im Trentino*, edited by Federico Steinhaus and Rosanna Pruccoli, 47–76. [Merano] (Bolzano): Comunità ebraica di Merano/Jüdische Kultusgemeinde Meran, 2004.

Pryłucki, Noah. "Sholem-Aleykhem (Part 1)." *Teatr velt*, no. 3 (October 16, 1908): 5–9.

Quilligan, Maureen. *The Language of Allegory: Defining the Genre.* Ithaca, NY: Cornell University Press, 1979.
Quint, Alyssa. "Yiddish Literature for the Masses? A Reconsideration of Who Read What in Jewish Eastern Europe." *AJS Review* 29, no. 1 (2005): 61–89.
R. "Ekspropri'irt Sholem-Aleykhemen!" *Der fraynd*, September 18 [October 1], 1908.
Raabe, Paul. *Klabund in Davos: Texte, Bilder, Dokumente.* Zürich: Arche Verlag, 1990.
Rabinovitsh, Binyomin. "Vegn Sholem-Aleykhems krankhayt." *Unzer lebn*, August 11 [24], 1908.
Rabon, Yisroel. *Di gas.* Jerusalem: Magnes Press, 1986.
———. *Di gas: Roman.* Warsaw: L. Goldfarb, 1928.
Radetsky, Ralph. "Denver Patient World Famous Playwright." *Post*, August 11, 1935. JCRS File 9698, Patient Record Halpern Leivick. JCRS Archive.
Raḥel. "Al ot ha-zeman (1927)." In *Shirat Raḥel*, 204–5. Tel Aviv: Davar, 1966.
———. *Ba-bayit uva-ḥuts.* Tel Aviv: Tamuz, 2001.
———. "Be-veit ha-ḥolim." In *Shirat Raḥel*, 32. Tel Aviv: Davar, 1966.
———. "Eni kovlah." In *Shirat Raḥel*, 63. Tel Aviv: Davar, 1966.
———. "Ets agas." In *Shirat Raḥel*, 30. Tel Aviv: Davar, 1966.
———. "Ḥaye nemalim." In *Shirat Raḥel*, 227–30. Tel Aviv: Davar, 1966.
———. "Ḥedri he-ḥadash." In *Shirat Raḥel*, 53. Tel Aviv: Davar, 1966.
———. "I Live High Up in a Sanatorium [IA zhivu vysoko v sanatorii]." In *Lakh ve-alayikh: Ahavat Raḥel u-Mikha'el: Mikhtavim, shirim, divre hesber*, edited by Binyamin Ḥakhlili, 79. Tel Aviv: Ha-Kibuts Ha-Meu'ḥad, 1987.
———. "Letter to Dvora Dayan," ca. 1921. Zalman Shazar Collection 248, Document 92307/1. Machon Genazim.
———. "Letter to Sara Milstein," n.d. Zalman Shazar Collection 248, Folder 29449-Kaf, p. 12. Machon Genazim.
———. Letter to Shulamit and Yitsḥak Klugai," n.d. In *Raḥel: Shirim, mikhtavim, reshimot, korot ḥayeha*, edited by Uri Milstein, 98. Tel Aviv: Zemora Bitan, 1985.
———. "Letter to Shulamit Klugai (#4)," n.d. Arkhiyon ha-Medinah [Israel State Archives]. Accessed December 8, 2013. http://www.archives.gov.il/NR/rdonlyres/B3713D18-FFC3–40CA-9BA7-BEE3CFD20C96/0/Rachel04.pdf.
———. "Letter to Shulamit Klugai (#6)," n.d. Arkhiyon ha-Medinah [Israel State Archives]. Accessed December 8, 2013. http://www.archives.gov.il/NR/rdonlyres/D9D726A6-F674–4EC9–8B2A-85E9F9CB96E4/0/Rachel06.pdf.
———. "Letter to Shulamit Klugai (#12)," n.d. Arkhiyon ha-Medinah [Israel State Archives]. Accessed December 8, 2013. http://www.archives.gov.il/NR/rdonlyres/313D8E87-C7A0–4D83-B75D-85AD6F72DFC0/0/Rachel12.pdf.
———. "Letter to Shulamit Klugai (#23)," n.d. Arkhiyon ha-Medinah [Israel State Archives]. Accessed December 8, 2013. http://www.archives.gov.il/NR/rdonlyres/BB354F0B-0A8D-4A9F-803C-1EC96650B0C1/0/Rachel23.pdf.

———. "Lo go'el—ve-karov kol kakh." In *Shirat Raḥel*, 91. Tel Aviv: Davar, 1966.

———. "Rak al atsmi." In *Shirat Raḥel*, 128. Tel Aviv: Davar, 1966.

———. "Yom ha-shanah ha-shishi le-mot Raḥel." *Davar*, April 15, 1937.

Ramras-Rauch, Gila. *Aharon Appelfeld: The Holocaust and Beyond*. Bloomington: Indiana University Press, 1994.

Ravitch, Melech. "David Fogel." In *Mayn leksikon*, 5:332–33. Montreal: Aroysgegebn fun a Komitet, 1958.

———, ed. *Toyt-tsiklus*. Vienna: Der Kval, 1920.

"Rebi Mendele Moḥer Sfarim (hirhurim u-maḥshavot le-yovel shenat ha-shiv'im shelo be-yom dalet tet"vav tevet), I." *Hashkafah*, January 23, 1907.

"Rebi Mendele Moḥer Sfarim (hirhurim u-maḥshavot le-yovel shenat ha-shiv'im shelo be-yom dalet tet"vav tevet), II." *Hashkafah*, January 25, 1907.

Reed, T. J. *Thomas Mann: The Uses of Tradition*. Oxford: Clarendon Press, 1996.

Reeder, Roberta. *Anna Akhmatova: Poet and Prophet*. New York: St. Martin's Press, 1994.

Rekhev, Gustah. "Al Raḥel ha-meshoreret." In *Raḥel ve-shiratah: Mivḥar divre zikhronot ve-he'arot*, edited by Mordekhai Snir and Shim'on Kushner, 58–59. Tel Aviv: Davar, 1971.

Reuveny, Yotam. *Yomam lailah*. Tel Aviv: Kadim, 1987.

———. *Yomam lailah 2*. Tel Aviv: Modan, 1988.

———. *Yomam lailah 3*. Tel Aviv: Nimrod, 1989.

Revell, Peter. *Paul Laurence Dunbar*. Boston: Twayne Publishers, 1979.

Rivesman, M. "Der stil: A briv in redaktsiye." *Der fraynd*, September 25 [October 8], 1908.

Ro'i, Natan. "Bet-hamishpat: Uri Milshteyn lo neheneh mi-tamluge Raḥel ha-meshoreret." *Davar*, February 27, 1987. Folder: Raḥel. Degania Archive.

Rokem, Freddie. "Hebrew Theater from 1889 to 1948." In *Theater in Israel*, edited by Linda Ben-Zvi, 51–84. Ann Arbor: University of Michigan Press, 1996.

Rokem, Na'ama. "German-Hebrew Encounters in the Poetry and Correspondence of Yehuda Amichai and Paul Celan." *Prooftexts* 30, no. 1 (2010): 97–127.

Ron, Amos. "A Rachel for Everyone: The Kinneret Cemetery as a Site of Civil Pilgrimage." In *Sanctity of Time and Space in Traditions and Modernity*, edited by Alberdina Houtman, Marcel Poorthuis, and Joshua Schwartz, 349–59. Boston: Brill, 1998.

Ronch, I[saac] E. "Dray liderbikher." *Der oyfkum* 2, no. 7 (1927): 46–47.

Rosenblat, H. "Bikher: Ofene toyren fun L. Mates." *Mayrev* 1 (February 1925): 52–55.

Rosenfarb, Chava. *Briv tsu Abrashen*. Tel Aviv: Y. L. Perets Farlag, 1992.

———. "Te-be-tse balade." In *Di balade fun nekhtikhn vald*, 19–24. London: Narod Press, 1947.

Rosenfeld, Morris. "A trer afn ayzn." In *Gezamelte lider*, 14–15. New York: International Library, 1906.

———. "Di greste tsedoke." *Der teglikher herold*, n.d. JCRS Records, Box 197, JCRS—Newspaper Clippings 1904–1906. JCRS Archive.

———. *Lieder des Ghetto*. Translated by Berthold Feiwel. Berlin: S. Calvary, 1903.

Rosenkrantz, Barbara Gutmann, ed. *From Consumption to Tuberculosis: A Documentary History*. Vol. 1. New York: Garland Publishing, 1993.

Roskies, David G. *A Bridge of Longing: The Lost Art of Yiddish Storytelling*. Cambridge, MA: Harvard University Press, 1995.

———. "Introduction." *Prooftexts* 6, no. 1 (1986): 1–5.

———. *The Jewish Search for a Usable Past*. Bloomington: Indiana University Press, 1999.

Rothman, Sheila M. *Living in the Shadow of Death: Tuberculosis and the Social Experience of Illness in America*. Baltimore: Johns Hopkins University Press, 1995.

Rozenfeld, Yoysef. "Sholem Aleykhems yubileum in Toronto, Kenede." *Der arbayter*, November 14, 1908.

Rubinstein, Rachel. *Members of the Tribe: Native America in the Jewish Imagination*. Detroit, MI: Wayne State University Press, 2010.

Rutberg, Ḥayah. "Raḥel ve-goralah." In *Raḥel ve-shiratah: Mivḥar divre zikhronot ve-he'arot*, edited by Mordekhai Snir and Shim'on Kushner, 29–31. Tel Aviv: Davar, 1971.

———. "Zikhronot." In *Raḥel ve-shiratah: Mivḥar divre zikhronot ve-he'arot*, edited by Mordekhai Snir and Shim'on Kushner, 25–28. Tel Aviv: Davar, 1971.

Salem. "Me-are ha-medinah: Odessa." *Hed ha-zeman*, December 28, 1908.

Sandbank, Shimon. "David Fogel, Georg Trakl—veha-tseva'im." In *Shete berekhot ba-ya'ar: Kesharim u-makbilot ben ha-shirah ha-ivrit veha-shirah ha-eropit*, 70–92. Tel Aviv: Ha-Kibuts Ha-Me'uḥad, 1976.

Saussy, Haun. "In the Workshop of Equivalences: Translation, Institutions, Media in the Jesuit Re-formation of China." In *Great Walls of Discourse and Other Adventures in Cultural China*, 15–34. Cambridge, MA: Harvard University Asia Center, 2001.

Savurai, Raḥel. "Morashtah shel Raḥel." *Ha-daf ha-yarok*, September 10, 1985. Folder: Raḥel. Degania Archive.

Scarry, Elaine. *The Body in Pain: The Making and Unmaking of the World*. New York: Oxford University Press, 1985.

Schachter, Allison. *Diasporic Modernisms: Hebrew and Yiddish Literature in the Twentieth Century*. New York: Oxford University Press, 2011.

Schnitzler, Arthur. *Dying*. Translated by Anthea Bell. London: Pushkin Press, 2006.

———. *Fräulein Else*. Translated by F. Y. Lyon. London: Pushkin Press, 2013.

Schulte, Bärbel. *Max Lazarus: Trier, St. Louis, Denver: Ein jüdisches Künstlerschiksal.* Trier: Stadtmuseum Simeonstift Trier, 2010.

Schwartz, Daniel B. *The First Modern Jew: Spinoza and the History of an Image.* Princeton, NJ: Princeton University Press, 2012.

Schwartz, Yigal. *The Zionist Paradox: Hebrew Literature and Israeli Identity.* Translated by Michal Sapir. Waltham, MA: Brandeis University Press, 2014.

Scott, Virginia. *Molière: A Theatrical Life.* New York: Cambridge University Press, 2000.

"The Scribe's Pinkes: Denver, Colorado." *The Sanatorium* 1, no. 3 (1907): 58.

Seelig, Rachel. *Strangers in Berlin: Modern Jewish Literature between East and West, 1919–1933.* Ann Arbor: University of Michigan Press, 2016.

Segal, Miryam. "Rachel Bluwstein's 'Aftergrowth' Poetics." *Prooftexts* 25, no. 2 (2005): 319–61.

Segal, Oren. "Sisyphus in Tel Aviv: AIDS in Yotam Reuveny's *Night Diary.*" *Prooftexts* 32 (2012): 115–40.

Seidman, Naomi. *A Marriage Made in Heaven.* Berkeley: University of California Press, 1997.

Sered, Susan Starr. "A Tale of Three Rachels, or the Cultural *Her*story of a Symbol." *Nashim* 1 (1998): 5–41.

Sh. "Le-yovelo shel Shalom Alekhem." *Hed ha-zeman*, October 7, 1908.

Shaked, Gershon. "David Fogel." In *Ha-siporet ha-ivrit, 1880–1980*, 93–101. Tel Aviv: Ha-Kibuts Ha-me'uḥad and Keter, 1988.

"Shalom Aleichem." *Jewish Chronicle*, December 11, 1908.

"Shalom Alekhem." *Ha-tsevi*, July 2, 1909.

"Shalom Alekhem be-Erets Yisra'el." *Ha-tsevi*, January 31, 1909.

Shelley, Percy Bysshe. *Adonais, An Elegy on the Death of John Keats (1821).* London: Publication for the Shelley Society by Reeves and Turner, 1886.

Sheva, Shlomo. "Raḥel ba-aliyat-ha-gag." *Davar*, May 7, 1971, sec. Davar ha-shavu'a.

Shilo, Margalit, and Gid'on Kats, eds. *Migdar be-Yisra'el: Meḥkarim ḥadashim al migdar ba-yishuv uva-medinah.* Be'er Sheva: Universitat Ben Guryon Ba-Negev, 2011.

Shimel, Harold. "Ha-tsad shelanu—hayam shelanu." *Davar*, July 19, 1974.

Shlonsky, A[vraham]. "Al 'ha-shalom.'" *Ketuvim*, May 11, 1927, 1.

———. "Amal." In *Shirim*, 1:163–65. Merḥavyah: Sifriyat Po'alim, 1954.

Shmeruk, Chone. "Yisroel Rabon and His Book *Di Gas* ('The Street')." In *The Street*, edited by Chone Shmeruk, v–l. Jerusalem: Magnes Press, 1986.

Shmu'eli. "Ba-arov yomah." In *Raḥel ve-shiratah: Mivḥar divre zikhronot ve-he'arot*, edited by Mordekhai Snir and Shim'on Kushner, 50. Tel Aviv: Davar, 1971.

"Shmuel Shmelkes un zayn yubileum." *Der morgn-zhurnal*, January 4, 1909.

Shneur, Zalman. "Al Uri Nisan Genesin." In *Ḥ. N. Bialik u-vene doro*, 397–412. Tel Aviv: Devir, 1958.

Sholem Aleichem. *Blondzhende shtern, I.* Vol. 10, *Ale verk fun Sholem-Aleykhem*. Warsaw: Tsentral, 1914.

———. *Blondzhende shtern, II.* Vol. 11, *Ale verk fun Sholem-Aleykhem*. Warsaw: Tsentral, 1914.

———. "A briv fun Sholem-Aleykhem." *D"r Birnboyms vokhenblat*, September 25, 1908.

———. "A briv in redaktsiye." *Der fraynd*, September 9 [22], 1908.

———. "A briv in redaktsiye." *Unzer lebn*, September 12 [25], 1908.

———. "Cedars of Lebanon: Sholem Aleichem in Sickness, Letter from Sholom Aleichem to Israel Cohen (6 March 1909)." Translated by Israel Cohen. *Commentary*, October 1950, 381.

———. "Cedars of Lebanon: Sholem Aleichem in Sickness, Letter from Sholom Aleichem to Israel Cohen (19 Nov 1909)." Translated by Israel Cohen. *Commentary*, October 1950, 383.

———. "Di epitafiye fun Sholem-Aleykhem." Vol. 16, *Ale verk fun Sholem-Aleykhem*, 291–93. New York: Morgn-Frayhayt, 1937.

———. "From the Riviera." In *My First Love Affair and Other Stories*, translated by Curt Leviant, 303–7. Mineola, NY: Dover Publications, 2002.

———. "Fun der Rivyere." In *Monologn*, vol. 25, *Ale verk fun Sholem-Aleykhem*, 213–20. New York: Morgn-Frayhayt, 1937.

———. "Geese." In *My First Love Affair and Other Stories*, translated by Curt Leviant, 115–28. Mineola, NY: Dover Publications, 2002.

———. "Genz." In *Monologn*, vol. 25, *Ale verk fun Sholem-Aleykhem*, 27–44. New York: Morgn-Frayhayt, 1937.

———. "Der gliklekhster in Kodne." In *Ayznban-geshikhtes*, vol. 26, *Ale verk fun Sholem-Aleykhem*, 23–38. New York: Morgn-Frayhayt, 1937.

———. "Go Climb a Tree If You Don't Like It." In *Tevye the Dairyman and the Railroad Stories*, translated by Hillel Halkin, 269–74. New York: Schocken Books, 1987.

———. "Goles datshe." In *Zumer-lebn*, vol. 11, *Ale verk fun Sholem-Aleykhem*, 7–72. New York: Morgn-Frayhayt, 1937.

———. "The Happiest Man in Kodny." In *Tevye the Dairyman and the Railroad Stories*, translated by Hillel Halkin, 143–52. New York: Schocken Books, 1987.

———. "Home Away from Home." In *Stories and Satires*, translated by Curt Leviant, 308–49. New York: T. Yoseloff, 1959.

———. "In di varembeder." In *Zumer-lebn*, vol. 11, *Ale verk fun Sholem-Aleykhem*, 73–118. New York: Morgn-Frayhayt, 1937.

———. "Letter to Bal-Makhshoves (July 28, 1912)." In *Briv fun Sholem-Aleykhem*,

1879–1916, edited by Avrom Lis, 550–51. Tel Aviv: Beys Sholem-Aleykhem & Perets Farlag, 1995.

———. "Letter to Gershn Levin (November 12, 1908)." In *Briv fun Sholem-Aleykhem, 1879–1916*, edited by Avrom Lis, 476–78. Tel Aviv: Beys Sholem-Aleykhem & Perets Farlag, 1995.

———. "Letter to Gershn Levin (November 23, 1908)." In *Briv fun Sholem-Aleykhem, 1879–1916*, edited by Avrom Lis, 478–79. Tel Aviv: Beys Sholem-Aleykhem & Perets Farlag, 1995.

———. "Letter to Gershn Levin (January 15, 1909)." In *Briv fun Sholem-Aleykhem, 1879–1916*, edited by Avrom Lis, 488–89. Tel Aviv: Beys Sholem-Aleykhem & Perets Farlag, 1995.

———. "Letter to Gershn Levin," January 27, 1909. Folder mem-lamed 3/13. Beth Shalom Aleichem Archive.

———. "Letter to Gershn Levin (March 27, 1909)." In *Briv fun Sholem-Aleykhem, 1879–1916*, edited by Avrom Lis, 499–500. Tel Aviv: Beys Sholem-Aleykhem & Perets Farlag, 1995.

———. "Letter to Mendele Mocher-Sforim (February 20–March 5, 1909)." In *Briv fun Sholem-Aleykhem, 1879–1916*, edited by Avrom Lis, 491–92. Tel Aviv: Beys Sholem-Aleykhem & Perets Farlag, 1995.

———. "Letter to Mordkhe Spektor (October–November 1908) [*sic*]." In *Briv fun Sholem-Aleykhem, 1879–1916*, edited by Avrom Lis, 474–76. Tel Aviv: Beys Sholem-Aleykhem & Perets Farlag, 1995.

———. "Letter to Natashe Mazor (January 25 [February 7], 1909)." In *Briv fun Sholem-Aleykhem, 1879–1916*, edited by Avrom Lis, 90–91. Tel Aviv: Beys Sholem-Aleykhem & Perets Farlag, 1995.

———. "Letter to Shmuel Sharira," November 22, 1908. Folder mem-shin 12/1. Beth Shalom Aleichem Archive.

———. "Letter to Yankev Dinezon," October 18 [31], 1908. Folder mem-dalet 4/45. Beth Shalom Aleichem Archive.

———. "Letter to Yankev Dinezon (October–November 1908)." In *Briv fun Sholem-Aleykhem, 1879–1916*, edited by Avrom Lis, 474–76. Tel Aviv: Beys Sholem-Aleykhem & Perets Farlag, 1995.

———. "Letter to Yankev Dinezon (March 27, 1909)." In *Briv fun Sholem-Aleykhem, 1879–1916*, edited by Avrom Lis, 500–501. Tel Aviv: Beys Sholem-Aleykhem & Perets Farlag, 1995.

———. "Letter to Y. D. Berkovits," October 14, 1908. Folder mem-bet 32/85. Beth Shalom Aleichem Archive.

———. "Letter to Y. D. Berkowitz (November 23, 1905)." In *Briv fun Sholem-Aleykhem, 1879–1916*, edited by Avrom Lis, 50–51. Tel Aviv: Beys Sholem-Aleykhem & Perets Farlag, 1995.

———. "Letter to Yitskhok Yampolski (n.d.)." In *Briv fun Sholem-Aleykhem, 1879–1916*, edited by Avrom Lis, 486. Tel Aviv: Beys Sholem-Aleykhem & Perets Farlag, 1995.
———. *Marienbad.* Translated by Aliza Shevrin. New York: Putnam, 1982.
———. *Maryenbad.* In *Zumer-lebn*, vol. 11, *Ale verk fun Sholem-Aleykhem*, 119–292. New York: Morgn-Frayhayt, 1937.
———. "The Pot." In *The Best of Sholem Aleichem*, edited by Irving Howe and Ruth Wisse, 71–81. Northvale, NJ: Jason Aronson, 1989.
———. "Ruf mikh knaknisl." In *Ayznban-geshikhtes*, vol. 26, *Ale verk fun Sholem-Aleykhem*, 273–82. New York: Morgn-Frayhayt, 1937.
———. "Shmuel Shmelkes un zayn yubileum." In *Fun Kasrilevke*, vol. 19, *Ale verk fun Sholem-Aleykhem*, 203–37. New York: Morgn-Frayhayt, 1937.
———. "Shmuel Shmelkess and His Jubilee." Translated by Israel Cohen. *Jewish Chronicle*, November 27, 1908.
———. *Shmuel Shmelḳis ve-ḥag-yovlo.* Vilna: Zaldaski Dfus, 1909.
———. "Dos tepl." In *Monologn*, vol. 25, *Ale verk fun Sholem-Aleykhem*, 7–26. New York: Morgn-Frayhayt, 1937.
———. "To the Hot Springs." In *Stories and Satires*, translated by Curt Leviant, 350–78. New York: T. Yoseloff, 1959.
———. "Tsu Mendele Moykher-Sforims yubileum." *Der veg*, January 19, 1906.
———. "Di vibores." *Yudishes folks-blat*, October 19 [31], 1883.
———. *Wandering Stars.* Translated by Aliza Shevrin. New York: Viking, 2009.
"Sholem-Aleykhem: Algemeyne betrakhtungen." *Yidishe arbayter velt*, January 8, 1909.
"'Sholem-Aleykhem' darf hilf fun Amerike." *Der morgn-zhurnal*, December 9, 1908.
"Der Sholem Aleykhem fond." *Der morgn-zhurnal*, January 15, 1909.
"Sholem-Aleykhem in Nervi (Italiyen)." *Der shtrahl* 1, no. 2 (1910): 7–9.
"Der Sholem-Aleykhem-ovent." *Lodzher tageblat*, November 9 [22], 1908.
"Sholem-Aleykhem ovent." *Haynt*, November 18 [December 1], 1908.
"Sholem Aleykhem oventn in Denver, Kol." *Der morgn-zhurnal*, January 10, 1909.
"Sholem Aleykhem: Oyser gefer." *Der morgn-zhurnal*, September 2, 1908.
"Sholem-Aleykhems yubileum." *Der arbayter*, November 21, 1908.
"Sholem-Aleykhems yubileum." *Der arbayter*, December 12, 1908.
"Sholem-Aleykhems yubileum." *Der arbayter*, December 19, 1908.
"Sholem-Aleykhems yubileum." *Der arbayter*, December 26, 1908.
"Sholem-Aleykhems yubileum." *Der arbayter*, January 2, 1909.
"Sholem-Aleykhems yubileum." *Haynt*, September 5 [18], 1908.
"'Sholem Aleykhem's yubileum haynt in Thalia." *Der morgn-zhurnal*, December 28, 1908.
Shryock, Richard Harrison. *National Tuberculosis Association, 1904–1954: A Study of*

the Voluntary Health Movement in the United States. Public Health in America. New York: Arno Press, 1977.
Shvarts, Shifra. *The Workers' Health Fund in Eretz Israel: Kupat Holim, 1911–1937*. Translated by Daniella Ashkenazy. Rochester, NY: University of Rochester Press, 2002.
"Shvindzukht toytet milyonen mentshn." *Der morgn-zhurnal*, September 30, 1908.
"Siḥot." *Hed ha-zeman*, November 11, 1908.
Simon, Rachel. "Teach Yourself Arabic—in Yiddish!" *MELA*, no. 82 (2009): 1–15.
Singer, Isaac Bashevis. *The Manor and The Estate*. Translated by Joseph Singer, Elizabeth Gottlieb, and Herman Eichenthal. Madison: University of Wisconsin Press, 2004.
Snyder, Sharon L., Brenda Jo Brueggmann, and Rosemarie Garland-Thomson, eds. *Disability Studies: Enabling the Humanities*. New York: Modern Language Association of America, 2002.
Solly, S. Edwin. *A Handbook of Medical Climatology: Embodying Its Principles and Therapeutic Application with Scientific Data of the Chief Health Reports of the World*. New York: Lea Brothers, 1897.
Sontag, Susan. *Illness as Metaphor and AIDS and Its Metaphors*. New York: Picador USA, 2001.
Spektor, Mordkhe. "Sholem-Aleykhem (tsu zayn 25-yerign yubileum)." *Unzer lebn*, October 12 [25], 1908.
Spinoza, Benedictus de. *Barukh Shpinoza: Di etik*. Translated by William Nathanson. Chicago: Naye Gezelshaft, 1923.
Spivak, Charles D. "The Genesis and Growth of the Jewish Consumptives Relief Society (Part I)." *The Sanatorium* 1, no. 1 (1907): 5–7.
———. "The Jewish Press." In *First Annual Report of the Jewish Consumptives' Relief Society at Denver, Colo., 1905*, 25–26. Denver: Smith-Brooks, 1905.
———. "Letter to Zishe Landau," July 16, 1923. JCRS File 6361, Patient Record Morris Lune. JCRS Archive.
———. "Minutes of the JCRS Book 1," n.d. Box 299. Beck Archives Penrose Library.
———. "Minutes of the JCRS, Record of the Board of Trustees," March 6, 1907. Box 299. JCRS Archive.
———. "Secretary's Report: Press and Propaganda" *The Sanatorium* 2, no. 2 (1908): 57–64.
———. "Secretary's Report: Yehoash and His Jonathan." *The Sanatorium* 3, no. 2 (1909): 66–67.
———. "Sekreters Berikht." *The Sanatorium* 3, no. 2 (1909): 145–53.
———. "Sekreters Berikht: Unzer baredevdiker meshulekh—der sanatoriyum." *The Sanatorium* 3, no. 2 (1909): 145–46.
Spivak, Charles D., and Yehoash (S. Bloomgarden). *Yidish verterbukh: Enthalt ale he-*

breishe (un khaldeishe) verter, oysdruken un eygnemen, velkhe vern gebroykht in der yidisher shprakh, mit zeyer oysshprakh un aktsent, un mit bayshpilen fun vertlekh un shprikhverter in ale velkhe zey kumen for. New York: Farlag Yehoash, 1911.

Sprecher, Thomas. *Auf dem weg zum "Zauberberg": Die Davoser Literaturtage 1996.* Vol. 16. Thomas-Mann-Studien. Frankfurt am Main: V. Klostermann, 1997.

———. "Kur-, Kultur- und Kapitalismuskritik im Zauberberg." In *Literatur und Krankheit im Fin-de-Siècle (1890–1914): Thomas Mann im europäischen Kontext*, 187–249. Frankfurt am Main: Vittorio Klostermann, 2002.

Stout, Cynthia Kay. "A Consumptives' Refuge: Colorado and Tuberculosis." PhD diss., George Washington University, 1997. ProQuest (Order No. 9726673).

Sufian, Sandra M. *Healing the Land and the Nation: Malaria and the Zionist Project in Palestine, 1920–1947.* Chicago: University of Chicago Press, 2007.

Tanenboym, A. "Lev Tolstoy: Zayn lebn un zayn virkn." *Der morgn-zhurnal*, September 13, 1908.

Taubenfeld, Aviva. "'Only an L': Linguistic Borders and the Immigrant Author in Abraham Cahan's *Yekl* and *Yankel Der Yankee*." In *Multilingual America: Transnationalism, Ethnicity, and the Languages of American Literature*, edited by Werner Sollors, 144–65. New York: New York University Press, 1998.

"Telegramen: Baranovitsh (spetsiel tsu 'Unzer Lebn')." *Unzer lebn*, August 7 [20], 1908.

"Telegramen: Spetsiel tsu 'Unzer lebn.'" *Unzer lebn*, July 30 [August 12], 1908.

Teller, Michael E. *The Tuberculosis Movement: A Public Health Campaign in the Progressive Era.* New York: Greenwood Press, 1988.

"Ten Leading Causes of Death in the United States, 1900, 1940, 1976." In *From Consumption to Tuberculosis: A Documentary History*, edited by Barbara Gutmann Rosenkrantz, 3–5. New York: Garland Publishing, 1994.

Tenenbaum, Shea. "Baynakht baym keyver fun Dovid Edelshtat." In *Hunger tsum vort: Miniyaturn*, 412–13. New York: CYCO-Bikher Farlag, 1971.

———. "Friling in Denver." *Tshernovitser bleter*, August 6, 1936.

———. "H. Leyvik—der mentsh." *Tshernovitser bleter*, June 24, 1936.

———. "Kinstler in Spivak Sanatoriyum." *Shikage kuriyer*, June 28, 1936.

———. "Letter to H. Leivick," n.d. (ca. 1934–35). RG 315, Box 29, Folder 54. YIVO.

———. "Letter to H. Leivick," March 11, 1935. RG 315, Box 29, Folder 54. YIVO.

———. "Letter to H. Leivick," April 25, 1936. RG 315, Box 29, Folder 54. YIVO.

———. "Letter to H. Leivick," July 1936. RG 315, Box 29, Folder 54. YIVO.

———. "Letter to H. Leivick," May 1937. RG 315, Box 29, Folder 54. YIVO.

———. "Lider fun gan-eydn." *Der yidisher kuryer*, June 16, 1940.

———. "Nyu-York—Denver (reportazh-notitsn fun a rayze)." *Nyu-Yorker vokhenblat*, June 5, 1936.

———. "Rokhl—di tsarte dikhterin fun Yisroel (1890–1931)." *Di naye tsayt*, November 28, 1950.

———. "Tuberkuloze." In *Bay der velt tsugast: Dertseyln un reportazhn*, 10–12. Warsaw: Literarishe Bleter, 1937.

"Ticket for Mr. and Mrs. H. Leivick as Delegates to the 37th Annual National Convention of the Jewish Consumptives' Relief Society of Denver, CO," March 29, 1941. RG 315, Box 65, Folder 74, YIVO.

"The Tolstoi Celebration." *Jewish Chronicle*, September 25, 1908.

Trachtenberg, Alan. "'Babe in the Yiddish Woods': Dos Lied Fun Hiavat'a." *Judaism* 50, no. 3 (2001): 331–40.

———. *Shades of Hiawatha: Staging Indians, Making Americans, 1880–1930*. New York: Hill & Wang, 2005.

Tsamir, Ḥamutal. "Ha-korban he-ḥalutsi, ha-arets ha-kedoshah ve-hofa'atah shel shirat ha-nashim be-shnot ha-esrim." In *Rega shel huledet: Meḥkarim be-sifrut ivrit uve-sifrut yidish li-khevod Dan Miron*, edited by Ḥannan Ḥever, 645–73. Jerusalem: Bialik Institute, 2007.

Ts[emaḥ], Sh[lomo]. "Be-vet ha-marpe." *Mozanyim*, 1929, 12–13.

Tsernikhov, Yankev. "Vos makht Sholem-Aleykhem? A briv in redaktsiye." *Unzer lebn*, September 3 [16], 1908.

Tshernikhov. "Fun der letster minut: Sholem Aleykhems krankyaht." *Haynt*, August 3 [16], 1908.

Tshernovitsh, Sh. "Le-yovel ha-sifruti shel Shalom-Alekhem." *Hed ha-zeman*, September 20, 1908.

Tsivyon. "Eyn ernst vort tsu Sholem-Aleykhems yubileum." *Yidishe arbayter velt*, December 4, 1908.

———. "Vider vegn Sholem-Aleykhem." *Yidishe arbayter velt*, December 25, 1908.

"Tsu Lev Tolstoys akhtsikyerikes yubileum." *Roman-tsaytung* 33 (August 28 [September 10], 1908).

"Tsu Sholem Aleykhems yubileum." *Der fraynd*, September 17 [30], 1908.

"Tsu Sholem-Aleykhems yubileum: A spetsiele telegrame tsum 'fraynd.'" *Der fraynd*, September 26 [October 9], 1908.

Tsur, Muki. "'Ba-bayit uva-ḥuts'—gilgulo shel sefer." In *Ba-bayit uva-ḥuts*, by Raḥel, n.p. Tel Aviv: Tamuz, 2001.

———. "Ke-ḥakot Raḥel: Kavim biyografiyim." In *Ha-shirim*, by Raḥel, 11–86. Bene Barak: Ha-Kibuts Ha-Meu'ḥad, 2011.

Tsvey-un-nayntsik. "Provints (fun unzere korispondenten): Minsk: Davke af yidish." *Der fraynd*, July 7 [20], 1908.

"Tsvishn yidn in oysland: A Sholem-Aleykhem ovnt." *Unzer lebn*, December 25, 1908.

"Tuberculosis Sufferers." *Palestine Post*, March 8, 1935.

Uchill, Ida Libert. *Pioneers, Peddlers & Tsadikim: The Story of the Jews in Colorado*. Boulder: University Press of Colorado, 2000.

Ug, Y. "Sholem-Aleykhem (tsu zayn 25-yeriken yubileum): I." *Lodzher tageblat*, October 13, 1908.

———. "Tsu Sholem-Alekhems yubileum." *Lodzher tageblat*, October 8 [21], 1908.

"An Urgent Appeal: To the Editor of the Palestine Post." *Palestine Post*, January 31, 1933.

"Vast Crowds Honor Sholem Aleichem." *New York Times*, May 16, 1916.

"Vaytere baytrage tsum Sholem-Aleykhem fond." *Der morgn-zhurnal*, December 15, 1908.

"Vaytere baytrage tsum Sholem Aleykhem fond." *Der morgn-zhurnal*, January 7, 1909.

"A vikhtike 'Sholem Aleykhehm' komitet." *Der morgn-zhurnal*, December 11, 1908.

Vilnai. "Al-yad mitato shel Shalom Alekhem." *Hed ha-zeman*, September 2, 1908.

Vladeck, B. C. "Letter to Mr. Rosen," June 15, 1932. JCRS File 9698, Patient Record Halpern Leivick. JCRS Archive.

Vogel, David. *Be-vet ha-marpe*. Tel Aviv: Ha-Kibuts Ha-Me'uḥad, 2008.

———. *Be-vet ha-marpe: Sipur.* Edited by Asher Barash. Jerusalem: Mitspeh, 1927.

———. "Dayar." In *Taḥanot kavot: Novelot, roman, sipur, yoman*, 265–68. [Tel Aviv]: Ha-Kibuts Ha-Me'uḥad, 1990.

———. "Degalim sheḥorim mefarperim." In *Kol ha-shirim*, edited by Aharon Komem, 80. Tel Aviv: Ha-Kibuts Ha-Me'uḥad, 1998.

———. *Ḥaye nisu'im: Roman.* Jerusalem: Mitspeh, 1929.

———. "Im Sanatorium." In *Im Sanatorium, An der See: Zwei Novellen*, translated by Ruth Achlama, 7–102. Munich: List Verlag, 2013.

———. *Ketsot ha-yamim*. In *Taḥanot kavot: Novelot, roman, sipur, yoman*, 269–326. [Tel Aviv]: Ha-Kibuts Ha-Me'uḥad, 1990.

———. *Kulam yats'u la-krav*. In *Taḥanot kavot: Novelot, roman, sipur, yoman*, edited by Menachem Perry, 65–197. [Tel Aviv]: Ha-Kibuts Ha-Me'uḥad, 1990.

———. "Letter 3 (Vienna, December 15, 1925)." Translated by Mikhail Krutikov. *Jews and Slavs* 17 (2006): 99–100.

———. "Letter to A. Broides," October 29, 1937. David Vogel Collection 231, Document 43957/1. Machon Genazim.

———. "Letter to Melech Ravitch," January 16, 1925. ARC. 40 1540, Folder D. Vogel. National Library of Israel Archives.

———. "Letter to Sh. Pollack," May 21, 1923. David Vogel Collection 231, Document 19227/1. Machon Genazim.

———. "Letter to Sh. Pollack," February 18, 1924. David Vogel Collection 231, Document 19243/1. Machon Genazim.

———. "Letter to Sh. Pollack," June 9, 1924. David Vogel Collection 231, Document 19241/1. Machon Genazim.

———. "Letter to Sh. Pollack," July 17, 1924. David Vogel Collection 231, Document 19293/1. Machon Genazim.

———. "Letter to Sh. Pollack," August 31, 1924. David Vogel Collection 231, Document 19242/1. Machon Genazim.

———. "Letter to Sh. Pollack," December 3, 1924. David Vogel Collection 231, Document 19240/1. Machon Genazim.

———. "Letter to Sh. Pollack," February 28, 1925. David Vogel Collection 231, Document 19244/1. Machon Genazim.

———. "Letter to Sh. Pollack," December 15, 1925. David Vogel Collection 231, Document 19247/1. Machon Genazim.

———. "Letter to Sh. Pollack," February 18, 1926. David Vogel Collection 231, Document 19248/1. Machon Genazim.

———. "Letter to Sh. Pollack," March 18, 1926. David Vogel Collection 231, Document 19249/1. Machon Genazim.

———. *Taḥanot kavot: Novelot, roman, sipur, yoman.* [Tel Aviv]: Ha-Kibuts Ha-Meʾuḥad, 1990.

———. "Y. Kh. Brener: A por verter tsu zayn 4th yortsayt." *Literarishe bleter*, no. 52 (April 30, 1925): 1.

Von Engelhardt, Dietrich. "Tuberkulose und Kultur um 1900. Arzt, Patient und Sanatorium in Thomas Manns *Zauberberg* aus medizinihistorischer Sicht." In *Auf dem Weg zum "Zauberberg": Die Davoser Literaturtage, 1996*, edited by Thomas Sprecher, 323–45. Frankfurt am Main: Vittorio Klostermann, 1997.

Warnke, Nina. "Of Plays and Politics: Sholem Aleichem's First Visit to America." *YIVO Annual* 20 (1991): 239–76.

Weigand, Hermann J. *Thomas Mann's Novel, "Der Zauberberg": A Study.* New York: D. Appleton-Century, 1933.

Weizmann, Moshe. "A briv in redaktsiye." *Der fraynd*, September 3 [16], 1908.

———. "A briv vegn 'Sholem Aleykhem.'" *D"r Birnboyms vokhenblat* 1, no. 6 (1908): 15–16.

———. "Sholem-Aleykhems yubileum." *Haynt*, September 5 [18], 1908.

———. "Sholem Aleykhems yubileum." *Der morgn-zhurnal*, October 15, 1908.

Werses, Shmuel. "Shalom Alekhem: Ha'arakhot ve-gilgulehen: Be-asplaklariyah shel ḥamishim shanot bikoret." *Molad* 17, no. 133–34 (1959): 404–21.

———. "Sholem-Alekhem: Ḥamishim shanot bikoret." In *Bikoret ha-bikoret: Ha'arakhot ve-gilgulehen*, 165–97. Tel Aviv: Hotsaʾat Yaḥdav, Iḥud Motsiʾim La-or, 1982.

Wessling, Robert Diedrich. "Semyon Nadson and the Cult of the Tubercular Poet." PhD diss., University of California, Berkeley, 1998. ProQuest (Order No. 9923103).

Winchevsky, Morris. "Cranky Old Ike." *The Social-Democrat* 4, no. 8 (1900): 253–56.

———. "Der alter krenk Ayk." Translated by Annie Goldstein. *The Sanatorium* 2, no. 4 (1908): 219–22.

Wirth-Nesher, Hana. *Call It English: The Languages of Jewish American Literature*. Princeton, NJ: Princeton University Press, 2006.

Wisse, Ruth R. *I. L. Peretz and the Making of Modern Jewish Culture*. Seattle: University of Washington Press, 1991.

———. *A Little Love in Big Manhattan*. Cambridge, MA: Harvard University Press, 1988.

———. *The Modern Jewish Canon*. New York: Free Press, 2000.

Wolitz, Seth L. "The Americanization of Tevye or Boarding the Jewish 'Mayflower.'" *American Quarterly* 40, no. 4 (1988): 514–36.

Woolf, Virginia. "A Room of One's Own." In *A Room of One's Own; and, Three Guineas*, edited by Morag Shiach, 1–149. New York: Oxford University Press, 1992.

World Health Organization. "TB: Reach the 3 Million." WHO Document Production Services, 2014. http://www.stoptb.org/assets/documents/resources/publications/acsm/WORLD_TB_DAY_BROCHURE_14March.pdf.

———. "Tuberculosis: WHO Global Tuberculosis Report," 2014. http://apps.who.int/iris/bitstream/10665/137094/1/9789241564809_eng.pdf.

"Yafo." *Ha-tsevi*, June 15, 1909.

Yedi'ot ha-ligah le-milḥamah ba-shaḥefet be-Yisra'el. Tel Aviv: Ha-Ligah Le-Milḥamah Ba-Shaḥefet Uve-Maḥalot Re'ah Be-Yisra'el, 1958.

Yehoash. "Abend-klangen, Part 2." In *Naye shriftn*, 1:110. New York: Ferlag Yehoash, 1910.

———. "Abend-klangen, Part 3." In *Naye shriftn*, 1:111. New York: Ferlag Yehoash, 1910.

———. "Amid the Colorado Mountains." In *A Century of Yiddish Poetry*, edited and translated by Aaron Kramer, 66–67. New York: Cornwall Books, 1989.

———. "At Quarantine." *The Maccabaean* 4, no. 6 (1903): 304.

———. "Barg-geviter." In *Naye shriftn*, 1:107. New York: Ferl, 1910.

———. *Gezamelte lider*. New York: A. M. Evalenko, 1907.

———. "Letter to Dr. Jacob Morris," March 23, 1907. Arc 116, Box 4, Folder: Dr. Morris. Jewish Theological Seminary Archive.

———. "Letter to Jacob Gordin," April 26, 1908. Arc 116, Box 1, Folder: Gordin, Jacob. Jewish Theological Seminary Archive.

———. "Letter to Rose Cohen," June 16, 1899. Arc 116, Box 6, Folder: Cohen, Rose. Jewish Theological Seminary Archive.

———. "Letter to Rose Cohen," October 7, 1901. Arc 116, Box 6, Folder: Cohen, Rose. Jewish Theological Seminary Archive.

———. "Letter to Rose Cohen," August 12, 1903. Arc 116, Box 6, Folder: Cohen, Rose. Jewish Theological Seminary Archive.

———. "The Phantom of Death." *The Maccabaean* 4, no. 6 (1903): 304.

———. "Der shterbender konsomptiv." *The Sanatorium* 1, no. 1 (1907): 11.

———. "The White Plague." *Colorado Medical Journal* 11 (1905): 434.

———. "The White Plague." *The Sanatorium* 1, no. 2 (1907): 30.

———. "Zununtergang in Kolerado." *Tsukunft* 1, no. 4 (April 1902): 186.

Yehoash (Lung-Fellow). "A literat-kandidat." *The Sanatorium* 2, no. 1 (1908): 39.

"Der Yehoash kontsert." *Der yidisher kuryer*, April 26, 1909. JCRS Records, Box 198, JCRS—Newspaper Clippings, 1909–1912. JCRS Archive.

"A Yiddish Literary Anniversary: A Character Sketch of 'Shalom Alechem.'" *Jewish Chronicle*, October 23, 1908.

Yidishe Patsiantn Komitet (Sanatorium Gauting). "Tazkir shel va'ad ḥole shaḥefet be-maḥane Fernvald-Germaniyah," October 1, 1952. VII-126–876. Machon Lavon.

"Yidn af der ufname bay shvartsn: Tolstoys hayntiker yubileum." *Haynt*, August 28 [September 10], 1908.

"Yubileum far Sholem Aleykhem." *Der morgn-zhurnal*, September 30, 1908.

"Yubileums: Sholem-Aleykhem." *Lidskis familiyen kalender: Almanakh*, 1909–1910, 128–32.

Yud-Alef. "Sholem-Aleykhem in Lodzh." *Lodzher tageblat*, June 29, 1938.

Zadoff, Miriam. *Next Year in Marienbad: The Lost Worlds of Jewish Spa Culture*. Translated by William Templer. Philadelphia: University of Pennsylvania Press, 2012.

Zagorodski, Y. Ḥ. "Ḥayenu ve-orekh yamenu: Etsot ve-ḥukim li-shemor beri'ut ha-guf." Warsaw: Schuldberg, 1898.

Zakim, Eric. *To Build and Be Built: Landscape, Literature, and the Construction of Zionist Identity*. Philadelphia: University of Pennsylvania Press, 2006.

Zederbaum, Adolph. "Letter to Yehoash," September 22, 1908. Arc 116, Box 5, Folder: Dr. Tsederboyn. Jewish Theological Seminary Archive.

Zeitlin, Hillel. "Sholem-Aleykhem: Etlekhe verter fun zayn yubileum." *Haynt*, September 11 [24], 1908.

Zhitlowsky, Chaim. "Vegn dem verte fun iberzetsungen." In *Dos lid fun Hyavata*, by Henry Wadsworth Longfellow, translated by Yehoash (Solomon Bloomgarden), iii–xxiv. New York: Farlag Yehoash, 1910.

Zierler, Wendy I. *And Rachel Stole the Idols: The Emergence of Modern Hebrew Women's Writing*. Detroit, MI: Wayne State University Press, 2004.

Zolotarov, H. "Tolstoy." *Di tsukunft* 13, no. 10 (1908): 3–8.

Zuckerman, Ghil'ad. *Language Contact and Lexical Enrichment in Israeli Hebrew*. New York: Palgrave Macmillan, 2003.

Zweig, Stefan, and Friderike Zweig. *Briefwechsel: 1912–1942*. Berlin: Alfred Scherz Verlag, 1951.

INDEX

STANFORD STUDIES IN JEWISH HISTORY AND CULTURE

Edited by David Biale and Sarah Abrevaya Stein

This series features novel approaches to examining the Jewish past in the form of innovative work that brings the field into productive dialogue with the newest scholarly concepts and methods. Open to a range of disiplinary and interdisciplinary approaches from history to cultural studies, this series publishes exceptional scholarship balanced by an accessible tone that illustrates histories of difference and addresses issues of current urgency. Books in this list push the boundaries of Jewish Studies and speak compellingly to a wide audience of scholars and students.

Sarah Wobick-Segev, *Homes Away from Home: Jewish Belonging in Twentieth-Century Paris, Berlin, and St. Petersburg*
2018

Eddy Portnoy, *Bad Rabbi: And Other Strange but True Stories from the Yiddish Press*
2017

Jeffrey Shandler, *Holocaust Memory in the Digital Age: Survivors' Stories and New Media Practices*
2017

Joshua Schreier, *The Merchants of Oran: A Jewish Port at the Dawn of Empire*
2017

Alan Mintz, *Ancestral Tales: Reading the Buczacz Stories of S. Y. Agnon*
2017

Ellie R. Schainker, *Confessions of the Shtetl: Converts from Judaism in Imperial Russia, 1817–1906*
2016

Devin E. Naar, *Jewish Salonica: Between the Ottoman Empire and Modern Greece*
2016

For a complete listing of titles in this series, visit the Stanford University Press website, www.sup.org.